Y0-BEK-519

WITHDRAWN
UTSA Libraries

Economic Strategies for Mature Industrial Economies

Edited by

Peter Karl Kresl

Bucknell University, USA

Edward Elgar

Cheltenham, UK • Northampton, MA, USA

© Peter Karl Kresl 2010

All rights reserved. No part of this publication may be reproduced, stored in a retrieval system or transmitted in any form or by any means, electronic, mechanical or photocopying, recording, or otherwise without the prior permission of the publisher.

Published by
Edward Elgar Publishing Limited
The Lypiatts
15 Lansdown Road
Cheltenham
Glos GL50 2JA
UK

Edward Elgar Publishing, Inc.
William Pratt House
9 Dewey Court
Northampton
Massachusetts 01060
USA

A catalogue record for this book
is available from the British Library

Library of Congress Control Number: 2010922149

ISBN 978 1 84980 404 2

Typeset by Servis Filmsetting Ltd, Stockport, Cheshire
Printed and bound by MPG Books Group, UK

Library
University of Texas
at San Antonio

Contents

List of figures   vii
List of tables   viii
List of contributors   x

1. Introduction   1
    Peter Karl Kresl
2. Global competitiveness and the role of higher education/
    community partnerships   22
    David J. Maurrasse
3. Montreal's technological and cultural clusters strategy: the
    case of the multimedia, and film and audiovisual production   37
    Diane-Gabrielle Tremblay
4. The knowledge base, research and development and
    regional economic policy: the US and UK experience   72
    William F. Lever
5. Government and governance – how to build and sustain a
    consistent focus: the case of three Italian cities   90
    Stefano Mollica, Marco Lucchini and Giovanna Hirsch
6. Economic structure and business organization in the central
    region of Mexico   112
    Jaime Sobrino
7. Cooperation and competition between cities: urban
    development strategies in Hong Kong and Shenzhen   132
    Jianfa Shen
8. A city loses its major industry – what does it do? The case of
    Turin   160
    Daniele Ietri
9. Northeastern US cities and global urban competitiveness   177
    Ni Pengfei
10. Industrial tourism: opportunities for city and enterprise   201
    *Leo van den Berg, Alexander Otgaar, Christian Berger and
    Rachel Xiang Feng*
11. An aging population and the economic vitality of
    Pennsylvania's cities and towns   232
    Peter Karl Kresl

12. The repositioning of cities and urban regions in a global
      economy   249
      Saskia Sassen

Index   289

Figures

2.1   Other relevant characteristics of higher education   27
2.2   Inherent convergence of local and higher education interests   29
2.3   Local effectiveness and wider value   30
3.1   Cluster model   40
3.2   Functioning of social capital   43
3.3   The cycle of inclusive local development   66
6.1   Differential urbanization: demographic performance by city
      size   113
6.2   Differential urbanization: territorial expression   115
6.3   Central region of Mexico   117
8.1   A map of the transformation in Turin   166
9.1   Output index system of global urban competitiveness   178
9.2   Input index system of global urban competitiveness   179
11.1 Population pyramids of Pennsylvania   234
11.2 Changes in age cohorts, Pennsylvania   234
11.3 Downtown Pittsburgh   239

Tables

1.1	Pennsylvania manufacturing employment	5
1.2	Pennsylvania's three largest MSAs are ranked (out of 75 US MSAs)	5
4.1	Global ranking of cities 2007, top ten	77
4.2	US cities and the knowledge base: world ranking	78
4.3	US cities in the top ten by dimension	79
4.4	Variables incorporated in the knowledge base	80
4.5	Knowledge base variables, US city ranking	80
4.6	Airport connectivity and quality of life	81
6.1	Central region: population, 1980–2005	118
6.2	Central region: gross domestic product, 1980–2005	119
6.3	Central region: gross domestic product by industry, 1993–2003	120
6.4	Competitiveness index for regional urban system, 1998–2003	123
7.1	Public opinion on possible policies to enhance Hong Kong airport's competitiveness (%)	139
7.2	Public opinion on possible policies on airport cooperation (%)	142
7.3	Do you agree that Hong Kong–Shenzhen governments jointly develop the river loop area of Lok Ma Chau?	146
7.4	Which function do you think should be developed in the river loop area? (multiple answers allowed)	146
7.5	Do you agree that the government should introduce the following special policies in the river loop area? (%)	147
7.6	Do you agree that the government should introduce the following special development measures? (%)	148
7.7	Who should play the leading role, government or enterprises, in the development of the boundary area? (%)	148
7.8	Are you satisfied with the progress and the performance of the government in the development of the boundary area? (%)	149
7.9	Public views on the development direction of the RLA	153
8.1	Vertical integration levels of Fiat Auto (%)	162
8.2	Auto production and manufacturing employment in the province of Turin	163

9.1 Top ten cities and Northeastern US cities among the 500 cities in terms of GUCI 182

9.2 Top ten cities and Northeastern US cities among 500 cities in terms of GDP (unit: US$ billion) 183

9.3 Top ten cities and Northeastern US cities in the 500 sample cities in terms of GDP growth rate (unit: percent) 184

9.4 Top ten cities and Northeastern US cities among the 500 sample cities in terms of GDP per capita (unit: US$) 185

9.5 Top ten cities and Northeastern US cities in the 500 sample cities in terms of GDP per square kilometer (unit: $ thousand) 186

9.6 Top ten cities and Northeastern US cities in the 500 sample cities in terms of employment rate (unit: percent) 187

9.7 Top ten cities and Northeastern US cities in the 500 sample cities in terms of productivity (unit: US$) 188

9.8 Top ten cities and Northeastern US cities in the 500 sample cities by number of international patent applications 189

9.9 Top ten cities and Northeastern US cities in the 500 cities in terms of the presence of multinational companies (unit: score) 190

9.10 Top ten cities and Northeastern US cities in the 500 cities in terms of ratio of nominal exchange rate to real exchange rate (unit: score) 191

9.11 Enterprise quality: world's top ten cities and Northeastern US cities in 150 cities 192

9.12 Industrial structure: world's top ten cities and Northeastern US cities in 150 cities 193

9.13 Human resources: world's top ten cities and Northeastern US cities in 150 cities 194

9.14 Hard environment: world's top ten cities and Northeastern US cities in 150 cities 195

9.15 Soft environment: world's top ten cities and Northeastern US cities in 150 cities 196

9.16 Living environment: world's top ten cities and Northeastern US cities in 150 cities 197

9.17 Global connectivity: world's top ten cities and Northeastern US cities in 150 cities 198

11.1 Pennyslvania age dependency ratios 235

12.1 Global immigrant cities: foreign born percentages and total population for selected cities 276

Contributors

Leo van den Berg, Department of Applied Economics Section Regional, Port and Transport Economics, and EURICUR, Erasmus University, Rotterdam, Netherlands.

Christian Berger, Consultant, Öar Regional Consultants.

Rachel Xiang Feng, Researcher, Erasmus University.

Giovanna Hirsch, Researcher, Aislo.

Daniele Ietri, Dipartimento Interateneo Territorio, Politecnico e Università di Torino, Italy and Institut de Géographie – Faculté des Géosciences, Universté de Lausanne, Switzerland.

Peter Karl Kresl, Charles P. Vaughan Professor of Economics and Professor of International Relations at Bucknell University (USA) emeritus, Lewisburg, Pennsylvania, USA.

William F. Lever, Professor of Urban Studies and Senior Research Fellow in the Department of Urban Studies emeritus, University of Glasgow, Scotland, UK.

Marco Lucchini, Senior Consultant, RSO.

David J. Maurrasse, President and Founder, Marga Incorporated, New York, USA.

Stefano Mollica, Presidente, Associazione Italiana Incontri e StudiDipartimento Interateneo Territorio, Politecnico e Università di Torino, Italy and Institut de Géographie – Faculté des Géosciences, Université de Lausanne, Switzerland sullo Sviluppo Locale, Milan, Italy.

Alexander Otgaar, Senior Researcher, Faculty of Economics, Erasmus University.

Ni Pengfei, Professor, Institute for International Trade and Finance, Chinese Academy of Social Sciences, Beijing, China.

Saskia Sassen, Robert S. Lynd Professor of Sociology, Department of Sociology and Committee on Global Thought, Columbia University, New York, USA.

Jianfa Shen, Professor, Department of Geography and Resource Management, Director, Urban and Regional Development Programme, Hong Kong Institute of Asia-Pacific Studies,The Chinese University of Hong Kong, Hong Kong.

Jaime Sobrino, Professor-researcher, Centro de Estudios Demográficos, Urbanos y Ambientales (Center for Demographic, Urban and Environmental Studies), El Colegio de México, Mexico City.

Diane-Gabrielle Tremblay, Canada Research Chair on the socio-organizational challenges of the Knowledge Economy, Director of the CURA Research center on work–life balance, Télé-université, Université du Québec à Montréal, Quebec, Canada.

1. Introduction

Peter Karl Kresl

Many mature industrial economies (MEIs) have not been treated well by the changes that have transformed the global economy during the past 30 years. Changes in technology have rendered many traditional locations non-competitive, the rise of emerging markets has posed a direct challenge to the vitality of these MEIs, and both capital and labor have moved to more congenial places of employment.[1] Since many states or provinces are composed of urban centers, towns of a variety of sizes, and agricultural spaces, some of which have survived these changes without much negative impact, we will focus our attention on the cities and towns that have been the heart of the industrial sector over the past century or two.

While it is true that researchers have found that some MEIs retain an endowment of assets that gives them advantages in the adoption of new technology-intensive production,[2] the experience of many others, if not most, has been one of a loss of competitiveness of their major economic entities, a decline in 'good jobs' employment, the migration of young, skilled and ambitious workers to more dynamic cities or even countries, declining tax revenues to support infrastructure maintenance and expansion as well as social services, and marginalization. The result is that these cities are characterized by: aging populations, deteriorating physical structures – be it residential, industrial or urban amenity – a loss of collective spirit and hope, and secular decline. The contributors to this book are of the opinion that it is possible for the overwhelming majority of MEIs to chart courses for their future development that will bring them much of the objectives their residents would choose for their city. It is in this spirit that we offer the elements of an economic strategy for a mature industrial economy.

ECONOMIC CHARACTERISTICS OF THE MEI

The debate about the fate of MEIs has been a feature of the discourse about urban areas for the past two decades. Much of the concern about their future was captured in the hearings of the US Senate Committee on Banking, Housing and Urban Affairs (1993) when senators, cabinet secretaries and other experts gave voice to the litany of failures and weaknesses of American cities at that time. Randall Bartlett captured this negative view of the future of US MEIs with his listing of their problems: (1) high crime rates, (2) high rates of poverty, (3) persistent unemployment and mediocre jobs, (4) deteriorating public services, and (5) geographic and social isolation (Bartlett, 1998, ch. 1). This was just over two decades after many of the MEIs experienced urban riots and after some of them were driven to or close to bankruptcy. At about this time I was in Minneapolis and listened to a radio discussion about the situation in that city. The concept being discussed was the 'hole in the doughnut'. Specifically, it was argued that if the per capita income in the center of the city fell to below 60 per cent of that of the ring around it, the city was in danger of a free fall into social pathologies and economic deterioration; the speaker felt that Minneapolis was heading in this direction. Such was the concern about US cities at that time.

More recently urban specialists have discussed the notion of the 'resurgent city', that is, a city that rises out of this deteriorated state into a new era of recovery, prosperity, and economic relevance. Allan Scott (2008, p. 549) sees globalization as 'helping to encourage the growth and spread of cities throughout the world'. Thus, much of his resurgence is taking place in Mumbai, Shanghai, Seoul and other cities in emerging economies, and when he examines this resurgence, presumably in MEIs as well, he finds an 'escalating contrast between its surface glitter and its underlying squalor'. So the resurgence tends to be captured by upper-tier workers rather than by society as a whole. Not a pretty picture.

A cautionary note with regard to the resurgent city is given by Storper and Manville (2006, p. 1269) who suggest that we should not 'see in every downturn a crisis and in every upturn a renaissance'. They urge us to differentiate between the metropolitan area or urban region and the central city itself. 'The revitalized central city needs not just a growing region but also some shift within that region that moves people towards city life.' City life is generally contrasted with rural or suburban life in its richness in 'urban amenities' such as museums, theaters, concert halls, high-scale shopping, restaurants, and major sports facilities – all in close proximity.

One of the major MEIs in the United States that has experienced the negative consequences of economic change is the Commonwealth of Pennsylvania. When Governor Ed Rendell took up his office seven years ago he immediately established the development of the economy of the Commonwealth of Pennsylvania as one of his highest priorities. One of the primary industrial states of the US until the OPEC oil price crisis of the 1970s, Pennsylvania became one of the most negatively affected economies in the Industrial Heartland – shortly thereafter the Rust Belt. Manufacturing jobs and young people with industrial skills continued to flow into other more expansionary regions of the US – the South and the West, of course, but also to other cities that were perceived to have more to offer. The same was true at the other end of the workforce. The Wharton School of Business of the University of Pennsylvania did a study several years ago and discovered that while over 65 per cent of MBA graduates of the Harvard Business School wanted to find employment in the Boston area, the percentage figures for Wharton and Philadelphia were in the mid-30s. Clearly there was something about the Pennsylvania economy that was not attractive either to young or to highly educated workers. Something had to be done.

In 2003 the Brookings Institution was commissioned to conduct a study of the Pennsylvania economy. They focused on 16 urban regions in Pennsylvania and noted, among other things, that the 16 urban regions accounted for 84 per cent of the Commonwealth's population and produced 92.3 per cent of its output. Unfortunately, they also argued, the Commonwealth had for decades overinvested in rural areas and deprived the urban areas of the funds they needed to become competitive in the modern economy. As a consequence of the structure of their study, the rural and agricultural areas of the Commonwealth were not studied. Two years later a second study was commissioned, this time from IBM Consulting Services (2005). This study accepted the notion that clusters are central to regional competitiveness and focused on 11 geographic regions and their strength in four industrial clusters: life sciences, high technology, advanced manufacturing and materials, and business services. While also a very useful study, IBM Consulting Services conceived of the Commonwealth as geographic in its make-up. In the Central region we find State College, Williamsport, Lock Haven, Lewisburg and Bloomsburg – cities for which there is no discernable commonality. What makes this a region other than geography?

It was in this context that the Global Urban Competitiveness Project (GUCP) proposed to the Department of Community and Economic Development that a third study be undertaken – not a better study but rather one that would have a different and distinctive basis to it. The Department accepted this proposal, and the presentations of that research seminar that are printed here are the realization of this initiative. The GUCP is an association of a dozen urban specialists from China, Korea, Mexico, the US, Canada, the UK and Italy.[3] It was proposed that this group should bring its collective understanding of the situation of cities and towns in various parts of the world economy to bear on a set of specific, major problems for the future development of Pennsylvania's cities and towns. While the initial focus was on the economy of Pennsylvania, the issues dealt with and the strategic responses that the GUCP brought to the discussion have relevance to the economic plight of MEIs in all parts of the industrialized world. Therefore, the focus of this book is far more extensive in its application than was the initial research seminar.

Data for 75 US Metropolitan Statistical Areas show that MEIs are 20 of the 26 urban areas with the slowest population growth, 15 of the 20 with the highest percentage of residents aged 65 and older, 14 of the 20 with the highest percentage of employment in manufacturing, half of the 20 with the lowest share of employment in professional, scientific and technical (PST) services, and 17 of the middle 30 with the highest percentage of residents with below poverty level incomes. To be sure many MEIs do not fit this pattern – New York and Baltimore have low employment in manufacturing and, along with Detroit, Bridgeport and Boston, high employment in the PST services; Boston, Balitmore and Minneapolis have low rates of poverty, and Washington, Minneapolis and Columbus have younger populations (Gaquin and DeBrandt, 2007). But for most, this pattern holds.

Pennsylvania, the initial focus of our research seminar, is a populous, slowly growing state with a population that is one of the oldest in the US. The fact that so many of its residents are seniors contributes to the low level of below poverty level individuals, since seniors receive Social Security and many also receive work-related retirement benefits. The Commonwealth is in the middle of US states in household income, the percentage of its population that is African-American and college educated. It has a high number of immigrants, but is below the average of US states when it comes to Hispanic residents and of residents with high school education.

The last decade has been hard on Pennsylvania's manufacturing employment, with 20 per cent fewer jobs in 2007 than in 1997 (Table 1.1). Gains in productivity have resulted in a continuing increase in manufacturing value added and output. In fact, during the recovery from the deindustrialization period following the OPEC petroleum price hikes, during 1986–2000 manufacturing output rose by almost 65 per cent while employment fell by over 10 per cent. Clearly important structural changes were taking place, both within manufacturing and within the workforce.

Pennsylvania has three large Metropolitan Statistical Areas, Philadelphia, Pittsburgh and Allentown-Bethlehem-Easton (A-B-E). Table 1.2 shows how different the three are. Philadelphia has a better educated population with fewer people aged 65 and older than the two other cities. Pittsburgh has less racial diversity, while A-B-E has a large population below the

Table 1.1   Pennsylvania manufacturing employment

1997	826 521
2002	715 453
2007	657 800
2007–1997	−168 721
2007/1997	0.796

Source: *Census of the United States*, Washington: Department of Commerce, various issues.

Table 1.2   Pennsylvania's three largest MSAs are ranked (out of 75 US MSAs)

	Philadelphia	Pittsburgh	Allentown-Bethlehem-Easton
Percentage 65 and older	18	3	6
Population change 2000–2005	60	74	29
Percentage White	37	1	6
Percentage college graduates	25	54	67
Median household income	21	25	65
Percentage of population below poverty level	40	43	73
Manufacturing employment/ total empl.	49	38	20
Empl. PST services/total empl.	13	29	70

Source: Gaquin and DeBrandt (2007).

poverty level, but it is growing more rapidly. Philadelphia is the least reliant on manufacturing and the most on professional–scientific–technical (PST) employment while the reverse is true for A-B-E.

As the above data indicates, Pennsylvania is not the most robust state economy of the United States. During the quarter century of the post-WWII period the Pennsylvania economy was doing deceptively well. However, lack of investment in new technologies in traditional industries such as steel making was slowly eroding the competitiveness of its manu-facturing industry. A variety of programs such as mortgage deductibility and the expansion of the highway transportation system undermined the vitality of large cities such as Philadelphia and Pittsburgh, inducing first residents and then jobs to migrate to suburbs and outlying areas.

Coal declined as a provider of jobs and local revenues and many of these regions found that their major export item had shifted from coal to young people. The *coup de grâce* for much of Pennsylvania's traditional economic strength was the increase in oil prices in 1973 and 1979 that turned the 'industrial heartland' into the 'rust belt'. The collapse of the steel industry in Pittsburgh, Bethlehem and elsewhere occurred fairly rapidly. In Pittsburgh the Homestead Steel Works of US Steel, that had produced more steel during WWII than all of the steel works in Germany plus all of those in Japan, finally closed its doors in 1986. The slow evolution from mighty steel works to derelict mills to shopping malls or vacant contaminated fields began. In finance, bank mergers, the rise of Charlotte, North Carolina as a financial center and the concentration of much of the high-level activity in New York reduced the status of both Philadelphia and Pittsburgh. Furthermore, when Pittsburgh lost Mellon Bank through a merger with the Bank of New York, employment in Pittsburgh increased but the jobs lost were high level managerial jobs and those gained were lower level back-office jobs.

One of the striking consequences of this economic evolution has been the inability of Pennsylvania to retain the thousands of graduates every year from its more than 150 colleges and universities. In addition to the working class young leaving declining coal towns, Pennsylvania has been losing its educated young workers. The Wharton Business School of the University of Pennsylvania referred to above was both a description of an existing situation as well as a clear warning signal with regard to the future of the city.

Recently, however, there have been signs of a reversal of Pennsylvania's fortunes. Philadelphia has emphasized in its economic strategy 'eds' and 'meds', that is, institutions of higher learning and research, and medical technology and health care. In Pittsburgh its two universities have focused their activities on two distinct sectors: Carnegie Mellon University has concentrated on robotics and computer science, and the University of Pittsburgh is gaining recognition as a center for medical technology and health care. There is some evidence that each of these two major cities has been successful in making itself more attractive to highly educated and skilled workers. The same is true of many smaller cities.

The story of Pennsylvania, both its decline during the last quarter of the 20th century and the recovery of some of its major cities, is duplicated in many other MEIs. Each has its own story but each has also been negatively buffeted by the same systemic forces of change.

POLICY OPTIONS FOR MEIs

From this we can see that some of the problems that confront the cities and towns of MEIs include:

- Retention of young workers and college/university graduates.
- Bringing economic vitality to many smaller towns in slow growing or declining regions.
- Introducing effective governance structures so as to mobilize more effectively local resources and talent.
- Refocusing the economic strategic thinking in major cities, as well as other cities and towns toward strategies that will be forward looking and will provide the residents of these cities with the lives they aspire to live.
- All US cities face the challenges of social exclusion, aging and economic deprivation and the challenges for some Pennsylvania cities and towns are more formidable than is the case elsewhere.
- In the current globalized economy all cities must attend to their competitiveness in relation to other cities in which they are in competition for jobs, plant and activity location.
- Technology is in a constant state of advancement and MEIs must continue to show that they have been participating in this exciting world of technology and finding practical employment in the latest technological advances.

Much of this confronts cities and towns everywhere, but Pennsylvania's economic history, its demographic and economic structures, and recent developments that are specific to it make it clear that the Commonwealth and other MEIs must chart their own individual course, one that is based on existing assets, additional assets that it is realistic to think can be put into place, and the aspirations of the residents of these MEI cities. This point is supported by Markusen and Schrock who wrote of the futility of

> try(ing) to match the competition elsewhere in terms of business climate (for example, tax, regulatory structure), subsidies to attract or retain business, or the provision of comparable land or infrastructure. This often-mindless groping for 'best practice' can be attributed in part to . . . the proliferation of economic development consultancies. (2006, p. 1319)

For them the best approach is that of playing to the city's strengths and developing new ones. One important aspect of this is to recognize a dynamic in which skilled workers go to the places with the multiple amenities they find congenial and then firms feel compelled to move there because that is where the workers are. 'Becoming more distinctive may be a survival strategy for an older industrial city. It may not increase overall employment, but it might countervail losses in uncompetitive functions.' Turok (2009, p. 27) endorses this approach and argues that: 'Cities need to develop capabilities for dynamic change that enable steady improvements over time through original analysis, creative thinking, enterprise, initiative, learning, and innovation. They also have to start from their existing position and inherited resources rather than some abstract high-end ideal.'

A rather similar conclusion is reached by Glaeser and Gottlieb (2006) whose research indicated that: 'The success and failure of big cities depends in large part on the urban edge in consumption, not production. Urban decline in the post-war period was caused in large part by changes in technology that made big cities less effective at catering to consumers' preferences' (p. 1297). The key elements in the subsequent resurgence has been declining crime rates and 'rising incomes and education levels which increase demand for urban amenities like museums, restaurants and concerts'. All of these are assets that are uniquely specific to an individual urban area.

Much of recent research on the resurgent city or MEI stresses this need to avoid the 'flavor of the day' and to develop assets that are indigenous to the MEI. There is no single approach or strategy that will work for all MEIs and there is a powerful need for a ground up development of a strategic response to economic distress or decline that is grounded in research done on the local economy, governance and society. The research seminar on Pennsylvania's cities and towns gave the urban specialists of the Global Urban Competitiveness Project the opportunity to bring their knowledge and experience from many countries and cities to bear on these issues of public policy. Specifically, we focused on the following eleven possible economic strategies that we believe should be considered by municipal leaders in MEIs in Pennsylvania and throughout the industrialized world.

1.   Higher Education/Community Partnerships

One of the principal assets of mature industrial economies (MEIs) is their rich endowment of universities and colleges. These higher educational institutions (HEIs) are ubiquitous in their location. Typically the largest universities are located in the MEIs, but smaller often excellent universities and colleges are situated in rural towns of little more than 10 000 inhabitants. In Chapter 2, David Maurrasse informs us that these 'anchored' institutions can form the basis of a local economy that is globally competitive. The key aspect of the relationship between an HEI and the community in which it is located is the creation of an effective 'multi-stakeholder, cross-sector' partnership. This means that the HEI is linked to entities in government, the business community and civil society. This is not an easy thing to initiate and even less easy to maintain in the long run. Maurrasse tells us that direct involvement of the leadership of these institutions is crucial, as is making explicit the mutual benefit that is available for all of the partners. HEIs are characterized by their unique combination of intellectual or knowledge capital, human capital and social capital. The fact that this capital is lodged in an institution that in most cases has been situated in a community for over a century, and is almost guaranteed never to relocate, makes HEIs powerful engines of economic growth. In effect the destinies of the HEI and its community are inexorably intertwined.

The relationships between HEIs and communities have not always been as mutually supportive and positive as Maurrasse argues it can be. Often the HEI and its faculty are focused on teaching and research activities that have little to do with the needs and reality of the local community. However, he argues that in all HEIs there are some faculty, programs/departments and administrators who do find inspiration and satisfaction in work that is tied to the community. Here he finds the kernel of mutual benefit that will create and sustain an effective HEI–community partnership. One such example he found in the University of Pennsylvania and its Anchor Institutions Toolkit for developing effective HEI–community partnerships, and this university's efforts to improve both its relations with, and the economic vitality of, the surrounding community in Philadelphia.

Maurrasse believes that MEIs in the US and other countries can become important laboratories for HEI–community partnership development. Our many HEIs that are located in cities and towns that range from the very competitive and successful centers of health care, consumer services and niche manufacturing to the de-industrialized, declining and abandoned can be mobilized as agents for town revitalization and competitiveness enhancement. The quality of the local environment is an important element in the success of the HEI, so there is a mutually beneficial result of a successful partnership that should be sufficient to mobilize the local resources and talents of all of these communities. Finally, it is argued that this is a propitious time for action since there is now in Washington a new administration that is interested in enlisting a wide array of federal agencies, in addition to the Department of Housing and Urban Development, in the effort to revitalize communities of all sizes.

The analysis of Maurrasse should give inspiration and hope to community leaders in all of the cities and towns in the Commonwealth that host one of the most powerful agents of economic change – one or more universities and colleges.

2. Technological and Cultural Clusters Strategy

It is typical for those who are involved in urban and regional economic development to speak glowingly about the potential for industrial clusters. While we have known about the potential benefits of clusters since Alfred Marshall wrote about them in the 19th century, in practice their impact is often somewhat short of what is promised. In actuality, clusters are organic, living structures that need certain conditions for their flourishing. Some industries are fundamentally uncongenial to them since the local firms are linked only to the parent firm, perhaps hundreds of miles distant, and they have no contact with other firms in the 'cluster'. In some other industries, local firms share a common asset, such as a pool of skilled workers, and have frequent contact with each other. In these latter situations we find true clusters, with all of the benefits of sharing tacit knowledge, common branding and marketing, and formation of working alliances and relationships. How many of the industrial 'clusters' identified in the IBM Consulting Services (2005) study of the Pennsylvania economy are true clusters, in actuality or in potentiality?

Diane-Gabrielle Tremblay examines in Chapter 3 how a strategy of technological and cultural clusters has been implemented and worked in Montreal. The predominant position of this city in the knowledge and innovation sectors of economic activity has its roots in the late 1980s when the provincial government introduced strategic policies to generate a 'technological turning' for its economic activity. This has manifested itself in the expansion of research and production in information-technology and multimedia activity. Today the city has strengths in multi-media, and in film and audiovisual production. In her examination of these clusters, Tremblay emphasizes the importance of consistency in a strategic policy thrust over decades, of supportive intervention by the state at crucial initial periods of development, of 'creating a sense of identity for the industry' and of branding the complex as being linked with the city of Montreal. This is needed for the mobilizing and bringing together of the creative individuals and private investors, and establishing links with the world outside of Montreal.

In many MEIs, the largest metropolitan areas have been developing economic strengths based on the cultural sector, both as a creative activity and in the sense of performance and display that will enhance their competitiveness. For development of clusters in design, fashion, film and audiovisual, video games and so forth, universities, colleges and schools of art are a necessary component of a successful strategic thrust. This suggests that there are many cities and towns, other than just the largest cities, that can be successful in creating clusters in the creative and innovative sectors of economic activity. The experience of Montreal, as detailed by Tremblay, should give inspiration and guidance to local leaders in these municipalities.

3. The Knowledge Base

Given the richness of the endowment of MEIs in institutions of higher learning and research, their cities and towns should have an advantage in developing economies based on the knowledge base and research and innovation. It is true that many MEIs have had difficulty in retaining their university graduates, but this just makes the challenge to local leaders all the clearer. Tax policies, public investment and public sector intervention may work on the supply of factors and on aggregate demand, but knowledge workers seek out congenial environments. These environments include factors such as education, quality of life, information infrastructure, airport connectivity, and access. In Chapter 4, William Lever sees Scotland as a typical MEI and he shows what has been done there to develop knowledge sector clusters and an economy based on research and development, and on knowledge spillovers. He notes that both Scotland and, among other MEIs, Pennsylvania have suffered from low population growth, an aging population, industrial decline and two major metropolitan areas – but also a disproportionate endowment of institutions of higher learning and technology. After decades of decline, now Scotland is experiencing a renaissance of its major urban economies; surely there are lessons here for other MEIs.

Using results from the Master Card World Centers of Commerce database, Lever shows that Philadelphia is ranked 18 of 63 cities throughout the world with regard to its knowledge base and has comparative strength in its medical schools. This is in line with the approach of Philadelphia's city planners of focusing on 'eds and meds', that is, on educational institutions and on medical technology and research. Scotland's policy approach has been to focus on biotechnology and creative media. The success of this focus gives guidance to Pennsylvania's municipal leaders with regard to developing university-based technology clusters and to introducing policies to attract and retain an educated knowledge sector workforce. Lever also shows how local authorities can take charge of their own economic development when the higher levels of government may be engaged in activities that have little to do with local development.

4. Government and Governance

Governance entails the coordination and mobilization of the human resources of an urban region – its people and its institutions – toward the objective of managing and directing the affairs in strategic planning and implementation. Thus governance goes far beyond just the activities of government, and includes the significant institutions of both the public and the private sectors: the firms that produce goods and services, the chamber of commerce, institutions of higher learning, skill development entities, labor unions, social organizations, citizens' committees, and so forth. However, in this world of globalization, restructuring, transition from manufacturing to services, development of local competences and branding it is clear that effective governance is a necessary condition of urban economic development. Effective governance is often an elusive goal in an environment of competing visions, sources of power, diffuse authority, little assessment of performance, and no consequences for failure. Sadly, it is utterly lacking in many of the industrialized countries as well as most of the countries of the Third World.

In Pennsylvania, some have memories of the effectiveness of the direction of some mayors or regional economic development entities. Decades ago when Allegheny County encompassed the municipalities and economic region of greater Pittsburgh, a strong Allegheny County Commissioner was able to accomplish the tasks of effective governance. Today, the regional economy extends beyond the county and many of the component municipalities and planning agencies have their own vision, plan and aspirations. Today most urban regions are like this, and effective governance has arisen as one of the principal challenges to our cities and towns. There are also many other examples of communities in which structures and relationships of effective governance are being put in place.

In Chapter 5, Stefano Mollica, Marco Lucchini and Giovanna Hirsch, uses the experiences of three cities in Italy to offer guidance to those who are charged with developing effective governance in the Commonwealth. Part of the story of these Italian cities is changes in the public administration system of the country. Laws and structures were changed to transfer responsibility and autonomy to local governments, improvement of mechanisms of citizen participation, and separation of the roles of politicians and managers. The other part of the story is actions taken in each of the three cities: Matera, Barletta and Pesaro. From these three examples Mollica et al. derive a set of nine conditions of effective governance.

There is much in the story of these diversely challenged cities that will give guidance to local authorities in MEIs elsewhere.

5.   Economic Structure and Business Organization

Jaime Sobrino in Chapter 6 relates developments in the economic and business activity of Mexico City to its demographic changes since 1980.

While the demographic changes in Mexico City do not parallel those of Pennsylvania, the similarities are important enough to make the experience of that city relevant to the situation of our cities and towns. Many MEIs have either lost population during the past 20 years or it has grown far more slowly than that of the nation or other major cities. Mexico City has seen its population grow but also at a rate that is significantly below that of other metropolitan areas of the country. Both Mexico City and Pennsylvania have also experienced net outward migration.

Population movements are importantly intra-national and have evolved from the rural to urban movements of the 1970s to urban to urban movement, in which neither Mexico City nor Pennsylvania's largest cities have been able to participate beneficially. A final common migratory experience has been significant intra-urban movement, often from the city center to outlying areas of the same city, and in Mexico City to new areas of development; both movements have generated needs for expensive urban transportation infrastructure investments.

In addition to demographic change, Mexico City was powerfully affected by an external event – the passage of the North American Free Trade Area (NAFTA) agreement between Mexico, the US and Canada. Pennsylvania was not significantly affected by NAFTA, although there has been some transfer of production and employment from some areas of Pennsylvania to Mexico since 1995, especially in textiles, manufacturing assembly, and woodworking. It is clear to Sobrino that, in addition to its acknowledged benefits, economic internationalization entails a reliance on external markets that, in a situation such as that which has been experienced throughout the world economy since 2007, also increases a city's vulnerability. This vulnerability can cause all strategic economic planning quickly to become diminished in its practical relevance.

The lack of diffusion of the benefits of NAFTA from the North Frontier area to the rest of the country, noted by Sobrino, makes clear the lack of interaction and linkage among Mexico's regional economies. He finds a similar lack of interaction in business organizations situated in the various regions of Mexico. As in many other MEIs, in Pennsylvania we make much of the divisive role played by the ridges that cut diagonally through the topography of the Commonwealth, the division of areas north and south, or east and west of major interstate highways such as I-80. The creation of a real, functioning sense of a Pennsylvania economy could bring substantial benefits in terms of coordination of initiatives and shared visions of the future. This is inhibited by the fact that local identities have become so powerfully comprehended during the past century or more. Surely, we could do more in this area of public policy.

6. Cooperation and Competition Between Cities

In our open, globalized and rapidly evolving economy cities and urban regions increasingly find themselves in relationships that are either cooperative or competitive in nature. Airport hubs are a good example. Recently, US Air made the business decision to concentrate its international and continental flights in Philadelphia to the detriment of Pittsburgh, which had for decades served as one of the airline's major hubs. In this industry there is room for only two to four such hubs in the United States. Here competition reigns, with a classic winner and loser. In rail transportation, however, for freight and passengers to flow smoothly, quickly and efficiently, cities all along the rail line must cooperate to facilitate the achievement of a common objective. Here Philadelphia and Pittsburgh, with the Pennsylvania Railroad, had a relationship of cooperation; a cooperation that extended to New York, Washington and Chicago. In other industries, firms that have carved out a niche, or have protection through patents or something similar, in effect can function in relative isolation from either competition or cooperation. This is hardly a typical situation.

In Chapter 7, Jianfa Shen uses the experience of two cities in China, Hong Kong and Shenzhen, to show how a relationship of dominance and subordinacy can evolve to one of competition; to one that combines both competition and cooperation. Hong Kong was a dominant economy under British rule but since 1985 Shenzhen has developed rapidly in areas of production that were complementary to Hong Kong but then took on a life of their own. Shen carefully demonstrates how the role of each city has changed since the 1970s and how they now support each other. The areas of cooperation include their two airports, which have had to discover their comparative advantages and to define their individual roles. Direct investment and a shared labor pool are areas in which there has been additional cooperation; however in much of the service sector competition reigns.

Philadelphia has this sort of relationship with regions in New Jersey and Delaware, as well as with New York City and Baltimore in areas such as finance and shipping. Pittsburgh is more linked with contiguous regions in western Pennsylvania. The third metropolitan area, Allentown-Bethlehem-Easton, is a rich area for study of this sort of inter-city dynamic. All towns and cities are in competition with other similar entities, but on a smaller scale we have regions within which relationships of cooperation have been and can be developed. Several of the smaller cities in south-eastern Pennsylvania, such as Lancaser and Reading, the Central Susquehanna Valley, the towns that border on New Jersey, those of the central Northern Tier, and others are all candidates for cooperative ventures in industrial clustering, tourism, joint marketing, and effective use of their universities and colleges, for example.

Shen makes explicit reference to cities and towns in Pennsylvania and concludes his chapter with a discussion of the similarities between them and Hong Kong–Shenzhen, and offers suggestions for us based on his study of these two very successful Chinese cities.

7.   Loss of a Major Industry

The economic history of much of Pennsylvania is dominated by the power of its manufacturing firms, especially those in steel, railroads, metal working and coal, as well as woodworking, textiles and food processing. The years since 1985 have been dominated by the restructuring of this sector. Much of it has been relocated to the US South or to lower labor cost countries in Asia and Latin America; much of the rest of it has been reconstituted with technologies that require less labor and that may have a reduced economic impact on its region. Throughout the 'industrial heartland' cities and towns have been struggling to find a new place for themselves in the new economic space and in the new urban hierarchy. Some cities, such as Chicago, have been marvelously successful, while others, such as Buffalo and Cleveland, are still struggling to accomplish this.

There is perhaps no non-US city that can provide a better lesson for our cities with regard to redesigning itself than Turin, Italy. This city that once was a powerhouse in the production of automobiles and office equipment saw its two dominant firms, FIAT and Olivetti, virtually collapse in a period of two decades. Given the news in the papers and television these days, it is clear that FIAT has made a very impressive turnaround – but what of Turin? Can our cities and towns learn anything from this city's experience with strategic rethinking and planning?

In Chapter 8, Daniele Ietri shows us that Turin can, indeed, demonstrate to our de-industrialized and restructured urban areas that rebirth is possible if local leaders are proactive and are effective in their efforts to reposition their urban economy. Part of the story is events that were part of the response of FIAT and part is the consequence of actions taken by the city itself. What interests us is the story of Turin's planning response. Turin had an early period of recovery dashed by a city-based political corruption scandal that was concentrated on both Turin and Milan. Then in the early 1990s they elected a mayor who was able chart a course for the city and to begin the actions that the major players would have to take. The strategic planning response was threefold: (1) the transformation of the economic functions of the urban space, (2) development of the city's education and innovation assets and potential, and (3) capturing the potential of the

Winter Olympic Games of 2006 and of the city as a cultural district, based on cultural institutions and on local cuisine and the 'slow food' movement. The point is to indicate that the city was able to take stock of its assets and potential and to design a strategic plan to realize their potential benefits.

Ietri takes from this experience two lessons that will be of interest to leaders of all MEIs. The first is the integration of the efforts of all residents from grassroots organizations to the policy elite. The second is the need to make explicit, functioning linkages between the city and the municipalities and firms of the surrounding urban region. In the case of Turin, many of the most innovative and internationally successful firms were in smaller towns in proximity to, but often ignored by, the city. Certainly an audit of the industrial landscape of other MEIs would identify several similar situations.

8.   The Competitiveness of Northeastern US Cities

In an extremely ambitious project, in Chapter 9 Ni Pengfei presents his calculations of the competitiveness of 500 cities throughout the world. Using the resources of the Chinese Academy of Social Sciences, he is able to include data for 144 variables in ten categories of elements of urban competitiveness. Since Ni's report is essentially the presentation of his results, focusing on cities in the Northeastern US, there is no need to put it in a context that shows its relevance to our cities and towns.

Ranking cities in terms of competitiveness, places to retire, centers of IT or some other industrial sector, strength as a learning region, cultural life, and so forth, is something of a growth industry, but none is as comprehensive as is this study by Ni. Two things make this a uniquely valuable exercise in benchmarking. First, is the sophistication and openness of his methodology. Second, is the fact that given his methodology he is able to go beyond the basic ranking to show the relative strengths and weaknesses. This latter aspect makes his study of use to city strategic planners as they are able to go beyond the local perception of a city's assets and potential to a realistic appraisal of what is actually possible.

The cities of the Northeastern US come out very well in this global comparison of urban competitiveness, but those of Pennsylvania are not uniformly so – Philadelphia is ranked 19 but Pittsburgh is 108. It is when nine other individual indices are presented that the cities of Pennsylvania and Northeastern US fall behind in some of the rankings. This suggests that while Northeastern cities are quite competitive overall, each has some areas that are in need of attention.

The full Global Urban Competitiveness Report is a very rich and informative document, and the observations about Northeastern cities of the US put our situation in the broad context of competitiveness beyond the region or the continent that is so necessary in today's economy.

9. Industrial Tourism Opportunities for City and Enterprise

As is the case with most MEIs, Pennsylvania has both a history and a present that are rich in firms and industries that produce goods and services, and use processes of production that are of great interest to the residents of the Commonwealth, and to others as well. In Chapter 10, Leo van den Berg et al. provide us with examples of what has been done in four industrial locations in Europe and one in China to develop industrial sites into attractive opportunities for industrial tourism. These are quite varied in nature and include the Volkswagen headquarters in Wolfsburg, Germany; industrial input firms in Cologne, Germany; Aurora pens in Turin, Italy; food processing in Pays de la Loire, France; port-related activities and food processing in Rotterdam, the Netherlands; and steel factories and creative business parks in Shanghai, China. This suggests that almost any industry is a candidate for beneficial industrial tourism.

The past is replete with examples of industries that dominated our past, such as steel and other manufacturing sites, coal-mining villages, various sites of railroad activity, as well as agricultural production. Some of these sites are already being developed and marketed as sites of industrial tourism. The most prominent such site in Pennsylvania is, of course, the Hershey Chocolate Company that began with tours through the actual production facility and now consists of tours through an exhibition center that depicts and explains all of the stages in the production of its chocolate products.

Van den Berg et al. show that industrial tourism is of benefit to both the region and to the company, if production is still active. The firm is able to display the qualities of its product it wants the consuming public to know, it helps to build brand familiarity and loyalty, and it may make industrial tourists less critical or more supportive in its relations with government. The urban region is able to gain tourism revenues, but of equal importance it is able to present a favorable image of itself – branding. Examples given include the aligning of Turin with excellence and Pays de la Loire with economic discovery.

The study done of the Pennsylvania economy by IBM Consulting Services (2005) mapped out the strengths of 11 of the state's regions in life sciences, high technology, advanced manufacturing and materials, and business services. These 11 regions include all counties of the Commonwealth and explicitly suggest opportunities for industrial tourism just in these four areas of the innovative sectors of the economy of the future. In addition to the industries of the future, so to speak, there are many traditional industries, such as 'metal-bending', agricultural processing, inter-modal transportation and port activity, woodworking, and furniture. Finally, most of the Commonwealth's universities and colleges have a long experience with campus tours, presentations with regard to what takes place in typical classrooms, interviews with professors, administrators and students. In some way the institutions of higher learning are models for industrial tourism and their experiences and knowledge could be of great benefit to the cities of and towns of MEIs and to their firms as they initiate their own programs of industrial tourism.

10. An Aging Population

As the introductory chapter tells us, Pennsylvania is the state with the 6th highest percentage of residents who are above the age of 65; projections suggest that the aging phenomenon will, along with urbanization, be one of the dominant features of the global economy during the next 40 years. Starting from such a high base, Pennsylvania is certain to be confronted with the fiscal, labor market, social and economic consequences of its aging population to a powerful degree. Aging presents government with impending burdens for retirement income, health care and long-term care; while these are serious problems, they are largely problems that must be met at the level of the national and state governments. Cities will have concerns about their own employees and some facilities that they will have to see are built, but their problems are lesser than they are for other levels of government. In fact, as Peter Karl Kresl argues in Chapter 11, there are significant benefits that can be gained by city governments – if they plan properly.

Kresl sees seniors as behaving differently in the years to come due to their economic and social characteristics – healthier, wealthier, better educated and more mobile. What he expects a significant percentage of them to do is: (1) move from rural and suburban areas into a university town or the center of a major city; (2) devote time and money to lifelong learning (intellectual activities) and (3) participate in cultural and arts sector activities and provide financial support for these institutions. Each of these activities will bring important benefits to the economies of cities and towns.

Most MEIs, as well as smaller college or university towns, have the potential to attract the sorts of seniors who can bring these positive economic benefits. The challenge is to ensure there is a sufficient supply of the desired urban amenities to be attractive to these seniors, and then to do effective marketing of their attributes. Upon retirement many seniors are very mobile and there is no reason why our towns and cities should not be attractive to them. Many towns may lack world-class cultural and other amenities, but those in the eastern third of the Commonwealth are within two or three hours of New York, Philadelphia, Baltimore and Washington.

Given that the demographic changes are the result of actions that have been taken years or decades ago, this phenomenon and its consequences are certain to have their impacts. Local officials in our cities and towns can do much to ensure that their net effects are less negative than they need be and in many cases can actually be positive.

11. Urban Regions in a Global Economy

The final chapter in this book is an analysis of urban regions and their place in the global economy that is very rich in its implications for Pennsylvania's cities and towns. Saskia Sassen discusses the notion of an urban region with particular reference to its scale, that is, how extensive is the spatial reach of this type of entity? Similar to Daniele Ietri in his discussion of Turin and its place in the economic space of northwestern Italy, Sassen links the firms in a specific city to broader spaces that extend, in some cases, to the world economy. But Sassen argues that a firm operating in a mega region might find that it contains areas with the lower costs of operation they now find overseas; this would bring the added advantage of lower transport costs, which could then be a trade-off enabling regulations that prevent race-to-the-bottom wages. This possibility depends upon the specific activities of a firm.

During the recent past the forces of globalization have promoted an allocation of tasks that extends from the head office of the firm to affiliates located on other continents in which each office performs some task in a location that is optimally suited to it. This has led to the de-industrialization of traditional industrial economies, such as that of much of Pennsylvania. Porter's work on the competitiveness of the inner city and the recent increases in fuel prices both suggest that this division of labor will not be sustainable in the future. The consequence is that firms will have incentives to bring tasks back from low-wage Third World sites to lagging towns and districts that are in close proximity to the headquarters or main production site. This bodes well for towns in Pennsylvania that have suffered from loss of manufacturing jobs but which still have certain advantages such as a moderately skilled or trainable workforce, access to good truck or rail transportation, proximity to production centers of the firm, familiar legal and regulatory systems, and so forth. Both Philadelphia and Pittsburgh are such centers and beneficial relationships between them and nearby towns in the Commonwealth could be explored.

These relationships would be part of a mega region, the structure that Sassen argues is becoming dominant, along with global cities, throughout the contemporary global economy. A mega region would be more extensive than, say, Philadelphia, and could encompass the entire Boston–Washington belt. There would be major cities with global reach as well as many underdeveloped communities. Within this mega region Philadelphia could create a niche for itself, one that would also accommodate places for many of our smaller towns and cities.

The example of Chicago is argued by Sassen to offer an illustration to other cities with industrial pasts. Chicago was late to the knowledge economy that is so crucial to today's economy, but it built a modern globally important urban economy that was based on legal, financial, trading and transportation assets and talents that were developed for its agro-industrial economy of trading and production. Philadelphia and Pittsburgh have developed assets and talents in the agro-industrial economy that was developed in the 19th century. Cities such as Buenos Aires have remade themselves after an event such as national bankruptcy. Other cities such as Detroit and many of the English manufacturing cities have failed to make the transition. Sassen finds that Detroit did not succeed in this process because it was basically dominated by one major industry – auto manufacturing: this led to a largely vertically integrated sector rather than the multiple distinct sectors and the complexities this entails we find in other major industrial cities. For Chicago its industrial past was a crucial part of its transition and the complexity of that past economy allowed it to extract multiple forms of specialized knowledge.

In essence, Sassen tells us that in the advanced knowledge economies of today and the future there will always be a 'vast array of low-wage jobs, low-profit and low-tech firms and under-resourced economic spaces . . . but the objective has to be upgrading those jobs, firms and spaces'. This is an instructive and optimistic vision with which it is appropriate to conclude this book.

NOTES

1. For the down side see Balchin et al. (2000) and Bartlett (1998).
2. Two classic positive views are Markusen (1996) and Porter (1995).
3. See: <www.gucp.org.cn>.

REFERENCES

Balchin, Paul N., David Isaac and Jean Chen (2000), *Urban Economics: A Global Perspective*, London: Palgrave, chapters 1 and 2.

Bartlett, Randall (1998), *The Crisis of America's Cities*, London: M.E. Sharpe.

Brookings Institution Center on Urban and Metropolitan Policy (2003), *Back to Prosperity: A Competitive Agenda for Renewing Pennsylvania*, Washington, DC.

Gaquin, Deirdre A. and Katherine A. DeBrandt (eds) (2007), *2007 County and City Extra, 15th Edition*, Lanham, MD: Bernan Press.

Glaeser, Edward L. and Joshua D. Gottlieb (2006), 'Urban Resurgence and the Consumer City', *Urban Studies*, Vol. 43, No. 8 (July), pp. 1275–99.

IBM Consulting Services (2005), *Action Plan for Investing in a New Pennsylvania – Identifying Opportunities for Pennsylvania to Compete in the Global Economy*, Harrisburg, PA: Department of Community and Economic Development.

Markusen, Ann (1996), 'Sticky Places in Slippery Space: A Typology of Industrial Districts', *Economic Geography*, Vol. 72, No. 3 (July), pp. 294–310.

Markusen, Ann and Greg Schrock (2006), 'The Distinctive City: Divergent Patterns in Growth, Hierarchy and Specialisation', *Urban Studies*, Vol. 43, No. 8 (July), pp. 1301–23.

Porter, Michael (1995), 'The Competitive Advantage of the Inner City', *Harvard Business Review*, May/June, pp. 55–72.

Scott, Allan J. (2008), 'Resurgent Metropolis: Economy, Society and Urbanization in an Interconnected World', *International Journal of Urban and Regional Research*, Vol. 32, No. 3 (September), pp. 548–64.

Storper, Michael and Michael Manville, 'Behaviour, Preferences and Cities: Urban Theory and Urban Resurgence', *Urban Studies*, Vol. 43, No. 8 (July), pp. 1247–74.

Turok, Ivan (2009), 'The Distinctive City: Pitfalls in the Pursuit of Differential Advantage', *Environment and Planning A*, Vol. 41, pp. 13–30.

US Senate Committee on Banking, Housing and Urban Affairs (1993), *The State of Urban America*, Hearings, April, Washington, DC.

2. Global competitiveness and the role of higher education/community partnerships

David J. Maurrasse

In these complex and volatile times, it is increasingly important that cities and towns consider their global competitiveness. As industries and economies continually shift, and boundaries gradually wither across the globe, the market in which cities and towns are situated is both global and dynamic. How can cities and towns find some semblance of stability within an unstable context? And, how can cities and towns take the greatest advantage of their assets in order to compete internationally? What kinds of markets and industries best suit cities and towns, as they seek comparative advantages against cities and towns around the world?

LOCALITIES INTO THE FUTURE

Marga Incorporated,[1] a New York-based consulting firm, advises on the creation and strengthening of strategic paths to community and economic development. Many of these paths are taking form in multi-stakeholder, cross-sector partnerships. These efforts tap a combination of public and private resources in collaborative efforts to address any number of local concerns. The complex and expensive reality of today leaves municipalities unable to succeed alone. Subsequently, these strategic partnerships are necessary for cities and towns to survive and/or thrive. Silicon Valley, for example, could not have emerged in Northern California without the alignment of government, business, higher education, and civil society. The global competitiveness and impact of that region was aided by the creative harnessing of resources in multiple sectors.

Additionally, partnerships of this sort are not only necessary for creating and strengthening industries, they are also essential for improving social infrastructure and meeting community needs. No city, town, or region can sustain vitality without the ongoing livability of its people. Critical issues facing civil society, from education to health to economic standing, all require collaborative effort that strategically leverages local assets.

Subsequently, in order for cities and towns to bring about economic and social success over time, partnerships across sectors are necessary. As municipalities assess their potential to effectively tap local resources to strengthen their opportunities, it is critical to consider the value of anchor institutions – institutions with longstanding vested interests in their geographical settings. Indeed, the landscape of anchor institutions has shifted significantly in recent years, moving from grounded manufacturing capital to mobile knowledge capital.

In numerous environments, long-term geographic commitments are increasingly scarce, as industries are more able to spread their influence, operate out of numerous settings, transmit boundless information, produce through technology, and pursue the cheapest possible labor and operating costs in any part of the world. Cities and towns that have historically relied on a manufacturing base have experienced intense capital flight. Institutions that have lasted have tended to be universities, hospitals, and museums. These institutions have proven to be 'anchored' in that they have been 'sticky capital' that remains while other industries flow in and out like tides.[2]

Marga Incorporated has been developing a tool to assist municipalities in assessing their assets and successfully leveraging them to increase their competitiveness and vitality. In imagining which types of stakeholders and institutions are essential to effective partnerships, a number of possibilities come to mind. However, it appears that government, institutions of higher education, the corporate sector, private philanthropy, and civil society organizations can, combined, bring an effective package to any range of needs in cities, towns, and regions.

Living Cities[3] recently commissioned Marga to visit and analyze a number of citywide partnerships in urban areas throughout the United States. For the most part, these sites combine these elements, which can be found in any major city and in numerous smaller towns as well. Partnerships of this sort, such as STRIVE[4] in Cincinnati, have taken the pains to create an unprecedented table at which local leaders across the sector, who have previously maintained only polite and cursory relations, forged a joint strategy to improve educational attainment in their region.

Undoubtedly, a widely educated populace enhances the global competitiveness of any municipality or region in today's rapidly shifting knowledge economy. The competencies of those who can be successful in an advanced knowledge economy are those who can analyze, innovate, and communicate – all characteristics heavily correlated with educational attainment. Nevertheless, while STRIVE and numerous urban collaborations in other areas identify the need for partnerships' and bridge initial boundaries to initiate collaboration, sustaining these efforts over time becomes challenging and costly.

THE WORKINGS OF PARTNERSHIPS

Partnerships are new formations in themselves, with specific aims and, ultimately, particular governing structures. Partnerships cannot merely form and achieve success. Patterns have emerged with multi-stakeholder and multi-institutional partnerships. They tend to gather groups that have not worked together in depth previously. These new formations discover common needs and mutual interests over time, but often not readily. Building trust and communication could span a lengthy period.

Working across sectors means different modes and cultures of operating must find a common way of working together. Corporations may want to move quickly and government might emphasize bureaucracy and due diligence, for example. Because partnerships create new work, they require unique attention. Some partnerships are embodied in new organizations or housed in existing ones.

The development of infrastructure to support such partnerships requires funding. Early enthusiasm among partners might keep a partnership going in the beginning, but over time, each stakeholder's primary priorities may take over. The need for additional funding to keep the partnership going could create a strain on all partners involved and wither the will to continue.

No one perfect formula has emerged on the partnership landscape; every locality has its unique history and ways of doing business. However, some characteristics of effective partnerships have emerged. First of all, the direct involvement of leadership among partners tends to ensure that partnerships remain a priority to those involved. Inside of the respective institutional partners, the commitment of leadership to a partnership sends a message, suggesting the institution's participation in the partnership is critical to core institutional interests.

Partnerships are more likely to succeed when the mutual benefit of partners is apparent and addressed. The self-interest of institutions should converge with the broad interests of a partnership. If key institutional needs are not met through a partnership, involvement in the collaboration will serve only ancillary interests. Because partnerships create additional costs, and require new infrastructure, new resources are required. The involvement of philanthropic institutions and other forms of flexible private capital can be the difference between the success and failure of a partnership.

THE UNIQUE POTENTIAL OF HIGHER EDUCATION IN PARTNERSHIPS

Institutions of higher education play a particularly critical role in their localities. They bring a combination of resources unlike any other institutional asset. Colleges and universities bring *intellectual* or *knowledge capital*. Comprehensive institutions of higher education contain expertise in multiple fields of interest, providing a base of information and thinking that can be applied to virtually any need. This intellectual capital can be tapped and aligned to support or strengthen industries, solve social problems, or increase awareness around any number of areas. Applied research projects can open doors to collaborative opportunities and enhance the practical relevance of scholarship. Academic writing and analysis can increase understanding around social, political, economic, scientific, and human phenomena. Technical and community colleges bring focused expertise and training that can develop jobs, careers, and industries.

Additionally, institutions of higher education bring *human capital*. Students, faculty and staff are very present in the localities in which colleges and universities reside. They often live in or near campuses, bringing resources and vitality. Stakeholders at institutions of higher education tend to spend locally, circulating localized monetary activity and infusing economies with a steady base of resources. Students, faculty, and staff often contribute volunteer time in communities. The rise and evolution of service learning has demonstrated the appetite for civic engagement among young people, who are sometimes eager to be involved. Students can become interns and employees in their surroundings. Businesses often consider the presence of institutions of higher education when they assess location options, cognizant of the human capital benefits they can attain through prospective interns and employees, not to mention culture and character in neighborhood living, as higher education stakeholders can keep restaurants, the performing arts, museums, cafes, and other industries thriving.

Institutions of higher education also bring *social capital*. The voice of university faculty and their research can bring legitimacy and a sense of neutrality to commentary on and analysis of contemporary challenges. This kind of viewpoint is poised to influence policy, strengthen the claims or intentions of community-based organizations, and inform the public. As institutions, colleges and universities can be important conveners – able to bring various parties to the table. Being seen as spaces through which knowledge and data can be produced, disseminated, and explored, institutions of higher education can help others transcend boundaries, ideologies, and partisanship in order to focus on the issues at hand.

Finally, one key, often overlooked, added value of institutions of higher education is *economic capital*. Colleges and universities are economic engines in their localities.

INSTITUTIONS OF HIGHER EDUCATION AS ECONOMIC ENGINES

Particularly in traditionally industrial environments like Pennsylvania, the transition to a knowledge-oriented economy has shifted the balance of local economics. Whereas factories were once the core of localities and regions, providing employment and thereby stimulating tax bases, other institutions have to fill the void now that so many of those manufacturing-oriented resources have dissolved or departed. In many localities and regions in states such as Pennsylvania, the new 'anchor institutions' are the entities that never went away. Colleges and universities are among such institutions. Through many decades and even centuries, these institutions have remained grounded in their settings.

Additionally, with the growth in certain knowledge sectors, institutions of higher education have grown, requiring new resources, new grounds, new buildings, and thus new jobs. Anchor institutions like universities and hospitals are among the highest local employers in so many cities and regions, providing the kind of stability that was once almost entirely associated with large manufacturing corporations.

With expansion comes procurement, as institutions of higher education contract with local businesses. There is no guarantee that institutions of higher education will procure and hire locally, but they are committed to their localities, making it inevitable that agreements with employees and contractors will benefit the immediate surroundings. While online learning has gradually expanded, and numerous students commute to campuses, the culture of colleges and universities is still quite local and residential. Employees and contractors and students and guests tend to purchase local goods and services. Local restaurants, cafes and other establishments tend to be part and parcel of campus/community life. Not only does this vibrancy attract and engage stakeholders in higher education, but it tends to bring in others from elsewhere. College or university towns, when they are at their most vibrant, are destinations in themselves.

The economic ripple effects of institutions of higher education can be

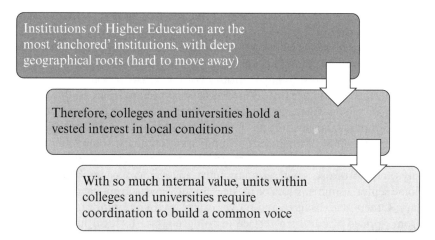

Institutions of Higher Education are the most 'anchored' institutions, with deep geographical roots (hard to move away)

Therefore, colleges and universities hold a vested interest in local conditions

With so much internal value, units within colleges and universities require coordination to build a common voice

Source: Created by Marga Incorporated.

Figure 2.1   Other relevant characteristics of higher education

quite extensive. The knowledge produced in colleges and universities informs innovation and entrepreneurship, as we have seen in northern California. Particularly in a knowledge economy, the resources and thinking present and nurtured in higher education spawns a wide range of new business opportunities that can not only stimulate host towns and regions, but resonate nationally and globally. National and global attention can only further enhance the attractiveness of the combination of particular institutions of higher education and their localities. Imagine Ann Arbor, Michigan without the University of Michigan.

The potentially tremendous economic catalyzing endemic in the pursuits of institutions of higher education can revitalize many miles of life and land. However, the ripple effects (see Figure 2.1) of higher educational growth can devastate populations that are not positioned to take advantage of certain advancements. Lower income communities often maintain tense relations with local institutions of higher education. Some colleges and universities have been continually cognizant of the economic conundrum of growing for a few to leave behind many, however, quite a number have not.

As, somewhat proudly, decentralized institutions, colleges and universities are hardly monolithic. Certain units on any campus might view their role as integrated with local interests and priorities, while others might take more of an 'ivory tower' approach to insular research and teaching without outside interference. The common interests between institutions of higher education and their surroundings are often very palpable. It is difficult for any institution to recruit students, faculty, or staff without being able to present and sell a full experience, which, ultimately, includes the relative vitality of the host town. The health of a surrounding town is continually of interest to any institution of higher education.

Nevertheless, this reality is not necessarily shared across the board within any given college or university. The town is never fully appreciated on a campus. If an institution of higher education is going to engage its town to the point of alignment around common goals, some attempts to strive for consensus must be pursued within any given college or university. Some professors will see community engagement as unscholarly, and some senior administrators or trustees might view such endeavors as ancillary. Others will disagree and move forward with any range of initiatives from applied research to service learning courses to local hiring provisions. Diversity in thought is fundamental in higher education. However, if colleges or universities can benefit from coordinated strategies with local stakeholders, then dialogue among internal constituents could be helpful. Some collective buy-in among internal stakeholders around the nature and scope of joint strategies with external parties could go far in sustaining mutually beneficial pursuits. The challenges presented by attempts to coordinate and legitimize attempts to expand community engagement within colleges or universities are well documented.

TAPPING THE RESOURCES AND INTERESTS OF HIGHER EDUCATION

Partnerships are necessary, but difficult. As the experiences of higher education/community partnerships illustrate, only deep communication and trust building can lead to mutually beneficial results. Colleges and universities have operated relatively independently of community voices over the years despite the mutually beneficial opportunities that can be attained (see Figure 2.2). In the short run, it is easier to operate alone; to plow ahead with an agenda and hope others fall in line. In the long run, however, collaborative pursuits bring greater benefit.

It is certainly not in the best interest of surrounding communities to merely follow the wishes of institutions of higher education even if they depart from theirs. Similarly, it is not in the best interest of institutions of higher education to be despised locally. As the experience of the University of Pennsylvania has reminded us, a climate of resentment in the local community creates an unpleasant experience for college and university stakeholders. This institution's story is an interesting case in turning

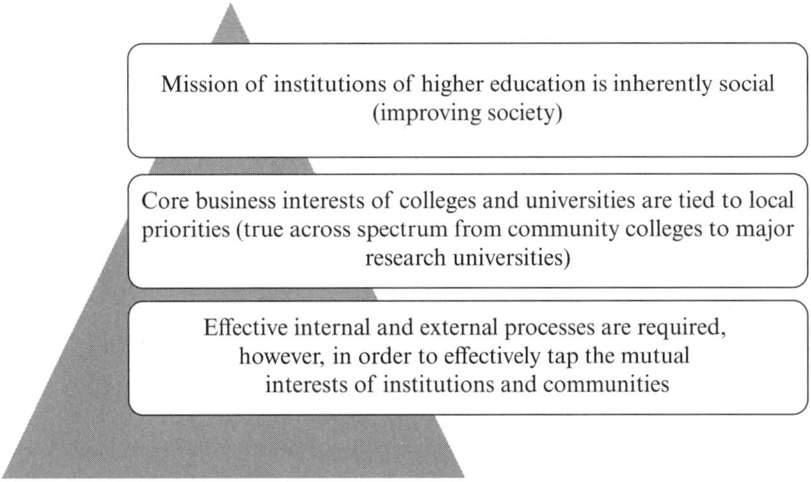

Mission of institutions of higher education is inherently social (improving society)

Core business interests of colleges and universities are tied to local priorities (true across spectrum from community colleges to major research universities)

Effective internal and external processes are required, however, in order to effectively tap the mutual interests of institutions and communities

Source: Created by Marga Incorporated.

Figure 2.2   Inherent convergence of local and higher education interests

a community that was perceived as a liability into more of a partner. This turnaround did not diminish the prestige of the institution; in fact, it strengthened it, and bolstered the neighborhood and city. The destinies of localities and institutions of higher education are intertwined.

The daily pains of partnerships are investments in the future. The institution of higher education that is willing to enter into difficult dialogue with a local school system, for example, can plant the seeds for a stronger municipality and region and institution. Undoubtedly, family locating choices are influenced by the conditions of schools. If schools are insufficient, families will not want to raise children in the area. If faculty and staff are being recruited by an institution, factors like the conditions of schools will be assessed. Safety will be assessed, as well as vibrancy and culture, air quality and housing, and opportunity. If numerous indicators of effective local environments are assessed in location options, then a college or university has a vested interest in improving upon those indicators as much as possible.

But, again, it is always important to remain aware of the combination of people and place. Too often, local higher education development strategies tend to emphasize improving the place for the sake of their people rather than improving the place and its people. Physical development strategies can go only so far when they are not complemented by significant attention to human development (see Figure 2.3).

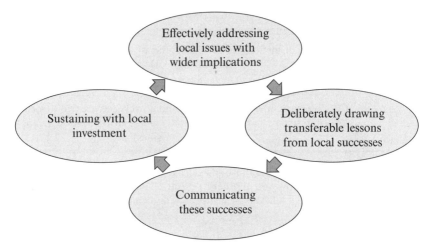

Source: Created by Marga Incorporated.

Figure 2.3   Local effectiveness and wider value

In thinking about how to stimulate sweeping change that encourages and strengthens mutually beneficial higher education/community partnerships, examples that demonstrate what is possible can be instructive to other environments. Great examples of successful higher education/community partnerships that are not communicated to broader audiences do not achieve their full potential. Due to the complexity of colleges or universities and the communities in which they are situated, genuinely successful partnerships are rare. Indeed, collaborations between particular units or classes and external parties are numerous, but comprehensive partnerships that reflect shared agendas across wider communities and significant cross-sections of institutions with the support of leaderships seldom appear. Subsequently, when exemplary partnerships emerge, it is important to tell the story. The University of Pennsylvania happens to be one such example; this institution was quite aware of the power of its story, most recently told in the *Anchor Institutions Toolkit.* This guide not only captures the peaks and valleys and milestones of the pathway to partnership, but it provides practical guidance to other institutions with similar goals.

When these examples of success are highlighted, the public is more aware of the potential of higher education/community partnerships, which do not necessarily share a glowing reputation. Higher education/community partnerships are often viewed as heavily driven by institutions, and highly self-serving. When examples transcend these characteristics, everyone has a better sense of what is possible. Because the global competitiveness of cities can be positively influenced by effective higher education/community partnerships, it is important to help localities throughout the world enhance their capacity to strengthen collaboration between colleges or universities and stakeholders in their localities and regions.

In imagining what others can learn from particular local examples, a continually arising challenge is the applicability of experiences in one environment to another. How can what works in Philadelphia influence anywhere else? Transferring lessons from one environment to the next is hardly automatic, but portable lessons can be extracted. Deliberate thinking about what can be instructive from one environment to the next can be an important strategic component in figuring out how to maximize the value of localized successes for broader purposes.

OPPORTUNITIES ON THE HORIZON

In the United States, the emergence of a new Federal Administration and the increased demand from states has created a complex yet vibrant dialogue about the bounds of higher education. Globally, a wider consensus around the significance of higher education to a knowledge economy is taking form. Whereas the United States was the dominant nation in producing postsecondary graduates, numerous countries have surpassed the United States in this respect.

Since, on the whole, the twenty-first century socioeconomic landscape requires exceptional analytic ability, adaptability, technical knowhow and overall literacy, greater exposure to higher education can position populations to advance more rapidly. Subsequently, national competitiveness in the global sphere is dependent upon institutions of higher education. This reality extends to the relative global competitiveness of localities and regions. Regardless of the nation in which a locality or region is situated, the globalized economy and society requires a degree of international linkage. In other words, what does a locality uniquely contribute to a global economy and society? Since markets are global, localities and regions have become more interdependent in the wider world than ever.

In the United States, local governments, states in particular, set a great deal of the policies that govern the lives of their citizens. Many of these states, however, have been underfinanced and differentially financed due to widely varied taxation. One area where resource limitations have been quite apparent is the financing of higher education. Moreover, in order for institutions of higher education to justify their continued levels of funding, they are required to demonstrate local relevance. This includes the application of knowledge to local challenges. While higher education spent much of the twentieth century strengthening its insular ability to produce and exchange knowledge, the more contemporary pressures are expecting institutions of higher education to engage externally.

While the curious interface between higher education and states might present challenges to colleges and universities to do more with less and change their modes of operating, this dynamic is a function of global shifts and demands. Institutions of higher education are expected to contribute to the global competitiveness of their localities and regions. And, in fact, they already do. From the revitalization of towns to the education of citizens who live and work in these localities to research with local and global implications, colleges and universities have continued to be engines of development and knowledge. However, now and into the future, the expectations are even higher, as colleges and universities are uniquely situated in a globalized and knowledge-driven society and economy.

As a new Federal Administration in the United States ambitiously attempts to simultaneously address a range of matters in complicated times within a short period, the role of higher education is very much in the dialogue. The President and First Lady have both expressed their interest in seeing greater engagement among institutions of higher education. Overall, the interest in civic engagement is quite high in this Administration, as exemplified in the new White House Office on Social Innovation and Civic Engagement.

Those who have advocated for greater Federal incentives for institutions of higher education to apply their research, involve their students, and more deliberately connect their resources to local economies are keenly aware of the new opportunities that have arisen with the advent of this new Administration. The Coalition for Urban Serving Universities, for example, recently emerged out of the common desire among leaders in public urban universities to raise awareness and funds in relation to the involvement of their institutions in localities and regions. This formation has designed comprehensive policy proposals that are currently circulating in the Administration. Additionally, the University of Pennsylvania convened a task force of experts to pose recommendations to the Department of Housing and Urban Development (HUD) around their inclusion of 'anchor institutions' in their agenda.[5]

This paper recommended HUD revive its Community Outreach Partnership Centers program from the Office of University Partnerships. This program had been providing numerous grants to colleges and universities to apply research and knowledge to solve problems in these institutions' localities. These grants not only strengthened the resources and support for local community partnerships and particular institutions of higher education, they created a field of advocates from institutions and neighborhoods nationwide. The annual meetings of these grantee institutions and their community partners connected those with mutual interests from across the United States, and began to craft a unified voice around the characteristics of effective partnerships.

The Association for Community and Higher Education Partnerships emerged out of these meetings. This formation promoted effective partnerships and provided technical assistance to strengthen various attempts to tap resources in higher education to transform communities.[6] As this Association dissolved and the grant program at HUD dissipated, momentum had been lost. Nevertheless, so many of those who have revived the discussion in more recent efforts were connected to these earlier efforts. The seeds had been sown for a new era of leaders in higher education, who have been explicitly highlighting the service or engagement aspects of their institutions' missions.

We are witnessing a convergence of those who have been practicing and promoting greater civic engagement in higher education with the interests of a new Administration, creating a unique opportunity to transform the very conception of higher education for these times. Interagency cooperation was one of the key themes in the recent report to HUD by the University of Pennsylvania's task force. As government re-imagines itself under President Obama's call for 'change', a key prerequisite will be the practice of policy formation and implementation. The kinds of social challenges in this complex world do not fit neatly in the pre-existing structure of Federal Agencies. For example, health and education may be distinct societal concerns, but they are quite intertwined when viewing indicators of health outcomes or educational attainment.

The harnessing of resources in higher education to improve society is hardly a HUD concern or the domain of the Department of Education. All Federal Agencies should view the ways in which they engage higher education. The National Science Foundation, for example, in recent years, seeks direct impact from its research grants to colleges and universities. In their view, it is not enough to fund studies that return interesting findings. For this agency, the breadth of relevance of research to society has to be explored. Indeed, great potential rests in any wide range of studies, which have not been tested for their application. Between research that has yet to be applied, student learning not challenged to connect to real social concerns, and physical and economic resources yet to be harnessed for growth, institutions of higher education are sleeping giants.

It only makes sense that Federal and local policies are poised to move in step with the latest chapter in higher education's evolution. Additionally, private wealth and philanthropy stand to gain from greater alignment with higher education and relevant policies. Because colleges and universities contain extensive resources that can be leveraged to take on key issues, philanthropic dollars can go far with appropriate partnerships with institutions of higher education. However, colleges and universities have not always been good stewards of private dollars intending to be applied in mutually beneficial partnerships with communities. The way of doing business in higher education tends to take grants for research, leading to written findings and analysis consumed by peer academics. The reward system in higher education is tied to this paradigm.

Incentives in higher education have generally not been aligned with the value of research to solving problems in localities and regions. Subsequently, external dollars and policies geared toward the practical application of higher educational resources must be explicit and even vigilant in encouraging a cultural shift. While colleges and universities have been slow to change historically, external incentives have been critical drivers in encouraging shifts in the ways in which institutions of higher education do business.

To this day, applied research, teaching, and learning can be dismissed as unscholarly in some circles. However, the wider context of the varied social demands on higher education is designing a more urgent scenario. If higher education does not change to adapt to altered societal demands, these external demands still stand to change higher education. It is in higher education's interest to demonstrate greater willingness to engage. Proactively, examples of effective higher education/community partnerships should be highlighted and analyzed for their ingredients of success. It is critical to demonstrate what is possible.

Philanthropic investments can catalyze models of effective local practice that could be instructive in other environments. Alliance between institutions of higher education, external local stakeholders, and local philanthropists such as community foundations can create unique mutually beneficial partnerships. When these efforts can demonstrate progress their learning can be consumed by others in order to inform how such collaborative pursuits can achieve greater success. The University of Pennsylvania's toolkit is a good example of an actual teaching tool that is based on the success of a local partnership in order to educate others with similar desires.

OPPORTUNITY FOR PENNSYLVANIA

With numerous institutions of higher education in both urban and rural areas, and a history of civic engagement infused into the philosophy of the state and its colleges and universities, Pennsylvania appears uniquely positioned for leadership in demonstrating the potential of instructive models of economic and community development. The urban model of the University of Pennsylvania has become well known, as representatives from institutions around the country and world continue to visit and seek greater understanding of how the University and West Philadelphia simultaneously grew and strengthened.

As in most states, the wider swaths of land are in rural areas. Increasingly, the rural model of development is one that is more regional than local. Pennsylvania's Keystone Innovation Zone program enables multi-stakeholder partnerships in regions that deliberately leverage the resources of major anchor institutions like universities and hospitals.

While much of the contemporary energy around the civic engagement of higher education has been urban in orientation, the concept of higher education extending its resources for local benefit has rural roots. The Land Grant College Extension Programs that emerged from the 1860s through the Morrill Act continue to function. However, higher education and society have evolved around this effort. The community college system emerged, providing vocational education and building skills in both rural and urban areas. Moreover, the United States and much of the world has become more urban.

On the one hand, the need for an urban Land Grant concept is evident. On the other, a common contemporary understanding around appropriate forms of local engagement for rural institutions of higher education has not been adequately designed. Work is required around both the urban and rural engagement of higher education. In rural areas, the Extension concept requires a more thorough review under the lens of current application and relevance. Additionally, numerous private colleges and universities have emerged in such areas over the last couple of centuries; this is very much the case in Pennsylvania. Small private colleges have garnered capital by emphasizing self-contained safe spaces for learning. However, the economic significance of such colleges to their surrounding towns and regions has become more apparent. In these areas where steel mills and other manufacturing industries flourished, the critical remaining resources are in hospitals, institutions of higher education, and government agencies. These are the places that bring employment, business contracts, local innovations and entrepreneurs, not to mention culture and vitality.

With a blend of urban and rural, public and private institutions of higher education, Pennsylvania can become an important lab for the rest of the US and other parts of the world. Fortunately for Pennsylvania, an extensive and diverse higher education industry remains a key asset for the State's global competitiveness. However, given the many challenges associated with forming and sustaining effective partnerships, efforts to create and improve collaborations involving higher education will require deliberate effort. Remaining cognizant of the successes and challenges of partnerships, attempts to tap higher education for local purposes can be better positioned.

The future of localities and regions in States like Pennsylvania partly rests on the ability to successfully harness the presence and value of a vast range of institutions of higher education. While awareness around the significance of higher education to global competitiveness has grown, the challenge is to determine the most appropriate ways to actualize effective partnerships. Given the complexity and even unwieldiness of partnerships, it is important to view these collaborative efforts as investments in the future. The laborious nature of these efforts can be distasteful, but the requisite hard work can tap knowledge and resources toward competitive advantage that could be the difference between vitality and decline.

NOTES

1. This firm was founded by the author of this chapter.
2. The idea of tapping institutions of higher education's deeply rooted investments in localities is a critical feature of discussion of higher education's stake in community partnerships in Maurrasse (2001).
3. A national effort in the United States, pooling the resources of major philanthropic institutions and corporations to enhance urban vitality.
4. A citywide effort that aligned higher education, the local school system, local philanthropy, local corporations, and local nonprofit organizations to revamp education from early childhood to post secondary education and beyond.
5. *Retooling HUD for a Catalytic Federal Government: A Report to Secretary Shaun Donovan* is the title of this report, which was the result of the efforts of a task force organized by the University of Pennsylvania during the winter of 2008 and 2009. One chapter within the report focused on 'anchor institutions', which was prepared by a subgroup that was organized by Ira Harkavy, Director of the University's Netter Center. Harkavy's anchor institutions task force continues to meet and organize a strategy to influence policy.
6. The Association for Community and Higher Education Partnerships (ACHEP) captured its overview of the characteristics of effective partnerships in *Real Partnerships*, a report arranged by Marga Incorporated in 2007. The idea for the paper came from the Carnegie Corporation's challenge to ACHEP to demonstrate what is possible when higher education/community partnerships are employing promising practices.

REFERENCES

Association for Community and Higher Education Partnerships (ACHEP) (2007), *Real Partnerships*, New York.
Maurrasse, David (2001), *Beyond the Campus: How Colleges and Universities Form Partnerships with Their Communities*, New York: Routledge Press.

3. Montreal's technological and cultural clusters strategy: the case of the multimedia, and film and audiovisual production

Diane-Gabrielle Tremblay

INTRODUCTION

Metropolitan Montreal is witnessing economic renewal. In the past, Montreal's economy flourished on traditional manufacturing activities and today the economy has successfully shifted in the direction of knowledge and innovation, after a certain number of years and various programs oriented towards the new sectors. According to PricewaterhouseCoopers (2000), the Montreal region ranks fourth among North American cities for hi-tech employment per capita, behind San Francisco (including Silicon Valley), Seattle (with Boeing and Microsoft) and Boston. In the Canadian aeronautics sector 70 per cent of R&D is done in Montreal and 60 per cent of employment is in Montreal.

The IT and multimedia sectors have also contributed to Montreal's economic industrial and territorial reconversion, especially in the aftermath of the dispirited 1980s crisis. Multimedia typically belongs with Montreal's hi-tech sectors on the same footing as aerospace, telecommunications and biopharmaceuticals.[1]

Montreal's multimedia sector is still relatively young, even if the gaming industry has become quite well known. It appeared in the 1990s with the expansion of the Internet and not until the mid-1990s could it be identified as such. Its specific contribution to innovation and territorial reconversion was then observable in Montreal and to some extent in Quebec City (Manzagol et al. 1999; Tremblay and Rousseau 2005; Tremblay et al. 2004). In more recent years, the film and visual effects sectors have also gained attention in the creative high-technology sectors.

The ascent of the multimedia sector fostered other advances as well. As concerns urbanism, the thrust fostered the revitalization and re-qualification of several former industrial or commercial zones, for example Faubourg des Récollets and St Lawrence Boulevard in Montreal and St Roch Borough in Quebec City. This phenomenon is not unique to Montreal, but is of interest to many old industrial cities which are having to move in new directions. San Francisco's South Market, New York's Silicon Alley or Le Sentier in Paris are other exemplars of urban re-appropriation and re-qualification (Manzagol et al. 1999). The ascent of the multimedia sector also caused the comeback of hi-tech activities in the city's timeworn core. While at one time hi-tech businesses had left the city center for newer quarters in the suburbs, this appears to be the indication of a general trend reversal. Hence businesses in the multimedia sector prefer old, open-space industrial buildings in which a more convenient working climate may be established for workers who need to exchange and interact extensively. This type of set-up is preferred by many entrepreneurs in the multimedia sector, but also more and more in the IT and life sciences as well. Indeed the multimedia sector has had a tangible impact on the territorial reconversion of the city center.

In this chapter I will try to present the policy elements that have led to a reorientation of the economic strategy of Montreal, and will concentrate on two sectors which I have studied in more detail, and that are of importance to Montreal's reconversion, that is the multimedia and the film–audiovisual sectors, or clusters.

I begin by defining the concept of clusters in more detail because I consider it important to develop a precise view and highlight the recent debates on this concept. I then define the cluster policy of the City of Montreal, especially as concerns the film and audiovisual production sectors, and analyse the process of cluster development in this sector, highlighting the difficulties and challenges encountered in this process of cluster creation. I then turn to the multimedia sector, or City of Multimedia project, which was also supported by the City of Montreal and Government of Quebec, with a special program. The chapter will thus center on the cluster strategy now put forward by the city on the process of cluster creation, as well as on the conditions that appear to facilitate or to impede the development. For this, I will start by highlighting the theoretical views on these issues related to cluster creation to better understand why these cluster strategies are seen as interesting for economic development and also better understand what is at stake in the concrete development of the clusters.

THE CONCEPT OF CLUSTERS

Theoretical Framework: Agglomeration and Clustering

Theories of regional specialization, agglomeration and clustering have existed in some form for quite some time, over 100 years, if we go back to the Marshallian district (Marshall 1889). However, these theories seem to have been rediscovered in recent years. There has been much interest over the last two decades on behalf of researchers, but also from government and public policy analysts in the search for modes of local regional development or re-conversion of de-industrialized zones. As Cassidy et al. (2005) indicate, many governments and public policy organizations are very interested in the concept of clusters and many have adopted it as a public policy instrument in order to increase local and regional (and eventually even national, in some cases), competitiveness, innovation, and growth (OECD 1999, 2001).

Why this interest in clusters? It is largely because of the importance of innovation and creative capacity, which are seen as fundamental factors of economic development and prosperity in the knowledge economy. Over recent decades, theories of innovation systems and clusters have put forward the idea that the territorial dimension is important in shaping innovative and creative capacities (Gertler and Wolfe 2005).

As Cassidy et al. (2005, p. 7) also remind us:

> The development of clusters promised a seemingly easy answer to the challenges created by increased international competition and the growing importance of innovation in the knowledge economy – particularly for smaller regions tied to traditional industries. Policy analysts, academics, and industry were happy to follow as it simplified their task of explaining and promoting regional development economics. This enthusiasm was further fuelled by the significant amounts of public money that flowed to cluster development initiatives.

This surely explains much of the interest in clusters. However, despite the interest, there has been some criticism over the years, some considering that this strategy is overexposed and sometimes seen as a 'magic recipe' (Andersson et al. 2004). Beyond this criticism, and beyond the possibly overplayed public policy attraction, researchers have in our view highlighted elements of interest over recent years. Indeed, the concept remains useful and it is important to go beyond the general definitions of clusters and highlight the elements that this strand of literature has contributed to as sources of competitiveness and socio-economic development.

Both clusters (single sector) and 'innovative milieux' (multi-sector agglomerations) are geographical concentrations of firms and supporting

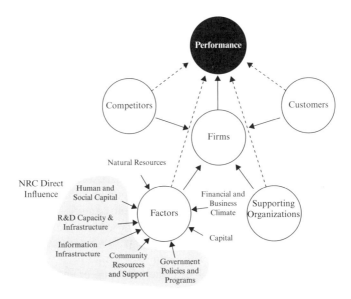

Source: Cassidy et al. (2005, p. 7).

Figure 3.1   Cluster model

organizations that 'trust' one another and frequently exchange knowledge. The theory of innovative milieux emphasizes the role of the milieu as
a source of innovation and industry growth: the proximity of competencies promotes the creation of new innovative firms (Camagni and Maillat
2006). This accent on competencies appears all the more important to us
in the context of creative industries and, in our view, the development of
competencies is one of the main sources of success for a cluster.

Let us recall that the cluster model developed in Canada (by the
National Research Council as well as the Innovation Systems Research
Network) is centered on the performance of firms and attempts to demys-
tify the various factors that might explain this performance. The success or
performance of a cluster is seen as being dependent on the performance of
the individual firms that are part of the cluster, and this performance has
been moderated by cluster conditions and the environment of the firms.
Amongst the factors which are seen as having an impact on the firms, let
us mention human and social capital, R&D capacity and infrastructure,
information infrastructure, community resources and support, as well as
government policies and programs. This model has been presented in a
figure by Cassidy et al. (2005) (see Figure 3.1), but many authors have
the same or very similar views (Julien 2005; Holbrook and Wolfe 2002;

National Research Council 1998; Padmore and Gibson 1998; Wolfe et al. 2005). Cassidy relates the model to the various factors included in the Porter Diamond of performance, but highlights the fact that Porter's definition of related and supporting industries has been enlarged to include public and non-profit organizations that support cluster development; these are known as supporting organizations. This is similar to the industrial districts and innovative milieux literature, since these writings include many organizations that can act as supporting organizations (Camagni and Maillat 2006).

In most writing on clusters, it is recognized that cluster development is a long-term process that is based on the mobilization of key stakeholders in the community, or local or regional territory. In this context, Cassidy et al. (2005) have identified four stages: latent, developing, established and transformation. While many writings on clusters are centered on established, long-existing clusters, there is now a recognition that clusters can be at different stages, and particularly that many are in the latent or developing stage in the new media or new creative industries (for example, in the new media industry in Canada; see Britton and Légaré 2004; Britton et al. 2009; Smith et al. 2004; Tremblay et al. 2004; amongst others; also, more generally, on other clusters, see Gertler and Wolfe 2005).

It is also interesting to see how the various concepts present in cluster theory have been operationalized in different research projects. The Innovation Systems Research Network (ISRN) is probably the most important source of operational research on the subject of clusters in Canada (Holbrook and Wolfe 2002; Wolfe et al. 2005). While the bulk of publications on the parent concept of innovative milieux is centered less on operationalization, the work by Julien (2005) is very much centered on operationalization of the concept of endogenous development and it complements the work presented by the ISRN group (Wolfe et al. 2005).

The main difference between this cluster view and other views of economic development or growth is the fact that it highlights the social and territorial nature of the innovation process; that has elsewhere been called 'socio-territorial capital' (Fontan et al. 2005a, b). This socio-territorial capital is seen as playing as important a role as economic or financial factors (price, financial support, and so on). The territory is seen here as being more than a simple repository for economic activity and the role of social relations of production and interactions is highlighted. This explains that our analysis of the birth of creative clusters is largely centered on the analysis of social relations and interactions between actors.

The Contribution of Human and Social Capital to Clusters

It is one of the main functions of clusters to provide human capital and social capital, as well as financial capital and resources (although this is more commonly recognized in economic theory), in order to support firms that are part of the cluster. Beyond the human resources necessary for production, firms need moral and general support for their activity, and this often comes through social capital. Indeed, it is through interactions that representations and ideas are exchanged, and this supports firms and entrepreneurs in a given cluster (Julien 2005, p. 170).

The concept of human capital is well known, but that of social capital is less well known. In Bourdieu's work, social capital is defined as the set of resources that are related to the possession of a durable network of relations, more or less institutionalized, with 'interconnections' and 'inter-exchanges'; in other words, this capital is related to the fact that one belongs to a group, a group of agents who are not necessarily character-ized by common properties, but by permanent and useful links (Bourdieu 1980, cited in Julien 2005, p. 170).

Some refer to the image of 'glue' to indicate how these links and 'inter-connections' function, since they can reinforce the relationships among members of a group or a cluster; others refer to the idea of a 'lubricant' that accelerates the interrelations by instituting a climate of trust between the actors and imposing specific rules that are known and accepted by all. When there is a rich source of information (especially implicit or tacit information, as is often the case in film and audiovisual production, as well as other creative industries, rather than explicit, codified knowledge), interrelations and exchanges offer an excellent way of transferring this information to various actors; this facilitates the production of meaning, since knowledge is shared in a more or less diffuse way. In this context, the cluster is seen as a very efficient mode of access to information and to learning (Julien 2005, p. 171).

As was highlighted in research on innovative milieux, industrial districts and clusters, these links can be stimulating and can contribute to innova-tion, but they can also limit creativity if they are too strong, and if cluster members limit themselves to the cluster rather than also being open to 'global pipelines' of information (Gertler and Wolfe, 2005; Julien, 2005). It is thus important for these links and relationships to be not only global and not only local, although there is no clear indication in any work or research of how the correct balance can be achieved to ensure fruitful knowledge flows within the cluster. This is an important issue for analysis and has brought us to try to identify the types of relationships important for our creative sectors.

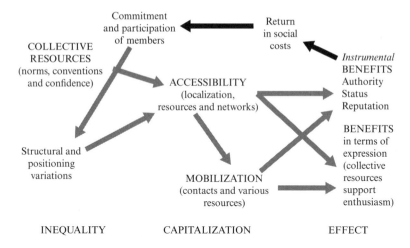

INEQUALITY   CAPITALIZATION   EFFECT

Source: Adapted from Lin (1999).

Figure 3.2 Functioning of social capital

On the basis of Lin's work (1999), Julien (2005) highlights how human and social capital function to support cluster development. Basically, the idea is that collective assets such as norms, conventions and confidence facilitate accessibility and exchanges, and that these will in turn favor mobilization of cluster members. Accessibility and mobilization bring various benefits to cluster members; as is indicated in Figure 3.2, benefits can take the form of status or reputation effects as well as collective resources or support for given projects. This in turn will favor commitment and participation on behalf of members and, hopefully, development of the cluster. It is thus interesting to analyse the development of the film and audiovisual production cluster to see how precisely this process happens, and what difficulties lie along the way. As mentioned above, much research has celebrated established clusters (Andersson et al., 2004), but the challenges related to their development often remain hidden.

The Impact of Networks and Clusters on Learning and Human Capital Development

In the context of the knowledge economy, knowledge and learning are seen as determinants in the economic development and prosperity of regions and nations, as well as in the competitive success of firms. Learning is thus considered as one of the main social processes that provides access to knowledge. Acquisition of knowledge through traditional means (buying licenses or patents, and so on) is also possible, but does not provide access to a constantly renewed knowledge stock as learning does. Learning is an ongoing process that enables individuals, firms or territories to change and adapt to the constantly changing conditions of their environment and is particularly important in the creative high technology sectors.

Various works have analysed the varied impact of networks, districts or clusters on learning. The work undertaken by Jacob et al. (1997, cited in Julien 2005, p. 276) highlights four sources of learning that are related to the clustering process:

1. Clusters accelerate the circulation of information between members, especially when trust is important, and this both facilitates and accelerates the analysis of information, favoring business and cluster development.
2. Clustering helps firms to compare themselves, and this leads to a more competitive attitude between firms and to continuous learning and more innovation.
3. Clusters offer new and non-routine information and facilitate multiplication and exchange within the group. The observation of others and the concentration of information from many sources favor the active search for new information (especially tacit information) and multiply the new ideas that support innovation.
4. When useful or needed, the cluster can transform competitive relations into cooperative relations, without completely eliminating competitive relations (Julien 2005, p. 276).

Creative capacity and innovation are thus largely determined by interactions between socio-economic agents, that is, social learning in a given territory. Many authors highlight the fact that social capital should be varied, in the sense that learning will be much richer if members of the network come from different environments and different backgrounds (Tremblay, 2003). Also, for a cluster to be successful, it needs to offer a variety of sources of social capital, some contributing to financial start-up capital, some to psychological or social support, and others to new ideas and innovation.

In order for clusters to develop new ideas and innovation, they must be capable of adapting ideas according to their business needs. The ideas must also be compatible with the values and norms of the present and future members of the clusters, while being innovative and supportive of the evolution of values. Finally, the networks must be linked to other networks from other regions or localities in order to increase the richness and variety of information they offer and to help entrepreneurs join more complex networks (Julien 2005, p. 288). Here again, we find the idea that local buzz and activities are not sufficient, but access to global knowledge flows is important.

Research also highlights the fact that collective learning and the appropriation of rich information within clusters requires a specific atmosphere that is without uncertainty and ambiguity and that generates social capital, and a culture that supports creativity. Social capital is thus the basis for the territorial embeddedness of firms and clusters, which is why it can be referred to as socio-territorial capital (Fontan et al. 2005a).

THE CLUSTERS STRATEGY OF THE CITY OF MONTREAL

The policies espoused by the city of Montreal since the 1990s support the idea of a network-based local development (Rifkin 2004) or cluster strategy (Gertler and Wolfe 2005). The current mayor of Montreal, Gerald Tremblay, introduced the concept of industrial clusters in 1991, when he was the Quebec minister of Industry, Commerce, Science and Technology. He sees it as a model which, in his own words: 'is designed to stimulate the creation of conditions within which new ideas and processes can pass from embryonic to commercialized stages and provide returns for stakeholders' (CMM 2008a).

After almost 20 years since the first presentation of the concept in Quebec, and some experimenting with the concept at the provincial Industry Department, this strategy has brought the City of Montreal to adopt the clusters strategy as a strategy for innovation (Tremblay, G. 2008). But before we present this strategy and go into the specifics for the two sectors mentioned above, let us present a short history to situate this strategy in context.

A Little History

If one wants to trace the roots of the cluster strategy, one can go back some 40 years, as does the Mayor himself, in his presentation (Tremblay, G. 2008). It was with the Saucier Commission and Report, in 1985, that the Quebec government first looked at proposals for improving the financing of firms, including SMEs with good growth potential, and to Tremblay this was the first step in a series of '40 or so significant events that, one by one, marked the phases and influences of the concept first proposed in the early 1990s, which eventually resulted, 15 years later, in the Greater Montreal Innovation system and the creation of the first four cluster secretariats' (Tremblay, G. 2008, p. 24). In 1986, there was a crisis in the pharmaceutical industry and representatives from various Montreal business, political and scientific groups formed a united front and reiterated their support for Bill C-22, on patent protection. The pharmaceutical industry then threatened to cancel its investments of some 1.4 billion dollars. In 1986 also, the Picard Report was an important milestone: the Canadian government mandated a committee to write a report on revitalizing the regional economy. The Picard Report recommended targeting seven competitive economic sectors: international activities; high technology; international trade and finance; design; cultural industries; tourism and transportation. The Report mentioned that revitalization would require joint action from the public and the private sectors.

In 1991, after the economic recession and the important job losses, the then Minister responsible for economic affairs, Gerald Tremblay, now mayor of Montreal, gave a talk referring to the 'urgency' of acting and developing a 'value-added economy' and two months later proposed the industrial cluster approach to restructure the Quebec economy. In 1991 again, Michael Porter wrote a study called 'Canada at the Crossroads' and suggested a framework for understanding the determining factors of Canadian competitiveness and identifying the sectors that require change, in relation with low productivity growth and rising unemployment (Tremblay, G. 2008, p. 24).

Another element mentioned in the history of this concept (Tremblay, G. 2008, p. 24) was the first long-term social contract signed in Quebec in 1991, a contract that rested on a partnership approach based on a medium- and long-term vision of the company's future. The union and employer abandoned the traditional practice of three-year contracts for a more long-term view, considered positive for both parties. While not mentioned by Tremblay (2008), the development of the Forum pour l'emploi (forum for employment), a concertation-based approach to discussions between the large employer and union organization also appears important to us in this development of a consensus- or concertation-based approach.

In 1991, the Quebec government thus put forward its innovative industrial cluster strategy and in 1993, a sort of encyclopedia of Quebec's economic activity was published under the title '*L'atlas industriel du Québec*'. The book was prefaced by Michael Porter, with the support of Gerald Tremblay, and it put forward the ideas that would lead to the adoption of the CMM (Montreal Metropolitan Community) Economic Development Plan in 2005 (Tremblay, G. 2008, p. 25).

In 1993, a book called *Les grappes industrielles* (industrial clusters) was published by the Department of Industry, Commerce and Technologies. The book examined competitive economies, synergy amongst the players in key sectors, as well as the issues and challenges facing Quebec. In the same year, the Quebec government action plan proposed a dozen concrete measures to support the economy and job creation and try to compensate for jobs lost during the 1991–92 recession.

In 1994, the North American Free Trade Agreement (NAFTA) was concluded, replacing the Free Trade Agreement concluded in 1988 with the USA, adding Mexico to the agreement. In 1996, there was a Summit on the Economy and Employment, and also the government mandated a group of Montreal businesspeople to determine the problems of the Montreal economy and present solutions to revitalize the city. The task force on the revitalization of Montreal presented some 30 initiatives, grouped into three large categories: 'shifting to the new economy; modernizing established sectors; and improving overall development conditions' (Tremblay, G. 2008, p. 25).

In 1997, Montreal International (MI), a public–private partnership, was charged with the mission of contributing to the economic development of metropolitan Montreal and increasing the region's international status. MI was funded by the Canadian and Quebec governments, the City of Montreal, the Montreal Metropolitan Community and the private sector. It was created as a result of the Summit on the Economy and Employment of 1996 (Tremblay, G. 2008, p. 25).

In 2002, upon being elected Mayor of Montreal in November 2001, G. Tremblay proposed to convene some 3000 participants to a summit to draft a shared vision for the city's future. The New City of Montreal was created on January 1 2002 following the merger of all the municipalities of the island (a few of them would, however, leave the city later, following a referendum).

In 2002, MI worked with the industry to define an action plan to position the metropolitan region as one of the world leaders in the life sciences, and this cluster adopted a brand strategy in 2005, renaming itself InVivo. The ICT cluster developed an action plan in 2005 and many other activities supported the economic development strategy at various moments in 2005 (City of Montreal Economic Development Strategy; success@montreal; Imagining – Building Montreal 2025). In 2005, the CMM adopted its Economic Development Plan that included a metropolitan cluster development strategy and a Competitiveness Fund to provide financial support to cluster development.

The Cluster Strategy

In the CMM documents, the city identified four clusters: the aerospace industry, born in 2006 after a concerted effort spread over two years; health sciences, which emerged in 2002; the information technology and communications sector launched in 2002 and, finally, the film and audio-visual production cluster, when the Quebec Film and Television Council (QFTC) became the secretariat for the film and television industry cluster. Together, these clusters represented a total of 238 000 jobs distributed between approximately 6363 institutions, businesses and organizations belonging to these four sectors (Tremblay, G. 2008, pp. 14–15).

Who oversees the development of these clusters? The Montreal Metropolitan Community (or Communauté métropolitaine de Montréal, CMM) is responsible for the strategy and so serves as the coordinator of the three fundamental steps in the creation of a cluster: pre-start-up, start-up, and operation. One of the conditions for eligibility for the CMM and its governmental partners to lend financial support to the secretariat of the cluster is that all of the industries' stakeholders have to be part of one non-profit organization run by a board composed of the sector's professionals.

The CMM economic development plan (2005) identified four types of clusters: the competitive clusters, that is those that bring together internationally competitive segments (aerospace, ICT, life sciences, textiles and clothing); the emerging technology clusters, that is cross-sectoral technologies with high, long-term growth potential (environmental technology, nanotech and advanced materials); the manufacturing clusters, those with growth potential based on natural resources (energy, paper and wood products, bio-food, petrochemicals and plastics and metallurgy); and finally visibility clusters, defined as strategic sectors for a city region's socio-economic development and branding, which include film, culture, tourism and services (Tremblay, G. 2008, p. 12).

The approach to these clusters is considered a bottom-up approach in the sense that initiatives must come from firms (demand-led), and that the metropolitan cluster must indicate that it can organize itself and adopt a development plan. The MMC is responsible for the general planning and coordinating of activities but does not substitute itself for local actors and decision makers.

In order to get financing the clusters must develop a business plan with growth objectives, value-added projects and performance indicators and they must function with a consensus-based approach. They should develop a three-year action plan and a ten-year development strategy. The financing is normally ensured by the three government levels (municipal, provincial, federal) and the private sector, at 25 per cent each.

Once potential is identified in a given sector, there are three phases that follow. The pre-start-up phase is one where the cluster has to develop its business case and it is self-financed. Then, at the start-up phase, there should be confirmation from the private sector for some C$200 000 (Canadian dollars) minimum per year over three years, which will make it possible for the public sector actors to put up to C$200 000 each as well. There is the possibility to obtain seed money for a provisional cluster committee in order to prepare the long-term plan, the triennial plan and the private sector solicitation plan. This would be shared by the Quebec government and the MMC up to C$200 000 for 18 months (CMM 2008b).

Clusters are obviously at different phases and for the moment only four clusters are considered to be at the operations phase, as mentioned above: aerospace, ICT, life sciences and film–audiovisual.

This development strategy is based upon the individualization of the strategic sectors and the mobilization of the principal stakeholders around a leader or champion willing to rally the community around a common goal. The objective is to allow Montreal to project the image abroad of a city of knowledge, as well as a creative and prosperous city. The European Union's interest in these practices, which led to the development of CLUNET (Cluster Network) beginning on September 1, 2006, is considered by many to be proof of Montreal's influence. The international project aims to create a network of the most innovative regions with clusters. CLUNET is composed of 16 partners, including Montreal, the only non-European participant, and the main objective of the network is to launch pilot projects fostered by international cooperation 'to achieve a common agenda for Europe that will lead to the creation of world-class clusters delivering global competitive advantage in lead markets'.[2]

The internationalization of expansion into new markets demonstrates a willingness to explore all of the means necessary to prevent the cluster theory from becoming merely a regional development tool and, instead, bring renewed investment into the regions they represent through the strengthening of international ties and the exploitation of the theory's full potential. This stems from the recognition of the fact that clusters need to be based on international links as well as local relations. The first potential pilot program was launched at a conference held in Montreal in September of 2007 entitled 'Europe Meets America'. The conference focused on the cooperation between the aerospace industry clusters in Hamburg, Berlin and Montreal; a second alliance is based on a group of eight pilot projects based in both Tuscany and Montreal, which focus on transnational commercial incubation of businesses.

A NEW MODEL FOR FILM AND AUDIOVISUAL PRODUCTION IN MONTREAL

The film and audiovisual production cluster is one of the most recent and most interesting examples of cluster creation in Montreal and Quebec.

It highlights the interesting developments observed in the sector of creative clusters, which has become most active in recent years (Pilati and Tremblay 2007).

In the case of the film and audiovisual production cluster, the organization set up to oversee its activities is the Quebec Film and Television Council (QFTC), an independent body which receives monies from the CMM after having signed agreements outlining the allocation of funds for specific projects. The QFTC receives two equal instalments and a third, which represents 10 per cent of the allocated funds, is disbursed at the reception of the project report. The relationship between these two organizations remains independent, as it is the QFTC which has close ties to the field and which is solely responsible for the completion of the projects.

It is in the context of this cluster development in Montreal that we decided to study the film and audiovisual cluster's pre-start-up stage to explore how Montreal, a city which built its industrial strength upon the aerospace industry, health sciences and information technology and communications clusters, is now creating a cultural cluster. The objective is to develop a creative cluster based on stimulating the density and quality of the exchanges between the main stakeholders involved in the film and audiovisual sectors.

Film and audiovisual production have been evolving over recent years and are now often seen as part of the new media sector, one of the main sectors of the creative industries sectors. The sector has evolved from purely audiovisual techniques to various creative services used in television, advertising as well as film. Montreal has long been known as an important North American hub for film and audiovisual production, especially with the presence of the French and English production of the CBC (Canadian Broadcasting Corporation) and the National Film Board of Canada. This reputation has continued over recent years with important developments in visual effects, often related as well to the important developments in the multimedia sector and the multimedia city of Montreal, which has attracted important firms such as Ubisoft, Electronic Arts and others. However, the protectionist attitude of the Hollywood filmmakers at times, as well as the negative effects of the long screenwriters' strike in Hollywood on Montreal's production, have been amongst the factors that have spurred important preoccupations for the future of Montreal's film and audiovisual production. In this context, the City of Montreal has decided to develop a strategy to protect and develop the future of this creative industry in Montreal, in the context of increased competition in the sector from the US, but also from other Canadian provinces. It is in this context that efforts have been made since 2004 to try to develop a cluster strategy in this sector and ensure this creative industry's future. The birth and development of the multimedia cluster in Montreal (as well as Vancouver and Toronto – see Britton et al. 2009) is one interesting case, to which we will return further on, but the film and audiovisual sector also presents an interesting case of development of a creative sector; although this sector is not so strongly supported by the provincial government,[3] it illustrates the challenges related to the birth of a creative cluster called upon to contribute to the development of the Montreal economy.

The Forum métropolitain de l'industrie cinématographique (FMIC – Metropolitan forum of the film industry), which took place in Montreal in November of 2004, represented the first concerted move towards the construction of a common vision and drafting of a development plan. The objective of developing a strategy which would protect Quebec's interests on the international scene and ensure the development of local production was a fundamental move to try to counteract the weak position in which the industry found itself at the beginning of 2003. Indeed, the strong competition between Quebec and the other Canadian provinces and American states, as well as the strength of the Canadian dollar that in itself reduced the attractiveness of the Canadian market to American production teams, created the framework for some cooperation and recognition of the importance of participating in this forum.

The event was orchestrated by the Montreal Metropolitan Community, which had allocated funds in its 2005 budget to provide the necessary financial support to create the executive of the cluster and to foster value-added projects that were backed by a consensus throughout the industry. Other partners that took part in supporting the creation of this executive included the Government of Quebec, the Government of Canada and the private sector; each was to contribute 25 per cent to the total amount of 18 million Canadian dollars allocated to this project. However, in November of 2007, the project lost one of its main backers: the Government of Canada. The Conservative government issued a note that stipulated that it was to cease funding non-profit organizations directly. Thus, the executive of the film and audiovisual cluster, which had taken the form of a non-profit organization, lost one quarter of the funding necessary for its development.

An E&B DATA study (2004), which preceded the FMIC by a few months, reported on the health of the film and audiovisual production portfolio in Montreal and Quebec by highlighting that the industry, characterized by the great quality and breadth of its talent and technological knowledge, was on the cutting edge and, as such, had the potential to be positioned as one of the most dynamic sectors of the Quebec economy. The structure of the portfolio was quite complex as it included all production, for both film and television, arranged into four categories:

production; broadcast; institutional complementary activities (finance and training); and support (visual software or audiovisual equipment, technical services), which represented a total of 35 000 jobs and more than 500 businesses in the production and broadcast categories alone (E&B DATA, 2004). This multitude of localized stakeholders represented the critical mass needed to put the film and audiovisual cluster into action and fostered the needed synergies and pooling of strengths to ensure the creation of a collective force.

For the Montreal film and audiovisual actors, this cluster strategy was seen as crucial. The reunion of companies who cooperate and contribute to revitalizing their sector is a response to the new network-based economy; one in which companies have to demonstrate their ability to create alliances within their industries in order to assert their competitiveness in the market. To do so, they must undergo a transformation for several years until the beginning of a new project, thus beginning a larger process of change that will ensure that they never exist in the same form again (Rifkin 2004).

It is in this context that the Quebec Film and Television Council was given the mandate to act as the cluster for the sector. In 2007, the board of this organization created a consultative committee and gave it the mandate to study the dynamics and orientation of the cluster in order to provide a guide for the development of the film and audiovisual production industry along the lines defined above. This work to develop the cluster was divided into five areas: labor, foreign investment, innovation, image/visibility/outreach and strategic planning.

The Quebec Film and Television Council is an organization that has responsibilities at the level of the whole province of Quebec, but there are also three similar bureaus at the regional level: the Montreal Film and TV Commission, the Laurentians Film and Television Commission (BCTAL) and the Ottawa-Gatineau Film and Television Development Corporation (OGFT). The latter covers two provinces, Ontario and Quebec, and is not included in the Montreal cluster because of its obviously divergent interests. The Montreal and Laurentians Film and Television Commissions are on the contrary very active in the cluster development. Their main role is to give information to local and foreign producers, to support film projects in their region, to promote the City of Montreal and Laurentians region (close to Montreal) in the film industry and to support the international strategy of the QFTC.

This trend towards clusterization seems to touch upon many sectors of the economy, but is very critical in the striking example which Hollywood presents, because of its transition from a model encompassing companies vertically integrated to a model with a multitude of SMEs and independent producers who work together on a project basis, while improving their performance in terms of flexibility, specialization, continuous learning and inter-company cooperation (Friedman 1995). Salvemini and Delmestri (2000) define a 'third way' – a governance model based upon collaboration between stakeholders and coalitions, in opposition to the classical model of a limited number of forces in play and the 'invisible hand' which coordinates, in contrast, the specialized activities of a large number of smaller stakeholders. According to these authors, the 'de-verticalization' put in place by the Hollywood industry, in terms of advantages to the competitiveness of the sector, 'has also created a split between the different sectors of the labor market, between core and peripheral workers, between the privileged ones who control access to work and the people who are manipulated to accept bearing the increasing uncertainty of the sector on their shoulders' (Salvemini and Delmestri, 2000, pp. 68–9). However, according to Ferriani et al. (2005), when it comes to the nature of the collaborations which begin and end extremely quickly, within the context of 'temporary creative systems', the reiteration of contacts which takes place provides a certain stability and continuity in the context of latent networks, within which 'there is a relationship between shared experience, the emergence of a collective mind and the stock of collectively held tacit knowledge' (Ferriani et al. 2005, p. 274). It is clear that Montreal wants to follow in this line of cooperation and clusterization in the film industry, but it remains to be seen of course if this strategy can counterbalance the attraction of cities such as Toronto and Vancouver (to speak only of Canadian cities active in the film industry). There are of course important challenges related to the development of a cluster and it appears useful to develop a little on this.

Challenges in Cluster Creation

Since the film and audiovisual cluster is not yet fully established, we concentrate here on the creation of links between actors and knowledge flows within the cluster. To analyse these elements, we contacted several key stakeholders who took part in the creation of the cluster, as well as the Quebec Film and Television Council and a few other associations which have an important support role in the film and audiovisual industries: besides the QFTC, there are training organizations, unions, financing bodies as well as public institutions. We undertook a series of 14 interviews with persons who hold positions within the main governing organizations of the film industry. We have also undertaken a comprehensive review of the existing research relating to Montreal's film and audiovisual production cluster.

The interviews emphasize the importance to all of the stakeholders involved in the cluster, who must partake in inclusive and collective projects, of making sure that that the 'Made in Quebec' film and audiovisual production industry can take full advantage of this new organizational model. By recognizing the role of the cluster strategy in the process of developing synergies within the sector, they see an improvement in the relationship between different organizations over the last years, especially since the creation of the cluster.

Collective mobilization thus appears crucial, and according to stakeholders, it appears crucial to 'sell Quebec' first, and then the specific region. The relationships between the different Film and Television Councils present in Quebec are thus moving in this direction. The fact that the Quebec Film and Television Council has a mandate for international development has rendered it more neutral – as it represents everyone. In the past, there were only regional offices that functioned independently and competed with each other. This situation arose in a great part because of the diverse budgets available to the various offices that prevented the creation of any positive synergy.

What is clear from all of our interviews is that because the film and audiovisual production cluster in Montreal is still in the start-up phase, and is definitely not an 'established' cluster, the dynamics of the collaboration between the members of the Quebec Film and Television Council are not yet fully developed. Based on the interviews, there are still a few obstacles to collaboration and it is also possible that other actors should be brought to the table to collaborate, many of which are not yet active members of the Quebec Film and Television Council. The groups that are identified are important financial actors, for example those who are involved in the management of real estate, and the stakeholders who are closely involved with the tourism and other commercial sectors, since many believe there are interesting synergies to be developed with these groups in relation to the film industry.

There is a fairly relaxed climate in the cluster because of the stakeholders' decision to associate themselves with the film and audiovisual production industry in Montreal out of their conscious recognition that being at the table is important to creating synergy within the sector, or simply because they wish to imitate the leaders in the sector; participation is not compulsory and this seems to attract many players. This imitation effect is not negligible and had been observed as well in the aeronautics and health sciences sector. If the main actors are there, the others follow. The challenge in the film and audiovisual sector, as in multimedia, is that it is composed of many more small players. But cooperation has been building, even if some mention a few conflicts when some forget the general interest in favour of their own personal interest. However, several significant elements come to light when evaluating the possibility of a larger mobilization of the main players in the film and audiovisual production industry and these highlight some challenges in getting all players around the table, since many may have conflicting objectives at times, for example the film and television producers of Quebec (APFTQ), the artists' union (UDA), the unions and the producers, who often have conflicting objectives. The role of arbitrator of the cluster comes out strongly.

Within this framework, the dual role of the Quebec Film and Television Council becomes even more important: it must jointly assume the role of international promoter focused on championing Quebec's attributes in foreign markets in order to attract business prospects as well as acting as the executive of the film and audiovisual production cluster in Montreal. The QFTC thus has a twofold role: one which is at the international level and another which is a regional and economic development portfolio directly tied to the strategy of Montreal's industrial clusters.

There seems to be a stronger inclination towards cooperation in the young small businesses, but the greatest weakness in the visual effects and animation sectors in Quebec is the lack of recognition they receive from governments, especially in contrast to the amount of attention paid to another sector to which they often compare themselves: video game production. While this latter industry remains in the media spotlight and is often cited as a source of innovation by the city of Montreal, the visual effects and animation industry remains in the shadows.

This is due in part, according to our interviews, to the lack of promotional planning and activities, especially when compared to those of the video game industry. In the case of visual effects and animation companies, the development of the cluster is seen as an opportunity to be proactive and raise the profile of their industry, not only internationally, where their success is well known, but also locally, where it appears less known. By adding these elements to the inter-generational element, is becomes clear that those who joined the cluster early, other than the younger businesses, are those who need opportunities to create synergy within the industry and project a stronger, more proactive image.

The boundaries between these two creative sectors appear more and more permeable, in particular for firms of cutting-edge technology, and this complicates the start-up process of the film and audiovisual production cluster. It is not a simple task to instill a unified vision and sense of belonging within a cluster, particularly when all players have so many interests at stake and they lack confidence in the collaborative process and sometimes see it as an invasion of their territory. These are the main challenges that are observed in the context of the start-up phase of this cluster.

Let us now have a look at the multimedia city, which if not a cluster per se in the MMC's books, has benefited from a lot of attention and gained a reputation as a strongly developing cluster (Britton, Tremblay and Smith 2009).

THE MULTIMEDIA CLUSTER

The contours of the multimedia sector are difficult to determine. Because its boundaries tend to be vague, available statistics on the sector are often partial and incomplete. It is estimated that there are between 1200 and 1500 multimedia firms in Quebec. This is a clear regression since more than half of the firms appear to have disappeared, compared to 1999 data. The Institut de la statistique du Québec estimated that there were approximately 3200 multimedia firms in 1999 (Tremblay et al. 2004). The sector has certainly experienced a degree of local consolidation of firms through mergers and acquisitions. However, the sharp decline in the number of firms can be explained essentially by the large number of firms that have had to close down. According to data gathered by Alliance NumériQC in November 2003, there were between 11 000 and 13 000 jobs in Quebec's multimedia sector.

According to the various definitions put forward, the term multimedia refers to an information technology that can be used to simultaneously manipulate sounds, images and texts using one suite of software interactively (Tremblay et al. 2004). By extension, a multimedia product is the result of the integration or transformation of the contents of multiple sources, such as texts, voices, data, images, graphics and video. This integration takes place in environments of interactive communications which can be disseminated digitally using a fixed support (CD-ROMs, DVDs, diskettes, and so on) or via a network (Internet, Intranet or Extranet).

In Quebec as in Toronto or Vancouver (see Britton et al. 2009), multimedia should be viewed as an emerging sector. It has given rise to dozens of new multimedia occupations, that is, designers, computer graphics designers and writers, but it must also be recognized that a number of these occupations or jobs strongly resemble those found in the information technology sector. This is true of programmers, who are applying their knowledge in a new sector but whose work is nevertheless quite similar to what it would be in the information technology sector.

Four categories of organizations operating in the multimedia sector can be identified. First, the multimedia producers, who make up the core of the sector, are responsible for multimedia applications. Second, some firms in traditional sectors (media, telecommunications, creative industries, advertising agencies, and so on) are attributing more and more importance to the development of multimedia applications in the context of their activities, in both areas of production and dissemination of contents. Third, are manufacturers of the products and material needed for creation and dissemination, but also for the use of multimedia applications. Finally, an increasing number of representation, training and research organizations revolve around the multimedia sector. In Quebec, the best known organizations are Alliance NumériQC, Réseau Interlogiqc, Centre NAD, the Institut national de l'image et son, and the Regroupement des producteurs en multimédia. In our research, we centered the interviews of firms around firms that are active as multimedia producers, that is the core of the sector, and we excluded telecommunications or advertising firms that might have some activity in multimedia.

Part of the IT cluster, the multimedia sector is one of the high-tech sectors that have contributed greatly to revitalizing the economic base of the Montreal region. A relatively young sector, its many applications have created visions of sustained growth, arousing the interest of many public and private actors in the sector. The sector has fulfilled its promises in part and met a number of expectations, to such an extent that for a number of years it actually experienced labor shortage, raiding of workers, high wages, the creation of many firms and significant interest on the part of the financial community. In short, for a few years the sector was an unqualified success.

Unfortunately, today, the reality is somewhat different. Yesterday's euphoria has given way to a bit of disillusion as a result of significant changes in the multimedia landscape over the past years. Today the multimedia sector is facing many challenges, mainly since the Government of Quebec withdrew its support for the sector by eliminating its funding for job creation in the Cité du multimédia. The withdrawal of significant government support, which is attributed to the change of provincial government in April 2003, is an important element of uncertainty, one that is exacerbating the difficult economic situation that has affected the sector since the technological bubble burst in October 2000, and again difficulties resulting from the financial crisis started in 2008.

Arrival of Ubisoft and the Birth of Multimedia in Montreal

The arrival of the French firm Ubisoft[4] in the Montreal region was an important milestone in the development of the city's multimedia sector. The firm, which specializes in entertainment, more specifically recreational games that can be used on different consoles, was looking for a location where it could set up in order to position itself in the North American market. Although the firm's establishment was an important element in the construction of this sector, it would be wrong to credit it with the sector's birth. In fact, prior to the arrival of Ubisoft, a number of firms already existed, but the sector was viewed as marginal and enjoyed little recognition at the various government levels.

Sylvain Vaugeois, the well-known Quebec lobbyist, was the instigator and promoter of the project to establish Ubisoft. He developed a highly specific and original strategy, called the Plan Mercure. Instead of providing financial support to firms through tax credits or large investments in their fixed assets, the plan proposed that the government invest in the labor force (C$25 000 annually per employee for five years) in the promising multimedia sector. The Plan was presented to the provincial government but received little support because it was seen as too expensive from the point of view of public finance.

Despite this, Vaugeois was convinced that he had a good idea and therefore decided to find a concrete application for his Plan. He went to Paris of his own accord to meet with Ubisoft's senior management. Attracted by this tempting offer and under the impression that it came from the government and was a firm offer of partnership, Ubisoft's representatives made an exploratory trip to Quebec. During their visit, they were astonished to discover that this was not the case. Embarrassed by the media coverage blaming it for the possible failure of Ubisoft to set up in Quebec, the Government of Quebec met with Ubisoft's senior management to discuss the question.

The French firm pointed out that it could set up elsewhere, specifically mentioning the Boston area, and at this point the City of Montreal got involved and put pressure on the governments. Ubisoft was immediately approached by Frank McKenna's government in New Brunswick. From that moment on, the Government of Quebec was faced with the possibility of losing 500 jobs in a fast-growing sector and losing all hope of becoming a Knowledge City, as it had envisaged with the Vaugeois plan.

It was therefore necessary to come up with a plan that might interest Ubisoft while respecting the government's budget constraints. The solution was the Cyrenne Report. The Report proposed that tax credits be used to provide training for local young people and attract firms to Quebec. The Minister of Finance announced the introduction of tax credit measures for multimedia development. However, the measures announced appeared to be far less tempting to the French firm. To make up for the discrepancy between the measures announced by his government and those advanced by Vaugeois, the Quebec government turned to the federal government.[5]

The Minister of Human Resources Development at the time, Pierre

Pettigrew, agreed to subsidize the creation of 500 jobs over a five-year period, at a rate of C$10 000 per person per year.[6] The goals of the federal government in taking this measure were simple: it wished to strengthen the positioning of Montreal as a world multimedia center and make the most of the potential spill-over effect of the French firm's arrival. Ubisoft would finally benefit from a grant of C$25 000 per employee, as planned initially in the Plan Mercure. The Quebec government would contribute C$15 000 while the federal government would contribute C$10 000 per employee.

The incentives offered were so generous and tempting that they succeeded in convincing Ubisoft to choose the Montreal region as the location from which to launch its North American expansion. In return for setting up business in Montreal, Ubisoft undertook to create 500 jobs over a five-year period. In 1997, it set up on Montreal's Saint-Laurent Boulevard in the former offices of the firm Discreet Logic, which was going to relocate in Faubourg des Récollets in Old Montreal. As we shall see further on, this relocation was also important because it had significant effects on the sector's dynamics.

Today, Ubisoft is one of the major actors of the multimedia sector, and especially of the gaming sector. Over the years, the Montreal subsidiary has become the largest of Ubisoft's 12 subsidiaries. It was entirely responsible for the design of the game Splinter Cell, which has sold more than five million copies and is considered to be a formidable success according to this industry's standards. The French firm, the third ranking game publisher in Europe and the sixth in the United States, is considered to be a giant in the electronic games industry.[7]

It therefore appears that Ubisoft has made a major contribution, with the multimedia subsector helping to position the Montreal region on the world map. The arrival of the French firm has also created an atmosphere that is conducive to developing the sector. Thus, Ubisoft has greatly contributed to raising the profile of Montreal's video game sector.

Mobilization of Actors

The emergence of the multimedia cluster has been fueled by the appearance of new coalitions and associations that would not have existed within the old economy. Since 1995, the local community has become highly mobilized and many associational structures have been formed. Among the most important are the Forum des inforoutes et du multimédia (FIM, information highway and multimedia forum), the Centre d'Expertise et de Services Applications en multimédia (CESAM, centre for multimedia expertise and application services), and the Association des Producteurs du Multimédia du Québec (APMQ, Quebec multimedia producers' association). In reaction to the considerable advantages accorded to the French firm, the multimedia sector firms organized themselves, rallying all the local actors gravitating around it. The local community mobilized itself and asked for government assistance similar to what was offered to Ubisoft. That was the beginning of recognition for the sector and of the institutionalization of the relationship between the local multimedia sector firms and the Quebec government. From then on, the sector would be seen as a distinct sector with specific needs.

In terms of actors' mobilization, a distinction should be made between two movements that, of course, have definite points of convergence, but also somewhat different goals. The first movement can be described as having a sectoral vision, essentially seeking institutional recognition of the local industry. The aim of this institutional recognition is to receive assistance similar to what the governments gave Ubisoft. The second movement can be identified with a spatial vision, focusing on issues related to the ways of appropriating space and the desire to be part of the future mission of the territory. Both are closely intertwined in the mobilization and governance developments.

Spatial and sectoral mobilization can and often does play a crucial role in governance structures and governance outcomes. Three main associations played a role in the cluster development.

The Centre d'Expertise et de Services Application Multimédia (CESAM) was created in 1995 at the instigation of the Centre de recherche en informatique de Montréal (CRIM, Montreal center for research on information engineering). CESAM is not an association but a business group that hoped in this way to create a critical mass that would allow it to take a leadership position in this potentially fast-growing industry. CESAM's goals were, among others, to establish a technological watch center, to promote multimedia training, to incubate businesses and to make the influence of Quebec's multimedia industry extend further.

The second largest association was the Association des producteurs en multimédia du Québec (APMQ). It was created spontaneously in the wake of the controversy surrounding Ubisoft's arrival in April 1997. In fact, the arrival of Ubisoft was a good thing because it spurred the industry to take charge of itself and the Quebec government to demonstrate that it was sensitive to the sector's problems.

APMQ defended the interests of entrepreneurs. The association strove to defy international competition but was also interested in high visibility issues such as the protection of intellectual property in the new media and improving the working conditions of the artists. It was also on the front line over the Cité du multimedia issue. APMQ had argued in favour of the other firms – those located outside the designated zone and those that did not wish to move into la Cité to be able to benefit from funding. It wanted to reach an agreement that would allow producers who did not want to move into la Cité to benefit from advantageous though less generous conditions. However, it did not succeed.

The third player was the Forum des inforoutes et du multimédia. In June 1996, about 15 distributors, developers and others, concerned by the multimedia explosion, founded this forum. A non-profit organization, FIM's mission was to promote the digital content and interactive applications industry. Some 120 people attended the organization's first public activity. Unlike the two previously mentioned organizations, FIM was open to all individuals. It acted as a forum for debate and discussion on the important issues of the day. In particular, it initiated important discussions that took place during 1998 on the issue of the evolution of Internet advertising and was responsible for the creation of the Bureau de la publicité sur Internet au Québec (Internet advertising bureau in Quebec). In April 1999, it received funding from the ministère de la Culture et des Communications (ministry of culture and communications) to produce training tools and hold seminars aimed at getting advertisers to increase their use of the Internet as an advertising medium.

In December 2000, the members of the Association des producteurs en multimédia du Québec (APMQ), the Consortium multimédia (CESAM) and the Forum des inforoutes et du multimédia (FIM) approved a joint agreement to create Alliance numériQC, a merger of CESAM and FIM.

Alliance numériQC is a non-profit organization which is supported by the federal government (Economic Development Canada) and the provincial government (ministère de la Culture et des Communications du Québec and ministère du Développement économique et Régional). It counts over 200 members (variations with restructurings, closings of firms, and so on), 75 per cent of which are private firms. Most of these firms are micro-enterprises and SMEs operating in different niches, for example E-learning, games, Internet applications, and so on. The Alliance takes action in three main areas. The first is support to firms in their marketing, finance, and market watch and information activities. The second involves the development of skills, that is, the transfer of skills and knowledge, skills training and development and raising awareness among the different actors (governments, firms, educational institutions). The third area concerns relations with governments, and the role of interfacing with governments. Within this association, committees called Réseaux d'intérêt d'Alliance numériQC (RIAN, interest networks) have been created. These committees are intended for all stakeholders in the digital industry who are members of the association and form the main actors of the cluster. They are formed at the initiative of people who wish to discuss subjects of common interest, often by sub-sectors. It should also be mentioned that the alliance encourages networking among the firms themselves, but also with other stakeholders such as universities, research centers, and so on.

Government's Support: the Role of Exogenous Resources

Numerous actors within the governments and the ministries with an economic, technological, cultural and regional development mission were interested in the multimedia cluster development. This interest was based on two factors: first, the broad definition of multimedia allowed many firms to qualify for government assistance and, second, the sector seemed to have such a promising future in the context of interest for the knowledge economy.

The Government of Quebec made the multimedia sector an important element in its economic development policy and thus supported the City of Montreal's cluster strategy. The government foresaw an enormous potential for job creation in this sector, particularly for young people. Indeed, the speed at which the various measures were introduced appears to confirm the government's interest in this area – in less than two years, a definite economic policy was implemented in this sector. Through these various measures, the provincial government's intention was to promote the investment in local firms in addition to attracting foreign firms[8] to follow the trail blazed by Ubisoft. Numerous actors were thus involved in the implementation of a range of measures to support the development of the multimedia sector in the Montreal region.

The federal government also got involved. The multimedia sector fitted well into its national policy centered on the development of a knowledge-based economy. Moreover, the federal government wanted to position the Montreal region as a multimedia center on the world stage. Just like the provincial government, several ministries and government agencies were interested in the multimedia sector (Canada Economic Development, Industrial Research Assistance Program, and so on).

All this highlights the fact that while the City's strategy is important, the support of exogenous resources (other levels of government, the local actors, and so on) is essential in the development of a cluster.

Two major types of interventions to promote the development of this sector can be identified: general measures and specific measures. General measures, which are numerous and varied, are not directly intended for firms. For example, the provincial government invested in the introduction of multimedia training programs in colleges (CEGEPs). Preferential purchase measures were also introduced.[9] In more concrete terms, in its 2000

Budget, the provincial government invested C$343 million to turn Quebec into a wired society. This strategy was mainly based on three measures: first, a C$125-million budget to help connect 200 000 low-income families; and second, a 40 per cent tax credit granted to SMEs wishing to set up a transactional website (C$126 million over three years). Third, C$15 million were earmarked for the deployment of a fibreoptic network in the region to support local electronic trade activities. The federal government also introduced similar measures.

Specific measures are directly centered on the development of firms and can include two sources: public or private funding. Though fewer in number, private financing includes venture capital corporations (Fonds de solidarité of the FTQ) and private funds (Fonds Bell or the Fonds de Daniel Langlois – creator of Softimage). Public financing from the ministries makes up almost all of the assistance granted to firms. These measures include programs, grants, tax credits, investment in capital stock and loans offered to firms.

The various governmental measures have several goals and can be associated with the following government policies: sectoral policy, spatial policy and cultural policy. We will not go into details on this but it appears important for the cluster to be able to count on the support of various governmental measures and programs in order to develop into an established cluster.

For the multimedia sector, the most important program was that created in 1998, the Cité du multimédia, and put under the responsibility of the Bureau des Centres de développement des technologies de l'information, which broadened, in both the literal and figurative senses, the support to the multimedia sector. The goals of the Government of Quebec regarding Cité du multimédia were highly ambitious, since it hoped that the Cité would generate nearly 10 000 jobs over a 10-year period.

In April 2003, a new government was elected in Quebec, with the Liberal Party replacing the Parti Québécois, which had initiated the measures to support the multimedia sector. While the multimedia sector had been viewed very favorably by the PQ government, the LP government saw things differently. In the 2003 provincial budget, the Minister of Finance announced the termination of tax advantages granted to firms in the technology sector in the designated zones.[10] In his view, the maintenance of 12 000 jobs and the creation of 5000 other jobs in the designated zones would have required a total public investment, in the form of tax credits, of up to C$4.5 billion by 2010. Moreover, according to the Minister, out of the 17 000 jobs linked to the designated zones, 12 000 already existed. In light of this conclusion, the tax credit programs were not expected to last much longer.

However, it should be specified that the new government will respect the commitments made to firms already established in the Cité. Firms that had not moved into a site but had received their approval certificate could also obtain the tax advantages provided. Moreover, firms that were expanding would continue to receive tax credits on new employees' wages. However, the government reduced the leasable areas of eligible buildings on the various sites, so that the tax credit will no longer be available beyond a certain expansion. Three sites are targeted, including the Cité du multimédia. Its area was decreased by 110 000 square meters and Phase VIII (a huge building which went on sale) was cut. The Cité du multimédia was sold to a Toronto real estate developer in early 2004 (except for the building that corresponds to Phase VIII). Nevertheless, the Cité du multimédia has put Montreal 'on the map' for multimedia production and most actors in the sector recognize this is extremely important, not only for the firms located in the perimeter of the Cité, but for all multimedia firms in Montreal. The Multimedia City has to a certain extent functioned as a marketing strategy for Montreal.

Sectoral Policy

It is difficult to separate sectoral and spatial policy when one knows that 90 per cent of the multimedia sector is concentrated in Montreal. In addition to the Cité du multimédia measure, the Government of Quebec offers a wide range of new and existing assistance programs to firms that set up both within and outside the Cité. These include programs to assist with pre-start-up, start-up, capitalization, export, dissemination, distribution, production, international marketing, development and R&D. While these last measures are not exclusive to multimedia, they nevertheless play an important role in this sector.

According to Alliance numériQC, 11 provincial programs apply to multimedia firms. The main lending agencies are the Caisse de dépôt et de placement du Québec (Quebec deposit and investment fund) and its subsidiaries, the Société générale de financement et Investissement Québec (Quebec general finance and investment corporation).

A number of important programs have disappeared. For example, the Programme d'aide à la recherche et développement, à l'amélioration des compétences en science et technologies (PACST)[11] which was once in high demand, no longer exists. While there seem to be many measures both at the provincial and federal levels, our interviews indicate that they are difficult to apply in the multimedia sector. The eligibility criteria are high and do not necessarily correspond to the specificities of the sector.

Cultural Policy

Cultural policy can also be viewed as a manifestation theme of govern-ance in the multimedia sector. The policy has three main orientations: the individual (that is, the artist), the firm and the sector. I will restrict my examination here to measures that concern firms. Among the best known measures in Quebec are the SODEC (Société de développement des entreprises culturelles) tax credit, which encourages the release of multimedia titles in French for the general public, as well as a variety of funds: information highway, culture and communications, development of Montreal and of the national capital, and those associated with private investment growth and employment revitalization. The SODEC was men-tioned by many interviewees as having an important impact, especially in the edutainment or gaming sectors.

I must add to this list the Financière des entreprises culturelles (FIDEC), a financial organization for the cultural industries created in 1999. It was created by the association of nine firms of the cultural and financial sectors. Amongt the creators, we find the Société de développement des entreprises culturelles du Québec (SODEC), the Fonds de solidarité des travailleurs du Québec (FTQ), the National Bank of Canada, the TV group TVA, CINAR, Daniel Langlois (founder of Softimage), Remstar Corporation, France Film, DKD! Spectacle/Centre Molson and Rosaire Archambault. This new financial group has some C\$45.5 million in capital aimed at supporting Quebec firms on the international scene.

To conclude, I might propose to see the development of the cluster along the lines used to analyse the development of other local initiatives; I have used this image of cycle to analyse many social-economy initiatives and it appears it may be appropriate to study the development of clusters, and the role of associations that contribute to these clusters. Indeed, it seems that collective action is at the base of the development of the cluster. Associations contribute to developing resource mobilization and territo-rial (local or regional) awareness. This contributes to empowerment of the associations and groups associated with the initiative, some partnerships are developed and this contributes to creating collective learning, and in turn, stronger institutions to support the cluster initiative (Figure 3.3). In some cases the social economy per se may have a role and in others it may be professional or sectoral associations, depending on the case. Thus, the social economy component might be replaced by associations in the case of the film and audiovisual cluster, as was the case in the multimedia sector.

Access to resources is clearly an important challenge for developing a cluster and for innovative economic development projects. In this context, actors or associations will tap into what we have called 'socio-territorial

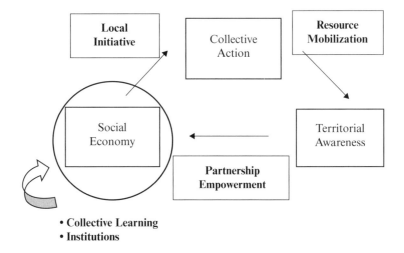

Source: Klein et al. (2009).

Figure 3.3   The cycle of inclusive local development

capital' in order to launch and develop its local initiatives such as the cluster. In order to succeed in deploying such collective actions as clusters, the associations and local initiatives must also tap into more comprehensive, global dynamics and resources. They have to establish links between social and economic actors, thus assuming their responsibility as a community intermediary organization (Klein et al. 2008; Klein and Tremblay 2009; Tremblay et al. 2009).

Access to resources is clearly an important challenge for developing a cluster and for innovative economic development projects. In this context, actors or associations will tap into what we have called 'socio-territorial capital' in order to launch and develop its local initiatives such as the cluster. In order to succeed in deploying such collective actions as clusters, the associations and local initiatives must also tap into more comprehensive, global dynamics and resources. They have to establish links between social and economic actors, thus assuming their responsibility as a community intermediary organization.

CONCLUSION

According to many actors in the sector, the film and audiovisual production cluster of Montreal as well as the multimedia cluster actors have managed quite well to mobilize actors around their project in order to develop the cluster. In both cases, as was seen, the support of the State (city of province) was quite important at some times, although over time their presence may diminish, as is the case with the multimedia cluster, which is now well known enough.

In the case of the multimedia, it is the MM City project which played the catalyst role, while in the film industry, it appears to be the Metropolitan Forum (Forum métropolitain de l'industrie cinématographique) which took place in November of 2004, and that put into motion the process of development of the cluster; it was mentioned in several interviews as a much appreciated effort, particularly by those who saw the need for a concerted effort throughout the difficult times the Montreal film and audiovisual industry was going through.

To return to the theoretical elements, I could say that social capital, as defined in Bourdieu's work as the set of resources that are related to a durable network of relations, with 'interconnections' and 'inter-exchanges', is only beginning to develop in the film sector, while it has clearly developed in an important way in the MM sector over the last decade. However, even in the film industry, many actors have seen enough common interests to start moving in the direction of cooperation and exchanges.

I mentioned earlier the image of 'glue' to indicate how these links and 'interconnections' can be useful, since they can reinforce the relationships among members of a group or a cluster; it is clear that to this day, the actors of the film and audiovisual cluster are not glued together, although some have started to develop connections and social relations.

In reference to the image of a 'lubricant' that accelerates the creation of relations between actors, we can say that the activities of the film and audiovisual cluster have contributed to an acceleration of the relations and connections by instituting a climate of trust between the actors and also by imposing some rules that reduce conflicts and favor cooperation, as well as by putting forward the general interest of attracting film produc-tions to Quebec, and then trying to distribute them in different regions.

We can thus conclude that the film and audiovisual cluster is at the start-up or development stage, that it has accelerated the circulation of information between members of the sector, and has contributed to some learning and innovation (innovation usually coming later, when clusters are more established and connections between actors more developed). There are still efforts to be made to ensure cooperation of many actors that are not directly in the cluster (tourism and film location actors such as real estate firms), as well as to ensure the transformation of competitive relations into cooperative relations throughout the cluster.

As for the MM sector, the MM City project has clearly played an important role in bringing the actors together, and in creating a sense of identity for the industry. It has also supported the territorial identity, by creating the image of Montreal as an MM city, but not only in the 'Cité du multimedia' perimeter.

My perspective situates the cluster initiatives in a context of innovation and the new economy, but also in a socio-territorial context, and this highlights the importance of the context in which the cluster is embedded. My approach thus highlights the importance of combining various types of resources and strategies, including various associations from the sectoral, professional local communities. At the same time, these clusters can of course not be separated from the global economy. Indeed, while socio-territorial awareness may be important to develop the cluster initiatives and rally people around them, it is essential to be connected to the rest of the industry and professional networks, in North America and around the globe. In this perspective, it is clear that both clusters analysed here have maintained strong connections with the global economy and the activities of their sector around the globe, but they connect themselves to the local territory to develop a sense of belonging or identity and to rally the main actors around their project of cluster development.

NOTES

1. According to Montreal International (2002), the Greater Montreal region ranks ninth in the IT sector, fourth in aerospace and eighth in biopharmaceutics among North American metropolises.
2. CLUNET Conference, Europe meets America, Montreal, September 20 2007.
3. The multimedia sector in Montreal benefitted from the Multimedia City program, which gave important financial incentives for firms to establish in the Multimedia City; if they did, they benefitted from financial contributions for each worker hired (Tremblay et al. 2004; Tremblay and Rousseau 2005). The program ended in 2008 and there is no similar program in the film and audiovisual sector.
4. The firm was founded in France in 1986 by the Guillemot brothers.
5. At the time, a rumor was circulating within the Quebec government to the effect that the Minister expected and even hoped to be turned down in order to be able to blame his federal counterpart for the failure to attract Ubisoft.
6. The formula chosen by the federal government was a discretionary form of assistance provided on an exceptional basis. Obviously the sector's actors contested this intervention. Faced with this dissatisfaction, Ottawa promised that firms with promising projects could obtain similar assistance.
7. In 2004, Electronic Arts also opened up in Montreal, which makes the gaming industry all the more important in Montreal.
8. They had hoped to attract a ratio of 50 per cent foreign firms/50 per cent Quebec firms.
9. According to the individuals interviewed, particularly in E-learning, the government completely abandoned this policy that had provided business opportunities and was highly appreciated by firms.

10. It should be mentioned that the biotechnology centres were spared but their tax credits were decreased.
11. For example, Discreet Logic has greatly benefited from this program.

REFERENCES

Andersson, T., S. Schwaag Serger, J. Sörvik and E. Wise Hansson (2004), *The Cluster Policies Whitebook*. Malmö: International Organisation for Knowledge Economy and Enterprise Development.

Bourdieu, P. (1980), Le capital social. Notes provisoires. *Actes de la recherche en sciences sociales* **31**, 8–19.

Britton, J. and G. Légaré (2004), Clustered beginnings: Anatomy of multimedia in Toronto, in *Clusters in a Cold Climate. Innovation Dynamics in a Diverse Economy*, edited by D. Wolfe and M. Lucas. Kingston: Queen's School of Policy Studies and McGill-Queen's University Press, pp. 139–64.

Britton, John, Diane-Gabrielle Tremblay and Richard Smith (2009), Contrasts in clustering: the example of Canadian New Media. *European Planning Studies* **17** 2, February, 211–35, http://www.informaworld.com/smpp/content~content=a9 08220372~db=all?jumptype=alert&alerttype=author,email.

Camagni, Roberto and Denis Maillat (eds) (2006), *Milieux innovateurs. Théories et politiques*. Paris: Economica.

Cassidy, E., C. Davis, D. Arthurs and D. Wolfe (2005), Beyond cluster – current practices and future strategies. Paper presented at the CRIC conference, Ballarat, Australia June 30–July 1.

City of Montreal Economic Development Strategy (2005), http://ville.montreal. qc.ca/portal/page?_pageid=5617,29759574&_dad=portal&_schema=PORTAL (last accessed 9 October 2010).

Communauté métropolitaine de Montréal (CMM) (2008a), *Les grappes et l'innovation: Libérer le capital créatif.*

Communauté métropolitaine de Montréal (2008b), *Cadre de financement des grappes métropolitaines*. Août. 7 p.

E&B DATA (2004), *Une filière d'envergure. La production audiovisuelle et les industries connexes dans la région de Montréal et au Québec*, March.

Ferriani S., R. Corrado and C. Boschetti (2005), Organizational learning under organizational impermanence: Collaboration ties in film project firms, *Journal of Management and Governance*, 257–85.

Fontan, J.-M., J.-L. Klein and D.-G. Tremblay (2005a), *Innovation sociale et reconversion économique. Le cas de Montréal*. Paris: Harmattan.

Fontan, J.M., J.L. Klein and D.-G. Tremblay (2005b), Collective action in local development: The case of Angus technopole in Montreal. *Canadian Journal of Urban Research* **13** (2), 317–36.

Friedman D. (1995), Why every business will be like show business, *Inc. Magazine.*

Gertler, M. and D. Wolfe. 2005. Spaces of knowledge flows: Clusters in a global context. Paper presented at the conference, 'Dynamics of industry and innovation', DRUID Tenth Anniversary Summer Organizations, Networks and Systems, June 27–29, Copenhagen.

Holbrook, A. and D. Wolfe (eds) (2002), *Knowledge Clusters and Regional*

Innovation: Economic Development in Canada. Kingston: Queen's School of
Policy Studies and McGill-Queen's University Press.

Imagining – Building Montreal 2025 (2005), http://montreal2025.com.

Jacob, R., P.-A. Julien, and L. Raymond. 1997. Compétitivité, savoirs stratégiques
et innovation; les leviers de l'apprentissage collectif en contexte de réseau.
Gestion **22** (3), 93–100.

Julien, Pierre-André (2005), *Entrepreneuriat régional et économie de la connaissance.
Une métaphore des romans policiers.* Québec: Presses de l'université du Québec.

Klein, Juan-Luis and Diane-Gabrielle Tremblay (2009), Social actors and their
role in metropolitan governance in Montreal: Towards an inclusive coalition?
Geojournal, **75**, 2.

Klein, Juan-Luis, Jean-Marc Fontan and Diane-Gabrielle Tremblay (2008),
Social entrepreneurs, local initiatives and social economy; foundations for an
innovative strategy to fight against poverty and exclusion. *Canadian Journal of
Regional Science* **30** (4).

Klein, Juan-Luis, Diane-Gabrielle Tremblay and Denis Bussières (2009),
Community based intermediation and social innovation. A case study in
Montreal's apparel sector. *International Journal of Technology Management*,
www.springerlink.com/content/102895/?Content+Status=Accepted&sort=p_On
lineDate&sortorder=desc&v=condensed&o=20.

Lin, N. (1999), Building a network theory of social capital. *Connexions* **22** (1),
28–51.

Marshall, Alfred (1889), *Principles of Economics*. London: Royal Economic
Society.

Manzagol, Claude, Éric Robitaille and Philippe Roy (1999), Le multimédia
à Montréal: Le high-tech à la rescousse des espaces fatigués, Montréal:
Département de géographie, Université de Montréal, www3.sympatico.ca/
eranlo.rob/multimedia2.pdf (last accessed June 2004).

National Research Council (1998), Supporting the knowledge-based economy in
the 21st century. Policy paper, National Research Council, Ottawa.

OECD (1999), *Boosting Innovation: the Cluster Approach*. Paris: Organisation for
Economic Cooperation and Development.

OECD (2001), *Innovative Clusters: Drivers of National Innovation Systems*. Paris:
Organisation for Economic Cooperation and Development.

Padmore, T. and H. Gibson (1998), Modeling systems of innovation, part II:
A framework for industrial cluster analysis in regions. *Research Policy* **26**,
625–41.

Pilati, Thomas and Diane-Gabrielle Tremblay (2007), Cité créative et District
culturel; une analyse des thèses en présence. *Géographie, économie et société* **9**
(4), 381–401.

PricewaterhouseCoopers (2000). *Étude du secteur du multimédia et des inforoutes
au Québec.*

Rifkin, Jeremy (2004), When markets give way to networks. . .everything is a
scrvicc, in *Creative Industries*, edited by John Hartley. London, UK: Blackwell
Publishing Ltd, pp. 361–74.

Salvemini S. and G. Delmestri (2000), Governance in the movie industry:
Alternatives to Hollywood?, *International Journal of Arts Management* **2** (2),
59–73.

Smith, R., J. McCarthy and M. Petrusevich (2004), Clusters or whirlwinds? The new
media industry in Vancouver, in *Clusters in a Cold Climate. Innovation Dynamics*

in a Diverse Economy, edited by D. Wolfe and M. Lucas. Kingston: Queen's School of Policy Studies and McGill-Queen's University Press, pp. 140–63.

Success@montreal (2005), http://ville.montreal.qc.ca/portal/page?_pageid=6037, 42239572&_dad=portal&_schema=PORTAL (last accessed 9 October 2010).

Tremblay, D.-G. (2003), New types of careers in the knowledge economy? Networks and boundaryless jobs as a career strategy in the ICT and multimedia sector. In *Communications and Strategies*. Montpellier, France: IDATE, pp. 81–106.

Tremblay, D.-G., C. Chevrier and S. Rousseau (2004), The Montreal multimedia sector: District, cluster or localized system of production? In *Clusters in a Cold Climate: Innovation Dynamics in a Diverse Economy*, edited by David Wolfe and Matthew Lucas. Montreal and Kingston: McGill-Queen's University Press, pp. 165–94.

Tremblay, D.-G. and S. Rousseau (2005), Le secteur du multimédia à Montréal peut-il être considéré comme un milieu innovateur? In *Géographie, Economie et société*. Paris: Lavoisier, pp. 37–56.

Tremblay, Diane-Gabrielle, Jean-Marc Fontan and Juan-Luis Klein (2009), *Initiatives locales et développement socioterritorial*. Québec: Presses de l'université du Québec. 353 p.

Tremblay, G. (2008), *Clusters and Innovation: Boosting Creative Capital*. Presentation at the 21st Annual Entretiens du Centre Jacques Cartier. October. 27 p.

Wolfe, D., C. Davis and M. Lucas (2005), Global networks and local linkages: An introduction, in *Global Networks and Local Linkages*. Montreal: McGill-Queen's University Press.

4. The knowledge base, research and development and regional economic policy: the US and UK experience

William F. Lever

INTRODUCTION

As the world becomes increasingly concerned about the onset of recession, whose depth and likely duration is uncertain, it may seem shortsighted or parochial to focus on local economic policy. Currently, national factors, and global processes, offer the most widely adopted explanations of the downturn. The fact that there are economy-based riots in Vladivostok and Moscow suggests that the whole of Russia has economic problems which stem from the two-thirds reduction in the price of oil. All Chinese cities seem to be suffering their share of the Chinese downturn in the economic growth rate from 10 per cent p.a. to 6 per cent p.a. So global has the economic downturn become that global unemployment rates are now being calculated and forecast at the global scale for the first time by the IMF and the ILO. Global unemployment rose from 180 million out of a total of 3 billion (5.6 per cent) in 2007, to 190 million (6.2 per cent) in 2008 and to 200 million (6.9 per cent) in 2009 (O'Grady, 2009).

In this context, however, there is still justification for examining economy at the local scale, either urban or regional. Successful local policy intervention may be able to ameliorate or offset the impact of national or global recession. Even if this does not happen, local policy can place cities or regions on a better footing to benefit when growth returns. The British government has been criticized for not putting its financial house in order during the long period of growth (by increasing financial regulation, by creating more efficient capital markets, by investing in labour training and infrastructure): it has been accused of 'failing to fix the roof when the sun shines'. This, however, is no justification for not trying to fix the roof when it rains.

If cities are, therefore, looking for ways to improve their competitive position even though the global and macro-economies are depressed, then there is a clear distinction between supply-side and demand-side consideration. If policymakers feel markets are constrained they are likely to focus on adjusting the supply of labour (by education and training), of capital, and of space (property and land). When the economy is depressed there is likely to be surplus of labour (unemployment) and space (vacant property and a depressed land market), but capital is likely to be short. When the economy is depressed there is likely to be an argument in favour of stimulating the demand side by public investment (a 'New Deal') and by encouraging private expenditure (by reducing personal direct and indirect taxation, and by reducing interest rates). Some of these approaches do lend themselves to local policy intervention, but most are amenable only to national (and even international) policy interventions such as interest rate changes and part-nationalization.

One set of policies designed to enhance urban/regional competitiveness focuses on the knowledge base and has elements of both supply side (such as human capital approaches and infrastructural investment) and demand side (such as public sector procurement). The remainder of this chapter looks at the generation and application of knowledge and IT.

THE THEORY OF KNOWLEDGE AND ECONOMIC COMPETITIVENESS

Theory links the development of the knowledge base with innovation and with economic growth in a Schumpeterian model. The recovery from earlier depressions has been linked to innovations such as road transport in the 1920s, television and plastics in the 1940s and information technology in the 1970s in long-wave Kondratieff cycles. OECD (1999) described how knowledge-based industries have been outpacing the overall rate of growth of gross domestic product for many years in most of its member states. OECD identified the knowledge-based sectors of a national or local economy as high and medium–high technology manufacturing industries and services such as financial services, insurance and communications which rose from 44 per cent of the total OECD economy in 1985 to more than 54 per cent in 2005. Within this group the services have now significantly outgrown the knowledge-based manufacturing. This knowledge base, theoretically, is generated by investment in research and development. This investment in software-writing, programming and publicly-financed higher education currently represents 10 per cent of all investment in the OECD and, as such, is marginally greater than investment in physical infrastructure – moving information is now more important than moving people and goods.

OECD defines knowledge in several ways. There is technical knowledge which contributes to the innovation of products, processes and services. There is customer-based knowledge which covers new markets, consumer choice and tastes and fashions, and is employed in the retail and distribution sectors (Wrigley and Lowe, 1996). There is knowledge which relates to financial inputs to the production or service process. Lastly, there is knowledge as human capital in the form of skills or creativity.

In terms of explaining economic growth and competitiveness however, what is critical is the distinction between codified and tacit knowledge (Feldman, 2000). Codified knowledge is widely available through telecommunications systems such as the internet. It facilitates most businesses' efficiency by widening supplier bases and access to markets, notifying the existence of producer services, widening labour sheds and labour fields, and providing financial information. However, as it is available to all at low or zero cost, is ubiquitous and is unambiguous, it confers no competitive advantage to its recipients (although lack of access may represent a disadvantage). Perhaps the most extreme recent example of the spread of codified knowledge is the development of the $10 laptop by the Sakshat company of India opening the internet to millions in the subcontinent. This is clearly radically cheaper than the MIT-produced Children's Machine costing $100, which has sold about one million units. In reality the $10 machine proved not to be a laptop but merely a specialized digital unit able to store specially produced educational materials which could be downloaded and printed from a regular computer (Buncombe, 2009).

Tacit knowledge, on the other hand, is available only to limited numbers of contacts, often requires to be passed on face-to-face because it is important that risk, ambiguity and fraud are minimized, it may be embedded in ways which are non-transferrable as in the case of creativity, and does confer competitive advantage on recipients. Because tacit knowledge often depends upon trust, risk minimization and face-to-face transmission it tends to advantage the largest cities where the highest levels of connectivity are to be found (Graham, 1999). It perhaps finds its antithesis in the recent Madoff scandal and fraud but more widely in the credit crunch and the subprime mortgage events.

There have been a number of empirical attempts to link statistically the knowledge base with the rate of economic growth and development at the urban scale. There are undoubtedly conceptual problems attached to the idea of a specifically local knowledge base. Information, particularly that generated by expensive research and development, tends to be transmitted within companies rather than by geographic proximity; knowledge generated within the public sector is likely to be disseminated as widely as possible within a nation state to maximize national productivity, and measures of absolute knowledge are difficult to calculate and calibrate in a way which makes them suitable for statistical analysis. Nevertheless, a number of studies have sought to correlate some measure of the extent of research and development with local economic performance. A study by Cheshire and Carbonaro (1996) used several multiple regression models to explain the economic growth of 117 Functional Urban Regions in western Europe. The independent variables were of several types including measures of population size, the impact of population potential with successive EU enlargements, economic structural variables (agriculture, coalmining, port-related activities) and, significantly, the number of research establishments per million inhabitants. In all the model specifications, the research and development variables were significantly correlated with the rate of change of GDP per head, or per worker. A similar study in the United States by Kresl and Singh (1999) produced similar results for 24 cities. Again, using the number of research centres per million workforce, the study correlated research with competitive success measured by the relative growth of retail sales, value added in manufacturing and business service receipts. A second variable, the engineering and research component of the labour force, was found to have a stronger relationship with competitiveness.

It has become clear that a wider and more multivariate definition of the knowledge base than that defined by the presence of research and development establishments is required, especially if this is being used to inform policymakers. Studies by Lever (2002a, 2002b) have expanded the measurement of the knowledge base to incorporate tacit knowledge, codified knowledge and knowledge infrastructure. As tacit knowledge almost certainly requires face-to-face contact in its transmission, the presence of major knowledge companies in the local economy will facilitate dissemination. A study by the World Cities Research Group (Taylor, 2009) used the presence of 74 major advanced producer service firms in accountancy, advertising, banking and finance and business law to rank cities and assess their global importance. A second way of measuring access to tacit knowledge is through the opportunities for travel and information exchange and measured by airport connectivity and specific sectoral events such as fairs and trade exhibitions.

Lastly within the category of tacit knowledge, the rate of new enterprise formation is used as a measure of innovation, although many knowledge-based innovations occur within existing enterprises. More crucially, a large proportion of registered new businesses do not reflect innovation but take the form of small wealth-absorbing consumer-oriented, personal services.

In seeking to measure access to codified knowledge, some studies use access to the internet, or the use by companies of e-commerce and e-trade. Codified knowledge is also measured by the extent of the local university-based research as this is assumed to be knowledge in the public domain. The volume of research is measured either by the absolute number of students in a city's universities or through the number of academic and scientific papers in refereed journals (with an emphasis on pure science, medicine and engineering) (Matthiesen and Andersson, 2000). Lastly, given the importance of telecommunications in the transmission of knowledge, a measure of telecommunications has been developed based on price, choice of physical infrastructure and the availability of more advanced systems such as broadband and darkfibre.

US CITIES AND THE GLOBAL ECONOMY

With the increasingly global dimension to the operation of the world's economy, the role of the world's major cities as economic drivers has been more and more the focus of study. Competition between cities, the operation of transnational companies, and the functioning of international entities such as the European Union and NAFTA, have reduced the role of the nation state in managing economies. One such study of competition between cities and the ranking of cities as global economic powers is the Mastercard Worldwide Centers of Commerce study (Mastercard, 2007). An index structure consisting of six dimensions based on 111 subindicators or variables was used. The six dimensions are (1) the legal and political framework, (2) economic stability, (3) the ease of doing business, (4) financial flows, (5) the business centre and, most importantly for this study, (6) knowledge creation and information flows. Collectively, these six dimensions cover the key functional characteristics of a city considered to be a world centre of commerce. Institutional factors are covered by 'the legal and political framework' dimension. The intensity of global connectivity and volume of throughput are captured by the 'financial' and 'business centre' dimensions. Risk factors associated with the city are covered by the 'economic stability' dimension.

The index also incorporates factors beyond those considered by traditional definitions of international financial and business centres. For example, in the 'ease of doing business' dimension, factors related to the quality of life are included and these, in turn, require some consideration of public policy challenges in urban development and related social policies (for example, crime, health and educational standards).

This index was applied initially to 50 and subsequently 63 cities worldwide. Table 4.1 shows the top ten cities globally, together with their overall

Table 4.1   Global ranking of cities 2007, top ten

Rank	City	Score
1	London	77.79
2	New York	73.80
3	Tokyo	68.09
4	Chicago	67.19
5	Hong Kong	62.32
6	Singapore	61.95
7	Frankfurt	61.34
8	Paris	61.19
9	Seoul	60.70
10	Los Angeles	59.05

Source: Mastercard Worldwide WCoC project.

scores. The scores are calculated so that for each indicator the highest/ best value is scored as 100 and the lowest/worse is scored as zero: intervening values are allocated proportionally and some variables are weighted. Thus, were a city to have the best value in each of the 111 indicators, its score would be 100: were it to have the worst of the 50 (or 63 subsequently) values it would have zero.

That London, New York and Tokyo are the top three worldwide centres of commerce is no surprise (although the fact that London outperformed New York was a surprise to some). The three Asian economic tigers, Hong Kong, Singapore and Seoul are amongst the top ten. In Europe, there was some surprise that Frankfurt outranked Paris, however marginally.

Nine US cities are among the top 50 cities and all of them are ranked in the top 25 (Table 4.2). US cities benefit from strong scores in the 'legal and political framework' and in the 'economic stability' dimensions, and interestingly they also score very high in the 'knowledge creation and information flow' dimension, although many of them score much lower in the other dimensions, such as 'ease of doing business', 'financial flow' and 'business centre' dimensions when compared with the leading European cities.

The ranking exercise was repeated in 2008. The number of cities was increased from 63 to 75, and Philadelphia was amongst the new entrants, and with a 2008 ranking of 18th was the highest of all the additional cities. The additional cities were included either to recognize world status which meant they should have been included from the outset (these included Philadelphia and Dallas in the US and Hamburg, Dusseldorf and Edinburgh in Europe), or to increase the geographic spread to reduce the

Table 4.2   US cities and the knowledge base: world ranking

	Overall		
	2008 Rank	2007 Rank	2008 Score Knowledge
New York	2	2	59.02
Chicago	5	4	46.31
Los Angeles	17	10	43.08
Philadelphia	18	*	37.80
Boston	21	13	40.58
Atlanta	25	20	38.21
San Francisco	28	18	36.34
Miami	29	21	32.19
Houston	34	22	36.09
Dallas	35	*	36.09
Washington	36	23	32.19

Note: *excluded from the 2007 ranking.

Source: Mastercard Worldwide WCoC project.

focus on North America and Europe (such as Buenos Aires, New Dehli, Jakarta and Rio de Janeiro).

Table 4.2 shows the overall ranking positions of the US cities. In general (with the exception of New York which retains its global second place by a significant margin) US cites lost some ground over the period 2007–08. This in part reflects the fact that some of the added cities were inserted at quite high levels in 2008 (including Philadelphia) but more importantly it reflects the relatively poor performance of the US economy nationally in this period, compared with the Far East, parts of Europe and parts of the Middle East. Cities such as Moscow, Singapore, Madrid, Shanghai and Sydney all did well in this period, for a variety of reasons. Moscow grew as a result of the rapid rise in the global prices of oil and gas, Madrid benefited from the growth of the Latin American economies for which it is the conduit into Europe, Shanghai has grown rapidly because of Chinese national urban planning and economic growth, and Sydney appears to have grown as a consequence of development for and after the Olympic Games.

Table 4.3 shows that in 2008 the 111 variables have been aggregated into seven dimensions rather than the six in 2006, and lists which US cities rank in the top ten in each dimension. From the table it is clear that some variables are only available at national level: hence the 'legal and political

Table 4.3   US cities in the top ten by dimension

Dimension	US cities in top ten
Legal and political	All US cities
Economic stability	None
Ease of doing business	New York, Chicago
Financial flow	New York, Chicago
Business centre	New York
Knowledge creation	New York, Chicago, Los Angeles
Livability	San Francisco

Source: Mastercard Worldwide WCoC project.

framework' which includes Moody's credit rating, the legal basis of grant-ing licences and registering property, and the ease of conducting interna-tional trade. None of the US cities rank in the top ten on the dimension of 'economic stability' which tends to be dominated by west European cities, reflecting the maturity of both their economic management institutions and their economies (although significantly London is not included in the top ten). New York and Chicago both make it into the top ten for the 'ease of doing business', the 'volume of financial flows' and 'knowledge crea-tion'. Only New York has a top ten listing in the 'business centre' dimen-sion which consists largely of airport connectivities, hotel availability and the functioning of the commercial property market. Los Angeles joins New York and Chicago in the 'knowledge creation and information flows' dimension. Lastly and uniquely only San Francisco among the US cities ranks in the top ten on the 'livability/quality of life' dimension along with Vancouver, Tokyo and seven west European cities.

THE KNOWLEDGE BASE

The worldwide centres project incorporates eight variables or indicators within the knowledge base dimension (Table 4.4). The overall dimension scores are listed in Table 4.2. Clearly New York is preeminent amongst the US cities, with Chicago second and Los Angeles third. The remaining cities are ranked very similarly to the overall ranking except that Boston seems to punch above its weight (presumably a Harvard–MIT–BU effect) whilst Miami and marginally Philadelphia have lower knowledge base rankings than their overall ranking amongst US cities.

Table 4.5 lists the rankings of the US cities on the eight individual indi-cators. Unfortunately, several of these indicators are not available at city

Table 4.4 Variables incorporated in the knowledge base

1. Number of universities
2. Number of medical schools
3. Number of MBA programmes
4. Patent applications per million people
5. Search engine hits
6. Researchers per million people
7. Scientific and technical journal articles per million people
8. Broadband access per thousand people

Source: Mastercard Worldwide WCoC project.

Table 4.5 Knowledge base variables, US city ranking

	Phil.	NY	Chic.	LA	Bost.	Atl.	SF	Mia.	Hous.	Dall.	Wash.
Universities	41	1	7	3	15	13	25	60	30	25	17
Medical schools	17	17	17	38	31	38	53	53	38	53	31
MBA programmes	14	10	11	26	14	26	20	47	20	61	14
Patents per mill.	7	7	7	7	7	7	7	7	7	7	7
Search engine hits	18	1	4	7	8	17	11	12	15	16	29
Researchers per mill.	26	26	26	26	26	26	26	26	26	26	26
Articles per mill.	16	16	16	16	16	16	16	16	16	16	16
Broadband access	19	19	19	19	19	19	19	19	19	19	19
Overall knowledge	18	2	7	10	19	17	23	23	24	30	10

Source: Mastercard Worldwide WCoC project.

level, and national averages are substituted here. In this case, separate data for the US cities would be available but, as this was part of a study of global cities worldwide, comparable data were not available for the listed cities in all the countries concerned. What we can conclude is that nationally, the US is strong on creativity, as measured by patents and on the production of scientific and technical journal articles (these two may be related) but rather poorer on access to broadband and has relatively

Table 4.6   Airport connectivity and quality of life

	Airport Con. Rank	Quality of Life
Philadelphia	19	29
New York	7	25
Chicago	2	26
Los Angeles	9	16
Boston	28	14
Atlanta	3	32
San Francisco	25	3
Miami	26	31
Houston	8	33
Dallas	6	28
Washington	11	21

Source: Mastercard Worldwide WCoC project.

few researchers per million inhabitants. At the city university level, Miami, Philadelphia and Houston do poorly although Philadelphia does relatively well on MBA programmes and medical schools.

Given the failure of the Mastercard study to pinpoint many specific factors in the knowledge base, two further variables are considered. As much of the knowledge base is vested in human capital and in face-to-face contact, the connectivity of the local airports becomes important. As expected the largest cities tend to have the most airline connections and volumes of passengers (Table 4.6). Chicago (2) and New York (7) are amongst the best connected US cities but the impact of hubbing shows up in the high placing of Atlanta (3) and Dallas (6), and the role of government in Washington (11). The least well connected of the US cities are Boston (28), Miami (26) and San Francisco (25). Philadelphia occupies a 'middle of the table' position in 19th place.

The second additional variable or dimension is quality of life or livability. As most of the knowledge base is generated by people in the form of human capital, for a local economy to be competitive it must offer an attractive location to innovative and creative people who may be highly mobile and very selective in where they operate. The term often used to describe the characteristics of such milieux is 'buzz' although definitions vary (Florida, 2002a, b). For some researchers buzz represents a community of like-minded businessmen and entrepreneurs whose actions and interactions are mutually supported. Whilst some have argued that such communities do not need to be based on spatial proximity, most authors see buzz in spatial clusters of creative activities where most of the rationale is in the face-to-face transmission of ideas and information (Asheim and Vang, 2005). Hall (2000) has described the locations most likely to generate or to appeal to a 'creative class' as those places which offer 'something to react to, cities in transition, a transition forward into new and unexpected modes of organization, societies which are in the throes of transformation in social relationships, in values and in views of the world'.

Whilst these are useful concepts they are difficult to measure or to confront with public policy. There are a number of wider concepts which seek to measure the quality of life. The most often quoted is the Mercer Index, designed by consultants to guide locational investment choices. This sets the value of New York at 100.0 and ranges for 215 cities worldwide from Zurich with a value of 106.5 to Baghdad, the least livable city with a value of 14.5. The Mastercard quality of life dimension is a composite of seven indicators. Four of these cover variables such as restaurants, museums and hotels, the other three are a measure of the quality of public sector provision in policing (crime rates), schooling and health care. Table 4.6 shows that for the ten US cities out of the global 75 in 2008, most are in the middle third, ranking between 25 and 35. The exceptions are San Francisco, which globally ranks third overall and Boston, Los Angeles and Washington. The lowest placed is Houston (33), and Philadelphia ranks 29th. At the global scale the range extends from Vancouver to Riyadh.

THE KNOWLEDGE BASE AND POLICY

Whilst the relationship between the knowledge base, competitiveness and economic growth is conceptually sound and empirically tested, it is less easy to draw practical policy conclusions. On the supply side shortages of capital, labour and space can be rectified by public sector interventions into the relevant markets: on the demand side, consumption may be stimulated by public investment, tax relief and procurement. No such solutions are available to remedy shortfalls in the knowledge base – the result is that governments, both national and local, must work on proxies and on correlated variables such as education, research, quality of life, information infrastructure and access.

The remainder of the chapter uses examples of public policy for the knowledge base drawn from Scotland. Scotland in some respects is an appropriate comparator for Pennsylvania, despite being rather smaller in population (six million compared with twelve million). Both have an economic base founded on old manufacturing industries such as steel and engineering, now rapidly being replaced by services both producer and personal. Both have a legislature with tax-raising powers, responsibility for delegated services such as health, social welfare and education (although Scotland's government has a minority party in power whose long-term objective is total independence from the rest of Great Britain). The two largest cities in each area are similar: Philadelphia and Edinburgh are the service centres with tourist industries and government; Pittsburgh and Glasgow are the old industrial centres which after a long period of decline and urban deprivation are now experiencing an 'urban renaissance'.

The first policy approach to building Scotland's knowledge economy has been demographic. Scotland has experienced a declining population since the 1960s, with brief respites in the mid 1970s and the early 1990s. Maximally, the net loss by the migration amounted to 25000 per annum and the worst population forecasts were a total population of 5 million. The 2000s have seen a rise in population to about 5.8 million currently. Disturbing as the population loss was, of greater concern was its selectivity, and a falling birth rate was leading to a rise in the dependency ratio (that is, the percentage of the population at work, or of working age is falling). The concern until recently has been that there will be insufficient labour available to fill the vacancies, and even currently specific skill shortages exist (construction workers, nurses, some personal services). The Scottish Government's response has been multi-faceted. Selective recruitment of overseas workers has addressed skill shortages, such as nurses from the Philippines and hotel staff from New Zealand, although there has been debate over the attraction of some workers such as health care workers from parts of the world where medical care is in relatively short supply. There has been a widespread acceptance of refugees and a policy change to enable them to seek employment in sectors such as construction (but more surprisingly doctors and dentists). The most recent enlargements of the EU (not including Bulgaria and Romania) has yielded a substantial flow of workers (Polish plumbers and tilers are a particular case in point), but the economic downturn has ironically raised concerns that their return to eastern Europe will leave further gaps in the labour force. Housing and social support has been made widely available and social networks have developed throughout Scotland in contrast to some of the larger English cities where the arrival of refugees has been seen as placing a high pressure on housing, health, education and social services. In Scotland the recent decline in the housing market, however, has cast refugees and EU members as a valuable source of demand for rental housing. In the most recent stage of the recession, many immigrant workers, especially those from the European Union, have returned home causing further problems in a very depressed housing and construction market. Many of the immigrant workers, such as political refugees, however, have been unable to return to their countries of origin, although in some cases they are prevented by law from gaining employment in the United Kingdom.

The current labour supply/demand balance in Scotland is unpredictable, but Robert Wright of Stirling University recently calculated that Scotland needs to import between 8000 and 12000 workers per year in order to make up the perceived shortfall of workers across a range of skills. The Scottish Government is also currently in discussion with the UK Home Office about easing visa regulations including the processing of visa applications offshore. A new Relocation Advice has been established to encourage immigrants to the UK to choose Scotland by stressing the problems of locating in the south east (housing, services, race relations). In terms of the knowledge base and innovation, the hope is that an increasingly multicultural population in Scotland will generate new ideas and enterprises particularly in personal and consumer services and the leisure sector.

In the changing financial and economic climate, increasing efforts are being made to manage the inflow of workers. Initially a points scheme was introduced for non-EU immigrants – workers with skills in demand were allocated higher levels of points and hence more rapid admission. More recently, a more graded system has been developed which offers automatic entry for immigrants with a higher degree for jobs with a salary over £25000, and other graduates may be recruited, but less skilled jobs must be advertised within the UK first before immigrants are sought and unskilled jobs may not now be filled by immigrants. This is clearly a UK-wide policy introduced by the Home Office, but there have been a number of instances where the differing labour market needs of Scotland and the south east of England have led to conflict between the Home Office and the Scottish Executive.

The attraction of immigrants and refugees to Scotland has a further advantage for the knowledge base. Richard Florida has advised the Scottish Government that knowledge workers are particularly attracted by the quality of life and diversity. The latter has been interpreted, at least in part, as multiculturalism and ethnic variety. Enhanced flows of immigrants will, it is hoped, increase the diversity of Scotland's cities not just in retail and leisure but in design (fashion, furnishings), in the creative arts (theatre, broadcasting, film), and in catering, food and drink. Five local authorities, including Glasgow, Aberdeen and Edinburgh, now have departments charged with assisting small business formation by immigrants.

The treatment of universities within the knowledge base in Scotland is quite distinctive. In addition to the Scottish Government's decision to waive student fees, in contrast to England, in order to attract more students, the foreign student cohort is set to rise beyond its current level of 13 000. Universities are actively encouraged to recruit overseas students, in part by the use of newly-created postgraduate scholarships. The result has been a rise of about 8 per cent in applications for 2009 admissions throughout Scotland with University of Glasgow applications up by 18 per cent. In part this is due to the onset of the recession (university applications always rise in recession as more school leavers choose not to try to enter employment, and some workers in employment seek to enhance their qualifications). Once graduated, foreign students are encouraged to stay by extending their visas for six months to two years beyond graduation. The fact that Scotland's government now has responsibility for all education, including both the vocational and academic post-school education, has enabled it to devise a system distinctively different from that in England where the vocational sector is run by a single national body. The Higher Education and Further Education sectors have access to a common pool of funding and have developed integrated programmes (for example 'access' courses delivered by FE colleges offer entry to first or subsequent years of HE universities' degree courses). This is of particular advantage to foreign students who may enter FE colleges and subsequently transfer to university courses. At the same time integrated courses have developed with both vocational and academic courses (for example Product Design and Engineering).

Scotland's position on graduates is that a higher percentage of school leavers go to university than in England but that the share of graduates in the workforce is lower in Scotland (17 per cent) than it is in the United Kingdom as a whole (20 per cent), although some of this differential is explained by the disproportionate share of graduate employment in London and the South East of England. The figures for graduates in the labour force, however, compare unfavourably with 31 per cent in the United States and 23 per cent in Japan. Attempts are now being made to increase Scotland's graduate retention rate. Some of this reflects the growing levels of devolution of government to Scotland, but even national functions are being moved such as defence procurement and even fixing a quota for the amount of public service television production which must come from Scotland.

Scotland's universities do have a good rate of spinout companies based on research. The Scottish Government and the Scottish Higher Education Funding Council's approach has been to concentrate on clusters of research-led companies focused on universities. The research cluster strategy has focused upon Glasgow (information technology, speech and face recognition security), on Dundee (biotechnology, both human and animal, including the notable animal cloning project) and Aberdeen (energy technologies with North Sea oil as a focus). Edinburgh, with its four universities, was originally omitted from the cluster strategy on the grounds that Edinburgh did not need further growth, but the Alba project, based on nanotechnology, has been located outside the city but based on research at Edinburgh and Heriot Watt universities.

The belief that knowledge-base clusters are a strong force for economic growth and innovation has been a significant element in Scottish Enterprise National's strategy (the regional development agency). The later 1990s saw a range of cluster-based policies usually comprising small firm support, contract registers, specialist scientific help, enhanced business services and labour market advice (Skills Development Scotland) in a specific area of Scotland. Evidence suggests that these clusters do not consist of firms which share or trade commercially sensitive knowledge but are composed of firms which share mutually advantageous external economies such as a skilled workforce, benign planning policies, a property development strategy and access to airports or other transport infrastructure such as the Euro freight rail terminal.

Two examples of clusters illustrate the Scottish Government's view on clusters and knowledge spillovers. The biotechnology cluster, most of it focused on Dundee, comprises about 460 enterprises of which about a quarter would benefit from assistance with growth. The essence now is to expand existing companies, or at least maintain the viability of companies rather than enhance the rate of new firm formation. The Biotechnology Association has identified capital shortfalls and reluctant lenders as a problem in moving into new market segments such as diagnostics, prosthetics and new therapies, and into new markets especially in Asia. Employment in the cluster grew from 12 000 in 1998 to 30 000 in 2007. The major asset for the cluster is the supply of trained graduate labour from universities such as St Andrews, Edinburgh, Dundee and Glasgow. There is little evidence, however, of transfers of knowledge or information between enterprises or in collaborative ventures, although recent developments in the fields of a cure for Alzheimer's, the creation of synthetic blood products and a new drug for HIV have been multi-firm because of the complexity of procedures and pharmacology involved.

The creative media complex in Glasgow, however, is assumed to exchange ideas, knowledge and techniques. It is focused upon a relocated centre for BBC Scotland on the former Garden Festival site, adjacent to which are the studios for Scottish Television, the largest commercial television station in Scotland. Film-making (with a range from *Braveheart* to *Harry Potter*) is now supported by Scottish Enterprise which maintains registers of available locations, casting agencies, and technical support, and has a development fund for companies involved in graphics, animation and special effects. There are further linkages with the creative art sectors such as opera, music (both classical and popular) and product design. In this cluster it is assumed that companies will interact by exchanging knowledge and ideas and engaging in joint ventures (Stirling and Leibovitz, 2002).

In the current economic climate, the role of the Financial Services Sector in Scotland is hardly an argument for job creation. The financial services grouping is largely based in Edinburgh where the Royal Bank of Scotland, Halifax–Bank of Scotland (now taken over by Lloyds–Trustee Savings Bank) and Standard Life, with 40 000 jobs jointly are located. The period of rapid growth led to market overheating (high property prices, high wage costs, congestion and skill shortages) which led to two relocation strategies. In the short run the opening up of the Edinburgh Business Park and its extension beyond the city limits has been facilitated by heavy investment in public transport. The longer distance transfer of financial services has been to the new Pacific Quay development in Glasgow utilizing the waterfront and an area of rundown commercial property. The global financial crisis has cast huge doubts over the sustainability of Scotland's financial services sector, especially the collapse of HBoS and RBS and the earlier mis-selling of insurance by Standard Life. However, the Glasgow segment has, to date, appeared more resilient with job creation in personal insurance, and in recruitment drives in the accountancy sector.

If one measure of the knowledge base is airport connectivity, then the Scottish Government has developed a modest strategy. The EU's Route Development Fund has been established to subsidize routes, and has been used in Scotland to subsidize marginal routes between Scotland's major airports to Europe and, to a lesser degree, to North America. Demand is currently divided between two major airports, Glasgow (70 per cent tourist) and Edinburgh (70 per cent business), and more minor airports such as Aberdeen (largely North Sea Oil traffic) and Prestwick (largely freight and some 'no frills' tourist). There has been discussion about the creation of a single central Scottish airport with the closure of Glasgow, Edinburgh and Prestwick to achieve scale economies and increase the possibility of interlinking (hubbing). Economic evaluation has indicated that such a development would not be economically viable and that capacity should be increased by adding a second runway at Edinburgh where business traffic is regarded as more important that tourist traffic (and tourist capacity at Glasgow can be improved by extending hours of operation and night flights: it is clear that the transport planners live under the flight path to Edinburgh airport and not Glasgow airport). The great majority of subsidized new routes are now operating out of Edinburgh, but the

European Union's concern about the public funding of unfair competition may adversely affect this development.

Lastly, a number of economic gurus, including Richard Florida and Ed Glaiser, have offered advice to the Scottish Executive on the attraction to Scotland of investment in the knowledge base. Their answers seem to lie largely in quality of life issues. To this end, the Scottish Executive, often through the agency of local authorities, has changed planning policies, service delivery and the consumer patterns within Scotland. The freeing-up of land in two sectors of Edinburgh, west and south-east, is designed to create new high income housing in attractive and accessible locations, rather than maintaining a strict and restrictive greenbelt policy. Glasgow has been assisted in its city centre renewal through urban renaissance grants and enhanced security so that it is now the second most significant centre in the UK after central London, having overtaken Manchester and Leeds. The tourist industry in Scotland has been radically restructured to encourage new leisure developments so that Edinburgh and Glasgow are now the second and third most population destinations in the UK (after central London). Hallmark events (European City of Culture, Commonwealth Games and currently the Scottish Homecoming) have been scheduled to raise Scotland's profile. Lastly, there have been major developments in the quality of public services including education and health as a consequence of the devolution of government. This latter does have the political advantage of winning votes from the indigenous population as well as attracting a new creative class.

CONCLUSION

The knowledge base is increasingly seen as the main asset in the economic competitiveness of cities and regions in the developed world of Europe and the United States, even in these difficult times. Much of the stock of knowledge is generated by research and development (R&D) investment but simple measures such as the number of R&D establishments per 100 000 inhabitants or patents do not adequately capture this concept. This distinction between tacit and codified knowledge stresses the importance of the former in explaining competitive success. It is possible to correlate a multifaceted variable to measure the knowledge with economic growth. The lessons for policymakers are less clear-cut but, using policy initiatives from Scotland, under the title 'Smart Successful Scotland', we focus on demographics, upon university spinoffs, upon knowledge-based clusters, upon access and technology and finally, and most generally, on quality of life to attract investment and creative and innovative people.

REFERENCES

Asheim, B. and Vang, J. (2005) 'Talents and innovative regions: exploring the importance of face-to-face communications', Mimeo.

Buncombe, A. (2009) 'Yours for £7, the laptop that will put India on line, and the £7 laptop that wasn't', *Independent*, February 2009.

Cheshire, P.C. and Carbonaro, G. (1996) 'Urban economic growth in Europe: testing theory and policy prescription', *Urban Studies*, 33, 1111–28.

Feldman, M.P. (2000) 'Location and innovation: the new economic geography of innovation spillovers and agglomeration', in Clark, G.R., Feldman, M.P. and Gertler, M.S. (eds) *The Oxford Handbook of Economic Geography*, Oxford: Oxford University Press, pp. 371–94.

Florida, R. (2002a) 'The economic geography of talent', *Annals of the Association of American Geographers*, 92, 743–55.

Florida, R. (2002b) *The Rise of the Creative Class*, New York: Basic Books.

Graham. S. (1999) 'Global grids of glass: on global cities, telecommunications and planetary urban networks', *Urban Studies*, 36, 929–49.

Hall, P. (2000) 'Creative cities and economic development', *Urban Studies*, 37, 639–50.

Kresl, P.K. and Singh, B. (1999) 'Competitiveness and the urban economy: twenty four large US metropolitan areas', *Urban Studies*, 36, 1017–28.

Lever, W.F. (2002a) 'Measuring the knowledge base and competitive cities in Europe', in Begg, I. (ed.) *Competitive Cities*, Bristol: Policy Press.

Lever, W.F. (2002b) 'Correlating the knowledge base of cities with economic growth', *Urban Studies*, 39, 859–70.

Mastercard (2007) *Worldwide Centers of Commerce Index*, Purchase NJ: Mastercard.

Mastercard (2008) *Worldwide Centers of Commerce Index*, Purchase NJ: Mastercard.

Matthiesen, G.W. and Andersson, A.E. (2000) 'Research gateways of the world', in Andersson, A.E. and Andersson, D.E. (eds) *Gateways to the Global Economy*, Cheltenham, UK and Northampton, MA, USA: Edward Elgar, pp. 17–31.

O'Grady, S. (2009) 'A world out of work', *Independent* 7-2-2009, p. 39.

OECD (1999) *Science, Technology and Industry Scoreboard: Benchmarking Knowledge-based Economies*, Paris: OECD.

Stirling, R. and Leibovitz, J. (2002) 'Creative-based clusters in Scotland', in Hardy, S. (ed.) *Regionalising the Knowledge-base*, London: Regional Studies Association.

Taylor, P. (2009) *Advanced Producer Services in Defining World Centres of Commerce*, Loughborough: WCRG.

Wrigley, N. and Lowe, M. (1996) *Retailing, Consumption and Capital*, Harlow: Longman.

5. Government and governance – how to build and sustain a consistent focus: the case of three Italian cities

Stefano Mollica, Marco Lucchini and Giovanna Hirsch

5.1 INTRODUCTION

The main objective of the chapter is to give evidence of some relevant experiences of Italian municipalities active in local development processes, looking at both the successful and unsuccessful sides of each of the cases presented. The chapter develops starting from the general hypothesis that, since the beginning of the 1990s, Italian local administrations have attempted to change their role by trying to become more active in local development processes. Some experiences can be considered successful, some others not. In any case, the administrations have had to face many difficulties in reaching their achievements and some inverted trends have occurred. The approach of our analysis is through case studies and historical analysis, also using *ad hoc* interviews with local actors to look at certain specific issues in more depth.

The chapter is organized as follows. In Section 5.2, the normative changes occurring in Italy since the 1990s in the public administration sector will be presented briefly showing the general framework in which some specific experiences took place. Section 5.3 will focus on the changes that particularly influenced the role and the organization of local governments. In Section 5.4, the case of three different Italian municipalities will be presented, paying particular attention to the role of public administration in the processes of local development undertaken. Section 5.5 will look at some policy implications and will open the general discussion on the role of local governments as local development promoters.

5.2 A CHANGING NORMATIVE FRAMEWORK: FROM SERVICES MANAGEMENT TO TERRITORY GOVERNANCE

In the 1990s, after decades of immobility, Italy, following many other OECD countries, started to undertake a series of reforms concerning its public administration system. A radical reform was needed not only because the administration was costly and obsolete, but also because in that period the institutional, economic and social contexts were changing. Those years, in fact, represent a particularly delicate and turbulent political season due to the Tangentopoli scandals that triggered a widespread public attitude against the waste of public resources; and due to the need for public debt realignment after a period of unstable equilibrium between relatively low levels of taxation, huge government debt and poor quality of public services. The need for change drove a large consensus for the implementation of a reform process.

After the first significant changes in 1990, a continuous set of policies followed one after the other until the early 2000s (see Box 5.1). The process of reform embraced both central and local government as well as the health care, school and university systems. The efficiency, responsibility and accountability of government, simplification of procedures, and the participation and empowerment of citizens were the guiding principles of the reforms. Some specific policies focused on making the administration more outward-looking and delivering better quality services while cutting costs. Several reforms took place in the management of public programmes, where the emphasis was put on performance and results instead of compliance and procedures (Marconi, 1997). The two key changes that occurred in the first part of the 1990s are: the reinforcement of performance orientation for managers and the introduction of a new accounting and control system. The responsibilities of politicians and those of managers were separated so that it was clear that politicians were responsible for policies and managers were responsible for administration.

The wave of reforms particularly highlights the new role of local governments. Since the 1990/142 Law, new principles and rules for the organization of local government have been put forward. Particularly relevant in the process of reform and in the definition of the changing role of local governments are the so-called 'Bassanini laws' which introduced the concept of 'vertical subsidiarity' and can be considered the basis for the following amendment of Title V of the Constitution. The following were introduced throughout this period:

BOX 5.1   CHANGES IN THE NORMATIVE
                FRAMEWORK

Some of the main changes in the normative framework since the
1990s are summarized below:

1990 L142:   local government reform.
This law defines the normative power of local governments and
introduces the Municipality Statute as a source of autonomy.
Different levels of government responsibilities are recognized:
European, national, regional and local. Each level has a regula-
tory autonomy; in particular local autonomy has been increased.
There is a problem with coordinating the different levels.
It found 'metropolitan cities', defining their role and functions.
It defines the forms of citizens' participation in local administrative
actions.
It redefines the role and competences of Municipalities and
Provinces.
It settles forms of local government cooperation.
It identifies private forms of local public services management.

1990 L241:   changes the relationship between public administration (PA) and citizens. PA does not only produce acts/proceed-
ings, but it also manages the territory. It develops participatory
strategies. It guarantees citizens' access to proceedings and their
participation in public sector decisions.
    It establishes 'the services conference' (Conferenza dei servizi)
that coordinates the decision taken by different administrations,
each responsible for a particular aspect of a problem. Before that,
each administration decided separately.
    It simplifies many unnecessary procedures and proceedings.

1993 L81:   Direct election of city mayors.

1995 DL 77:   Introduces the idea of economic accounting in the
public administration
Introduces the practice of budget in local public administration.

1997 L 59 (Bassanini Law I):   Has two objectives: strengthen
local autonomies and simplify public administrations' procedures.

It widens the regions' field of action. The three principles through which the reform is conducted are: the subsidiarity concept; administrative simplification; the pertinence concept.

1997 L127 (Bassanini Law II):   Introduces a wider separation between politics and administration, giving managers the responsibility to adopt administrative measures.

DPR 447/98:   This was the attempt, that failed completely, to create a unique local public interface to enterprises, with the aim of supporting their development processes.

DPR 286/99:   Internal control system in terms of strategy, management, legitimacy and managers' performance assessment.

1999 Introduction of private contract rules for local government officials.

2000 Testo Unico Enti Locali.

2001 Reform of Title V of the Constitution – Arts 117, 118, 119: Regions have a legislative power over every subject that is not expressly in the State's exclusive competence.
  Concurrent legislative power remains high despite Constitutional reform and in some specific cases it is not clear who is responsible for making decisions.

- more autonomy to local governments;
- simplification and more transparency of procedures;
- introduction of some forms of citizens' participation in local administrative actions;
- introduction of private forms of management in the public sector;
- introduction of private contract rules for public administration (PA) employees;
- vertical and horizontal subsidiarity;
- separation and distinction between politicians' and managers' roles.

An important effort has also been made in terms of enhancing coherence among policies, strategies, administrative structures and processes of public local governments. This is the period of local development and 'concertation' that envisages the participation of stakeholders in government decisions.

To sum up, local governments, according to the new normative framework, must not be just hierarchical structures and procedures, but they have also to become expressions of cooperation, values, strategic visions and organizational culture. Administrations must play an active role in local development processes, in the government of the territory, and in the promotion of democracy. Their responsibilities have become wider, more complex and more challenging.

5.3   THE ROLE OF MUNICIPALITIES IN LOCAL DEVELOPMENT PROCESSES

Much of the changing normative context outlined in the previous section was concerned with municipalities and their changing role. Cities and territories were the first and most important places where administrative changes occurred. In Italy, in both large and small localities, local public administrations had to face the issue of reforming their structures and rethinking the form and the content of the services they supplied. According to the changing general context and to the lines of the reform, local government bodies would not just be structures able to control and to regulate, but would also offer specific services in order to satisfy the needs of their citizens and the collectivity.

There are several innovative ideas aimed at de-bureaucratizing local public administration and curbing costs while improving the quality of services and providing more efficient management. Local governments have to become active and responsible subjects in local development and competitiveness growth processes, implementing policies and strategies to enhance local development trajectories. Institutional duties have become more complex and more interdependent, focusing less on simple managing activities and more on active government of the territory. The specific objectives of the reforms are to increase the quality of local government by developing its capacity to realize efficient policies and to supply efficient public services in a context where the needs of the collectivity are more and more complex, differentiated and prone to rapid changes. Municipalities are the focal promoters and suppliers of essential services for citizens and must become flexible enough to change rapidly according to what the society and the territory need. The idea is to operate according to market and competitiveness logic, with flexibility in structures, resources and solutions. However, the reform of local governments is not just an issue of optimization, efficiency and productivity enhancement, but (according to the direct experience of the authors) it is also an issue related to the need of changing the local administration organizational models and the need of changing the main goals to be achieved: from a local government body that produces acts and proceedings, to a system which produces and offers services, qualified policies, government initiatives and strategic visions in order to help to develop the territory.

There are many concrete examples of the changes outlined above. Several Italian municipalities started to introduce specific programmes and policies directly oriented to enhance and lead local development processes. For instance, some municipalities undertook urban regeneration policies; some others introduced citizens' involvement and participation mechanisms; some others introduced social budget practices; and recently more and more municipalities, for example, have promoted urban strategic planning processes.

In the next section, the experiences of three Italian municipalities involved in different local development and change processes will be presented and discussed, focusing in particular on the role of local public administration in activating and leading territorial transformation.

5.4 THE EXPERIENCES OF SOME SMALL–MEDIUM SIZED ITALIAN CITIES

This section presents three cases of small Italian cities (Matera, Pesaro and Barletta) that, during the mid 1990s, undertook some innovative and challenging experiences. The analysis focuses particularly on the role local administrations played in each of the different local development processes. Matera is an example of an extraordinary case of urban regeneration in the presence of a unique cultural and architectural asset; Pesaro is an example of a virtuous change in the internal organization and structure of a municipality, that has been able to positively affect the entire city; Barletta and the surrounding municipalities represent a case of a quite successful experience of inter-institutional cooperation. These three cases have been chosen because the authors had direct experience of those areas and because they believed that they could be an interesting starting point to stimulate a discussion and a debate with Pennsylvanian local officials in order to improve mutual knowledge and comparison. As we will see, in fact, these experiences were not free from contradictions and difficulties – sometimes public administrations were able to trigger virtuous circles of innovation and development, sometimes things happened regardless of local government intervention.

Matera: the 'Sassi' Case of Urban Regeneration

The urban regeneration project and the role of local public administration
The case of the urbanization of an ancient area of the city of Matera (that is located in the Basilicata Region in the South of Italy) is an impressive story of urban regeneration where the interaction between national and local interventions played a crucial role. The peculiarity of the case is, however, certainly determined by the existence of an extraordinary cultural and architectural asset: the Sassi – a belt of soft tufa rock-cut settlements, with two natural depressions. Matera is in fact the only place in the world where people can be said to live in the houses where their ancestors lived more than 9000 years ago. Natural caves were the first shelters for man (used since prehistoric times), who gradually transformed them into real houses taking advantage of particular inclinations and shapes able to protect them from heat in summer and cold in winter.

From the 17th century on, this area was left to the poor. At first they lived in the bare caves, later these were developed into house-like structures. In the first half of the 20th century, living conditions were extremely poor, with a high infant mortality rate that dramatically exceeded the national average.[1] First Palmiro Togliatti and then Alcide De Gasperi[2] a few years later, visited the area, and De Gasperi decided to sign a national special law in 1954 in order to evacuate all the inhabitants of the Sassi; that is, 15 000 people, living in extremely poor hygienic circumstances, had to be resettled in new quarters. Entire new boroughs (La Martella, Venusio and Picciano) were planned and built outside the Sassi area in order to host the displaced people. For this reason, Matera was one of the first Italian cities with town planning. In about 15 years, all the people living in the Sassi were placed in the new areas and the Sassi remained completely deserted, with living there being declared illegal. In exchange for the new houses where the rent was extremely low, the houses located in the Sassi area were expropriated and became government assets. As only richer people could afford to buy a new house and maintain estate property in the Sassi, most of the houses within the Sassi are now government-owned.

Therefore, Matera was a lively city but its historic centre was completely dead and crumbling. After decades of abandonment and a complete lack of public national or local interventions, a long process of regeneration and recovery of the area began. Over the course of years, a debate has developed on how to intervene to renovate the Sassi area. In 1986, the famous architect Renzo Piano proposed a refurbishing project for part of the area. This project, not actually put into practice, was based on providing lodgings, restaurants and meeting facilities in coherence with traditional building techniques. The actual recovery of the area started with the 'Sassi Law' (n. 771/1986), a national law which allowed financial resources for the project. The law gave local authorities the power to directly manage the project, recovering houses and churches in the area with public–private cooperation arrangements as many of the Sassi houses were government-owned. Law 771/1986 put aside 100 billion liras, and more money was added thanks to following national budget bills and European funding. The municipality of Matera had arranged two-year plans to enforce the law. A special technical office within the local administration organization was created in order to facilitate the management of the Sassi refurbishing. The mechanism for restructuring the properties worked as follows. With a request to the municipality, it was possible to receive a Sassi building under concession for 99 years, with the condition of refurbishing it. Between 40 and 60 per cent (depending on the destination) of the money needed for refurbishing was granted free by government. Property owners could also enjoy government funds. A huge part of the area has been restored thanks to this joint national–local level intervention and the refurbishing process is still ongoing.

In 1993, UNESCO acknowledged the Sassi area as a World Heritage site. Sassi was the first site to be named a 'cultural landscape' and it has been taken as a benchmark of a place where natural environment and man can mutually integrate. In a few decades, the Sassi, from being a 'national shame', has turned into a human heritage site known all over the world.

Positive impacts on the territory and emerging problems
The urban regeneration project carried out in the Sassi area of Matera had a significant impact on local development processes and on the territory's economy. UNESCO acknowledgement, together with the refurbishment intervention managed by the municipality, made Sassi one of the most important tourist attractions in the South of Italy and the first source of tourism in the Basilicata region. The project has certainly encouraged a series of activities linked with tourism that have affected the local economy positively: hotels, restaurants, meeting centres, art craft shops and private houses. Part of Sassi has in fact been transformed into residential properties, part into commercial activities, and part is developing into a museum network. Today, there is a project to transform part of the not yet refurbished part of Sassi into a system of museums (a demo-anthropologic museum, a farming culture museum, and so on) that aim to keep alive the past culture of this unique place thanks to exhibitions, seminars and dissemination activities.

An interesting aspect of Sassi development, not yet studied in detail, is the relationship between the renovation process of the area and the development of Matera's furniture industrial district. It seems that the two areas continued to develop in separate ways. However, recently, the furniture industrial district has placed its own representative office within the Sassi area, a sign that the municipality has recognized the importance and convenience of reciprocal support for local development. Some evidence in fact shows that the industrial district has helped to promote Sassi in the world thanks to its relations with international businessmen.

The overall perception about the urban regeneration process carried out in this city is that it has worked very well and produced important economic results for the territory. In the entire design, the role jointly played by national and local government has been crucial. In particular, local government has been able, until now, to handle and manage the entire process with a certain success. The technical office in charge of Sassi management in 1994 won the 'European urban and regional planning award' for the best refurbishment project of an urban centre.

However, in order to pass from a renewal start-up phase to a profitable and ongoing asset management phase, it is certainly necessary to have a forward-looking local political group able to continue to invest in local development in the absence of further national Sassi Law funding.

Barletta: the Case of Territorial Pact

The story of the 'Nord-Barese-Ofantino' Territorial Pact

'Territorial pacts' (*patti territoriali*) have been an interesting and innovative form of social dialogue that partially changed the Italian experience of 'social concertation'. The idea of territorial pacts was devised during discussions within CNEL (Consiglio Nazionale dell'Economia e del Lavoro) – which brings together representatives of the social partners – from 1993 onwards. The aim was to promote and coordinate various economic development projects in a particular area (for instance a province, a city or a neighbourhood) and to put them into an integrated framework, based on bargaining. The territorial pact was thus a means of gathering together all the resources present at the local level and directing them towards the realization of shared development objectives.

The 'Nord-Barese-Ofantino' Territorial Pact is often considered as one of the most successful pact experiences held in Italy (Cersosimo and Wolleb, 2006). The process that led to the implementation of the Pact has been long and complex. The idea of the Pact had been possible mainly thanks to a certain territorial homogeneity and productivity strength (mainly based on traditional productive sectors like footwear and textile industries), and a vital demographic dynamic. The Pact involved a series of medium-sized towns (Barletta, Andria), small towns (Trani, Corato,

Canosa di Puglia) and very small towns (Trinitapoli, Margherita di Savoia, Minervino Murge, Spinazzola).

Such territorial homogeneity encouraged the move for the creation of a distinct Province separate from the Province of Bari. However, the Pact project was both a factor of cohesion and a source of conflict among the different municipalities involved. Past experience was therefore characterized more by campanilistic conflicts than by cooperation experiences, and the Pact, in order to start and to survive, had to overcome adverse relationships among the bigger cities within the territory (namely Barletta, Andria and Trani). The Pact overcame its initial 'impasse' only when a new generation of city Mayors – younger, more autonomous in the management of their municipalities and eager to find innovative forms of local governance – found an agreement. Changes occurring in the Italian context in fact led local administrators to assess in a more careful way the opportunities and advantages coming from horizontal cooperation. The Barletta and Andria municipalities in particular were promoters of the Pact, able also to gradually involve other neighbouring towns.

In 1997, after many years of sensibilization and local concertation among public authorities, trade unions, civil society and the private sector, the Pact action plan was drafted, with the inclusion of nine municipalities in the territory north of Bari, and an in-depth debate about the initiatives for employment and social development to be carried out in the territory took place. The aim of the Pact was basically to support a transition from a disarticulated area to an integrated territorial system, able to integrate all its socio-economic components: culture, environment, tourism, infrastructure and production.

The Pact followed different steps of development:

1. Subscription (by Andria, Barletta, Corato and Trani municipalities, trade unions, the Bari industrial association, the SMEs coordination association) of the first local concertation document at CNEL (March 1997). All the subscribers committed themselves to implementing the necessary steps to obtain funds to start the Pact.
2. Transition from national to European Pact (towards a Territorial Employment Pact in coherence with European Union measures).
3. Application for European Community action (April 1997) and European Commission approval.
4. Setting up of a technical group for the creation of the Intermediary Local Subject (Soggetto intermediario locale – SIL). The governance structure of the Pact was based on two main pillars: the agency for employment and development, and the Territorial Pact Association for employment. The first was the technical body of the Pact that

worked as an intermediary local actor for the decisions concerning the use of the structuring funds. The Association, which included 68 subjects, represented the political body of the Pact.

5. Action Plan drafting for the years 1998–99. The approval of the Action Plan signified the passage from a concertation phase to a management phase.
6. Action Plan drafting for the years 2000–2006. This Action Plan set a new territory governance system that was organized in a system of different agencies, consortia and structures.
7. The Pact became a real Local Development Agency. The Agency became the main body responsible for the elaboration and management of all local public development policies in the area. The Agency handles the Agricultural and Fishing Pact, promotes Prusst (Programmi di Riqualificazione Urbana e di Sviluppo Sostenibile del Territorio), is committed to monitoring the minimum wage in the Pact area and participates in the PIT (Piano Integrato Territoriale).

Results, innovative experiences and effects on the territory
The experience of the Pact has certainly produced positive effects on the territory. It has been recognized as one of the most successful European pact experiences in terms of resource spending capacity. The Pact promoted economic redistribution in the area facilitating the start-up of a series of commercial and productive activities, motivating the implementation of some public works and helping municipalities and institutions that found themselves in bad financial conditions. This also had a positive employment outcome, even if probably to a lesser extent than it was expected.

Nonetheless, assessing the entire experience, the key question to address is: 'did the Pact effectively change local actors' cognitive schemes and behavioural models?'. It can be stated that some things have certainly moved in the desired direction. Local actors' capacity to think in terms of collective action has increased significantly, the degree of self-referentiality has diminished and partnership relationships have become more solid (Cersosimo and Wolleb, 2006). According to many, in fact, the most impressive effect of the Pact experience has been the increasing capacity for local administrations to work and plan together, often in a private–public team form. In fact, today, national and international scenarios are so vast and complicated that it is not possible to think that territorial institutions act independently and alone. Any kind of decision concerning employment, environment, culture, tourism, economy and so on, increasingly requires cooperative arrangements between public and private institutions on a wider scale than a single municipality. When a territorial common vision is outlined, it is easier to overcome egoistic and personal interests in favour of a positive and profitable integration. The Pact, after the first programming period, also worked as an incubator of local development projects and ideas that involved the whole area.

Limits and problems of the experience

The overall experience of the Pact can therefore be assessed as a positive one, even if, during the different phases, it encountered some difficulties. The resource spending ability of the Pact was accompanied by at least two main shortcomings: the not entirely successful partnership involvement in the elaboration and management of local development strategies, and the difficulty in the realization of local public assets thanks to collective action (Cersosimo and Wolleb, 2006). Then, from the Pact governance point of view, the organization in terms of a technical Agency and a more political Pact Association has not been an entirely successful story. Since the beginning, while the Agency has worked very effectively in implementing the Action Plan, the Association has turned out to be a useless and powerless political body. One of the reasons for such difficulties has been attributed, by different sides, to the unbalanced composition of the Association with the predominant role of bigger municipalities.

More recently, the passage from the Pact to a Local Development Agency has also shown some difficulties. The new structure, based on the creation of many different agencies, resulted in a decentralization process and in a fractionalization of the interventions and decision making. This in turn dampened the capacity to continue to develop and implement a common territorial vision and weakened inter-institutional cooperation arrangements between private and public actors. The new challenge has now started with the first election of the new Province in June 2009, which could provide the opportunity for the Agency to become the active local development body for the entire Province.

Pesaro: Municipality Internal Reorganization and its Impact on the City

The story of the internal reorganization of Pesaro municipality

In the early 1990s, Pesaro was a substantially well administrated town, providing plenty of servicing and cultural activities, with a sound economic background based on an industrial district system of medium and small enterprises. Nonetheless a radical reorganization of the municipality's nature and functioning was started. The main reason was to give a new stimulus to a local government model whose innovation capacity was decreasing. The city of Pesaro has always been run by left wing administrations experiencing innovative stages in the 1970s, as well as contradicting and static ones in the 1980s and early 1990s. The aim of the restructuring process was to show that the local administration was able to reinvent itself and to break from previous experiences, maintaining the same political colour. Another reason was to keep in tune with the rest of the country. In fact, as already pointed out in sections s.2 and s.3, the early 1990s saw the collapse of the so-called First Republic, the failure of the traditional political parties and a wide moral and economic crisis. Thanks to a national and international push, new ideas on public administration then emerged not only as pure management of procedures and services but also as an engine of innovation, dynamism and changing of the entire local system. This innovation was necessarily led by the introduction of managerial criteria within public administration, of results-oriented policies and the abandonment of bureaucratic schemes. The pursuit of results in terms of efficiency, money saving, effectiveness and transparency became then the leading rationale for changing local public administration organization. This was basically the background from which Pesaro's decision to restructure originated. The process was facilitated by the strong determination of the City Mayor, who, for the first time, was elected directly by the citizens and by the problems created by the opposing forces linked with old nepotistic administrative practices occurring between government and management.

Local government reorganization was based on different steps. A key aspect was the programme which, in contrast with past experiences, became central in the relationship between the City Mayor and the voters.[3] The programme became less generic and was assessed according to its actual feasibility. In order to correctly interpret the role of politics towards administrative management, programmatic priorities were defined, in turn shaping the organizational structure. This was the second innovative element: the local government organizational structure was no longer considered a static entity, completely separate from politics and from programme priorities, but it became a tool through which political commitments were implemented. Therefore, the centrality of the programme and politicians' responsibility to reorganize the administrative machine according to the programme's priorities (evolving from the concept that politicians pass and managers rest) are the basis of the restructuring of the municipality of Pesaro.

How could intervention in the reorganization be achieved? As the process started before the national legal context changed concretely, it was necessary to justify the process from a legal point of view. Therefore, it was necessary to find the right way to allow the municipality to undergo changes without objections and appeals from the trade unions, finding spaces for autonomy within the Municipality Statute. The 1995 City

Mayor election campaign was then based on the issue of local administration reorganization. This was considered an extraordinary innovative issue that created consensus among citizens and entrepreneurial associations and great expectations for a more efficient and modern administration.

After the elections, on the basis of the programme presented, the reorganization process started, focussing on the identification of professional figures able to pursue and process the objectives. First of all, it was crucial to strengthen coordination within the local public administration structure. Traditionally, local public administration was organized in well separated and often non-communicating specific sectors and areas. This model of organization could lead to the fact that quite often the left hand did not know what the right hand was doing. There was no communication between different branches of the organization, each official was jealous of his/her own procedure and not interested in the final overall results. The reorganization process aimed to change this structure by reinforcing coordination and interconnecting different skills that were useful to implement policies that were not necessarily integrated. For instance, if a policy which has an impact on citizens' health, environmental quality, education and culture has to be implemented, it is necessary to have a convergence of different skills within the administration. During past decades, incommunicability and shifting the blame onto each other became consolidated practices among local administration branches. Identifying coordination figures like 'Area Managers' who monitored the integration and cooperation among different branches and skills represented a real change within the organization.[4]

Another significant change was represented by the identification of professional figures linked to specific projects. Usually, the public administration managers' capacity was directly linked to the number of persons they managed and the complexity of the structure they controlled. In the idea of a new administrative organization, efficient policies became the key objective. Often policies are implemented thanks to specific projects and project managers do not necessarily need a huge number of officers, but they need to activate skills and knowledge already present in the administration and make them work together.

At the top of this structure, the General Manager was recognized for the first time as having a highly coordinating function. The General Manager was responsible for the efficient functioning of the organizational structure (in other words the relationship between human and financial resources and the attainment of the main objectives), while the old figure of Municipality Secretary was responsible for legal and procedural accuracy.

Such an innovative framework emphasized the intense debate within the administrative structure that involved internal officials, staff and trade unions. The reforming process promoted a drastic structural change that sometimes involved the need for new professional figures taken from outside the structure, and sometimes the functional restructuring of some other internal figures.

Results and positive effects on the city

Local government reorganization had impressive positive effects on the city of Pesaro. In particular, the changing model of budget planning released important resources that were then used either to implement new projects or to reimburse citizens. In the past, budgets were prepared by responsible managers simply claiming more resources than the previous year, without any economizing effort. With the introduction of a new budget planning system, it became practice that the General Manager, Area Managers and their officials conducted a bargaining process in order to optimize resources. This mechanism was a success and there are some concrete examples as evidence.

1. The first example refers to the important political objective of fighting fiscal evasion. At the time of the first steps of restructuring, in Pesaro there was a specific tax for garbage disposal. From that point, the office with responsibility operated in a repetitive way without applying any new examination to verify if there were tax evasion cases. The new administration then decided to launch a call for tenders, selecting a company that started to measure all property areas. This operation was criticized within the leading political party because of the fear that people were concerned about violation of their privacy. The administration promised that, if the operation produced any financial savings, these would be redistributed to citizens. The operation was rapidly concluded with the return of about 7 billion liras to the citizens of Pesaro.
2. The second experience that is worth mentioning refers to the different use of resources. In the past, resources were not usually handled in managerial terms, but often were exploited to favour private rather than public interests. The administration then decided to make a resource plan in order to free funds for boosting investments. Another complex operation was the transformation of municipalized societies into public–private ones with the selling of 25 per cent of public ownership to a private partner selected through a bid. This operation was able to restore the municipality's cash account, making it possible to build a new road (the Interquartieri road) without any support from either the Region or the State.

3. A third interesting and successful example was that of the changing management pattern of municipal chemistries. Municipal chemistries were an important resource for the city with the absurd paradox that private activities made good profits while public ones did not. So, the new economic and managerial perspective has also been applied to municipal chemistries, matching directors' payments directly to their effective results and not only to their role or educational qualification.

Innovations introduced by municipality reorganization therefore had important impacts on the development trajectories of the city of Pesaro. First, with the reorganization, local public administration gained the trust of citizens, and acquired a reputation that in turn made improvements in terms of efficiency and the simplification of procedures. In other words, reorganization changed the relationship between public administration officials and their jobs, and therefore the relationship between local administration and the citizens. Second, the containment of municipality expenses made it possible to convert part of the current spending on more and better services for citizens. This could also be possible thanks to the specific characteristics of Pesaro's entrepreneurial fabric which was mainly formed by a network of small firms. In such a typical industrial district context, the territorial environment was thought to deeply influence firms' performance. An efficient public administration, well functioning social service and education systems, a good cultural supply and no wasteful investment in public works, were, at the time, all perceived by entrepreneurs as concretely supporting factors of local industrial development. Third, reorganization made local public administration more prepared to respond to the economic system. The economic system had often lamented the indeterminateness of public administration and the length of its responsive capacity. Putting the citizen, the customer and the firm at the centre of the local administration activities made the timing of the response a priority, rather than the simple fulfilment of the procedure. In concrete terms, for instance, a Unique Office for Productive Activities (Sportello Unico per le Attività Produttive) was created to give prompt answers to the economic system. Fourth, the new emerging idea of local public administration has favoured the introduction of urban strategic planning in Italy. In other words, if local administration wanted to be a real engine for territorial development, it had to promote a local governance able to involve all the different actors in the territory, allowing them to cooperate and to address their actions towards a common vision. The urban strategic planning of Pesaro has been a direct result of the overall process of local public administration reorganization. An internal reorganization of the public administration body has occurred, then, little by little, a new mission for local administration has emerged.

All these changes and innovations do not necessarily protect the territory from the international financial market crisis or from Chinese competition, but they can be considered possible solutions to making local administration work more efficiently. Today, in fact, *vis-à-vis* the ongoing financial crisis, local public spending and infrastructure investment are again at the centre of the debate.

Limits and problems of the experience

These new managerial and planning processes have been supported by the introduction of other innovative mechanisms of management control and staff assessment systems. In fact, if all public officers are in general available to commit themselves to a more professional and efficient way of working, they also want to be reassured by selection and payment systems that reward merit and efficiency rather than political links, friendships or family relationships and so on. Otherwise, local public administration may become a strong factor of conservation that works against any innovation mechanism.

Most of the changes that the reorganization process brought about are still effective in Pesaro's public administration body. However, the enthusiasm of the first years of the reform and the strong political strategic vision have gradually weakened. One of the limits of the experience has been that it never reached a wider level, even if the administration tried to extend it to neighbouring municipalities. The difficulty in becoming a national benchmark was mainly due to the fact that sometimes politics fears changes and does not promote successful cases. Moreover, in Italy there are few arenas able to recognize successful experiences and share them with other municipalities.

However, Pesaro represents a successful experience of the changing role of local public administration that was characteristic of many other territories in Italy at that time. The relationship between local public administration and territorial development radically changed in two-thirds of the country. However, since 2001 the overall context has changed again, mainly showing a decrease in the innovative push that characterized the 1990s.

5.5   SOME POLICY IMPLICATIONS

From the three cases described above it is possible to draw some policy implications relative to the role local government and its structure can play in different local development processes. The main question that arises is: 'which are the most effective structures/forms/organizational models that allow innovation and changes to occur?'. First, what is common to all the experiences presented is that innovation processes need to be handled by specific structures and skills, separate from the ordinary local government bodies, coherent and dedicated to the specific mission. Often, the current branches of local government are in fact unable to trigger and to manage changes that break with the past. Only when innovation is finally integrated in current processes, can it be absorbed by the ordinary structure of local government. Another key issue that arises from the analysis of the cases reported is that effective changes must be triggered without stopping the ordinary functioning of local government units. New political and technical skills must be introduced while maintaining ordinary operations.

Each of the cases presented also suggests some interesting hints that can enhance the debate and open up the comparison with other national and international experiences. The case of urban regeneration in the Sassi area of Matera raises a series of discussions around the conditions of success of such a local development experience. The first condition of development is certainly linked to the presence of an extraordinary cultural and architectural asset, the Sassi. More generally, however, it can be assumed that a key step for a local government engaged in a local development process is, first of all, to identify a local asset – that can be tangible or intangible, cultural, architectural, archeological, and so on – and then to identify the right policy efforts to improve the asset and make it more visible. The second condition of success can be found in a productive cooperation between state and local governments in pursuing the urban regeneration project. In this specific context, cooperation between different government levels has been useful: (1) to find the right civic and political cohesion necessary to give a solution to a relevant national issue (the urban renewal of a profoundly downgraded area); (2) to agree a common cultural valorization strategy (identifying conditions, legal and political tools, organization patterns and so on); and (3) to agree a high level of devolving operative power to the local government (with the creation of a special office within the local administration structure, entirely devoted to the management of the national Law for refurbishing the Sassi). Ultimately, the Matera story tells us that it is not possible to make valuable and sophisticated assets the centre of a local development strategy without an administration able to deeply comprehend the value of the cultural heritage it wants to improve. In this sense, for the future of the Sassi, it is necessary to have an enlightened local administration able to continue to invest in the area (without or with less State support) and able to understand the complex relationship existing between the asset valorization and a development pattern.

To sum up, the success of Matera's story is due to a mix of specific conditions. National funds for the refurbishing project have been used efficiently and not lost on wasteful activities. The project has been carried out with the commitment of many actors, not least with the commitment of many citizens that believed in refurbishing the Sassi and invested in the area.

The second case presented in the chapter is the case of the 'Patto territoriale Nord-Barese-Ofantino'. The general idea of our study is that an integrated 'network of municipalities' (*area vasta*) may develop only in the presence of a governance pattern that promotes a well functioning inter-institutional cooperative arrangement. Basically, there are three conditions for the success of such an experience. First, it is necessary that local government has a strong political willingness. In other words, it has to be a powerful and skilled political leadership able not only to identify territorial needs, but also to overcome selfish interests in favour of more important common positive effects on innovation and the competitiveness of the whole area concerned. In order to reach this result it is also necessary that the local governments involved can easily manage the appropriate technical and political tools to implement the project. The second condition of success for an inter-institutional cooperation experience is the involvement of a motivated and committed private partnership. Again, the private counterpart has to be able to identify the long-term advantages coming from cooperation and not limit its vision to only the immediate results. In this light, it is important that private subjects have a clear idea of how to cooperate in the project (providing funds, human resources, knowledge, and so forth). The third key condition is undoubtedly the creation of an ad hoc technical and professional body well equipped to support policy decisions with specific knowledge and skills. In theory, if the aim is to develop a longlasting cooperation experience, it would also be hoped that all the municipalities involved would delegate some decision-making authority and some functions to a third neutral body. This is perhaps the most difficult step to tackle, because often specific, selfish and immediate interests from both the private and public sides prevail over common concerns.

Ultimately, from the last case presented in the chapter, the case of local public administrative reorganization in the municipality of Pesaro, we can gather that as local government bodies supply a series of strongly diversified services to citizens, local public administration improvement also occurs as a result of the integration of such multiple activities. Moving in the direction of improving integration, cooperation and coordination among different responsibilities and branches of the local public administration structure means creating a new and more effective public administration and therefore better and more efficient services to citizens. Another crucial precondition of any local development policy is the resetting of the complex relationship that characterizes Italian public administration, namely the relationship between political and administrative structures. According to the authors' experience of Italian cities, results often depend on the joint and strongly linked action between the Mayor and his General Managers. In Italy, Pesaro represents the first attempt to find a profitable reorganization of political and managerial responsibilities. Moreover, changes and innovations have been successfully pursued with strong support from stakeholders external to local government and basically by the electorate. This can be identified as a general condition of all kinds of processes of change, as a change often triggers a shift in the balance of power and those against the change are usually the more powerful. Therefore in order to promote innovation it is necessary to gain more consensus through the relationship with citizens. This occurred in Pesaro during the second half of the 1990s, thanks also to the introduction of the direct election of the City Mayor and a campaign mainly focused on the idea of restructuring the local public administrative body. Ultimately, as happened in the other two cases presented as well as in Pesaro, it is evident that innovation has been possible because the reforming process has been managed separately (at least initially) from the ordinary public administration structure. However, ad hoc structures then have to be integrated if the initial results are to be absorbed and endure into the future.

Then, from the cases reported and from the authors' direct experience (also in the management of many institutional and structural change processes), it is possible to argue that a proactive local government role is essential in promoting sustainable territorial development processes. However, this local government role is possible and effective only if administrations have appropriate decisional and operational capacities that fully match with the complexity of the required changes.

This in turn requires certain conditions:

1. Leadership and enough political strength in order to change. Continuous and strong commitments and push are needed to avoid change and innovation becoming just procedures and bureaucracy. Politics must recognize the role of a new administration not only able to produce acts and services but also able to 'direct' and 'manage' development. In other words, it has to be a powerful and skilled political guide.
2. Commitment and knowledge of the issue. A set of laws and regulations is needed in order to justify changes and a full commitment of those who have the responsibility to take decisions.

3. Support of change management experts. Skilled and motivated managers and professionals are needed to implement changes and new policies. New public managers, in particular General Managers, are needed to ensure a profitable coordination among policies and processes.

4. An appropriate 'organizational model'. Structures coherent with the objective and with the importance of the changes occurring are needed. Innovations and new policies have to be handled by specific structures and skills, separate from the ordinary local government bodies, coherent and dedicated to the specific mission. Effective changes must be triggered without interfering with the ordinary functions of local government units. New political and technical skills must be introduced, while maintaining ordinary operations.

5. Strong cooperation between political officers and managers, although maintaining their specific roles and responsibilities.

6. Cooperation and subsidiarity between national, regional and local government levels. A productive cooperation between state and local governments has to be established in order to pursue the change and to sustain development: (i) to find the right civic and political cohesion necessary to provide a solution for a relevant national issue; (ii) to agree a common cultural valorization strategy; and (iii) to agree a high level of devolving operative power to local governments.

7. The idea of a 'network of municipalities'. This may develop only in the presence of a governance pattern that promotes a well functioning inter-institutional cooperative arrangement.

8. A clear and challenging vision of the main issues to be dealt with, that is, to be able to recognize and improve the appropriate assets and skills that local development needs.

9. Involvement and participation of private (economic) partnerships and of citizens. The involvement of a motivated and committed private partnership is needed. It is important that private subjects have a clear idea of how to cooperate in the change project (providing funds, human resources, knowledge, and so forth). It is very important that citizens may also participate in the change process, both through participatory democracy means and through an active role in the implementation of public functions.

ACKNOWLEDGEMENTS

The authors want to acknowledge Oriano Giovanelli (former Mayor of the City of Pesaro); Francesco Salerno (former Mayor of the City of Barletta); Tito Di Maggio (former public local officer of the City of Matera) for sharing with us their direct evidence, giving us important information about the case studies and offering their thoughtful contribution and suggestions.

NOTES

1. The situation got worse until the 1940s. At that time, Carlo Levi (an Italian novelist) visited the Sassi and described them in his novel *Cristo si è fermato ad Eboli*, reporting on the dramatically poor living conditions.
2. Palmiro Togliatti was the leader of the Communist Party, while Alcide De Gasperi was the leader of the Christian Democrats Party and at that time the Prime Minister.
3. Before the direct election of the City Mayor, the process of programme definition was much longer and complicated: the date for the local council election was fixed, political parties were presented, city councilmen were elected, and then the campaigning started to build the majority. After a few months, the City Council was established and the City Mayor was elected. Then, the programme was elaborated as a synthesis of the political parties' equilibria. With the direct election of the City Mayor, the programme was submitted together with the mayoral application and became a real pact with citizens.
4. This reflected the general cultural changes somehow confirmed by DL29/1993 that, for the first time, distinguished between political and managerial roles.

REFERENCES

Cersosimo D. and Wolleb G. (2006), *Economie dal basso: un itinerario nell'Italia locale*, Roma: Donzelli Ed.
Marconi P. (1997), 'Public administration reform and government responsiveness to citizens in Italy', Public Management Service, OECD.
List of websites consulted:
http://www.sassiweb.it/unesco/
http://www.worldheritagesite.org/sites/isassidimatera.html

6. Economic structure and business organization in the central region of Mexico

Jaime Sobrino

INTRODUCTION: DIFFERENTIAL URBANIZATION AND METROPOLITAN REGIONS

In 1993, a paper by Hermanaus Geyer and Thomas Kontuly appeared in the *International Regional Science Review*, the purpose of which was to propose a graphic and territorial model on the demographic performance of cities based on population size (Geyer and Kontuly, 1993). Based on the available literature until that date, and with some empirical exercises undertaken by themselves, they concluded that the model could be applied both to developed and developing countries.

That model was called differential urbanization and assumed that the cities of a national urban system, divided according to population size, experience successive periods of high and low demographic growth. These differences in demographic growth are attributed to the pattern of migration flows that occur inside the nation.

From a graphic perspective, the model of differential urbanization presents three phases: (i) primary city; (ii) polarization reversal, and (iii) counterurbanization (Figure 6.1). During the first phase, most of the population growth inside the urban system occurs in the main city, generally the capital of the country, where most of the population and of the national economic activity are concentrated. The second phase is when intermediate cities have a major rate of population growth, in relation to the primary city, and at the same time they work as alternative nodes for economic activity location; internal migration is not for the primary city but for intermediate urban areas.

Finally, the third phase, counterurbanization, occurs when the smaller urban areas are the major attractors of a migrant population and receptors of productive investment. The origin of these migration flows could be from rural areas, from mobility characterized by internal migration

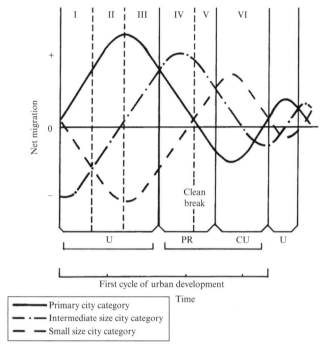

Note: Generalized stages of differential urbanization. I, Early primary city stage (EPC); II, intermediate primary city stage (IPC); III, advanced primary city stage (APC); IV, early intermediate city stage (EIC); V, advanced intermediate city stage (AIC); VI, small city stage (SSC). U = urbanization; PR = polarization reversal; CU = counterurbanization.

Source: Geyer and Kontuly (1993).

Figure 6.1   Differential urbanization: demographic performance by city size

in the phases of primacy and polarization reversal, or from larger urban areas.

This model of differential urbanization is a result of a series of factors, such as the diseconomies of agglomeration that face urban areas (Moomaw, 1981; Prud'homme and Lee, 1999); changes in the structure of the urban labor market associated with the neoliberal stage of capitalism (Balchin et al., 2000; Gordon and Turok, 2005); an increase in the educational levels of the population (Polèse, 2005; Smith, 2000); the search for environmental amenities from the migrant population (Barbiero, 2007; Boyle et al., 1998) and changes in the age pyramid associated with demographic transition (Clark, 1987; Cliquet, 1991). It is important to mention, however, that in the design of this model, and in the causes that explain the transit from one phase to another, the economic behavior of the country is not included, and therefore this variable is assumed as a catalyst that eventually would accelerate or delay the process of change.

From a territorial point of view, in the phase of polarization reversal, the intermediate cities that are generally located near to the primary cities are those that experience, in the first instance, a population and economic boom, in relation to the total of these areas in the national urban system (Figure 6.2).

That dynamic is explained by the generation of centripetal forces from the primary city, an aspect that is reinforced by the concentration of infrastructure and technological advance in that part of the national territory (Malecki, 1997). This means an intraregional decentralization of population and economic activity. The intermediate cities that are part of this intraregional decentralization are, in a way, independent, that is they have their own urban labor market. Likewise, the urban continuum in these areas is not contiguous to the primary city.

This kind of territorial concentration and economic activity, and the interactions generated among urban areas of different sizes and between them and the rural areas, are called megalopolis (Gottman, 1961), metroplex (Meltzer, 1984) or polycentric urban regions (Champion, 2001). In this chapter they will be called metropolitan regions.

A metropolitan region is a vast territory that contains a large metropolitan zone and smaller neighboring urban areas in a radius of 150 kilometers, or a number of cities with no dominant one among them. In this territorial configuration a series of interrelations and interdependencies occur and are shown by the redistribution of population and economic activities, the productive specialization of each population center and complex social processes.

Champion (2001) established three major problems in the identification of a metropolitan region: (i) the spatial scale to which it belongs (metropolitan, regional or megalopolitan); (ii) the degree of interaction and interdependence needed to become a region of this type (the productive specialization of urban areas and daily mobility of their population), and (iii) the way in which it is formed (diffusion, incorporation or fusion). Again, in the models of metropolitan region formation the evolution of the national or regional economy is not included. Likewise, it is a fact that economic growth operates primarily at the national/societal level and not at the city/regional level (Polèse, 2005).

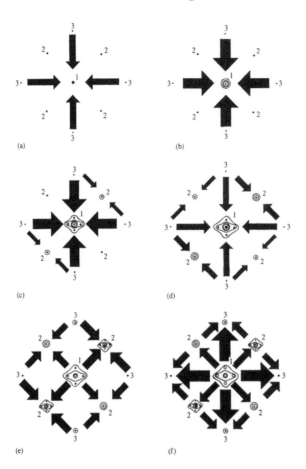

Note: A graphic model of the phases of differential urbanization: mainstream movements; (a) early primary city stage, (b) intermediate primary city stage, (c) advanced primary city stage, (d) early intermediate city stage, (e) advanced intermediate city stage, (f) small city stage.

Source: Geyer and Kontuly (1993).

Figure 6.2   Differential urbanization: territorial expression

CENTRAL REGION OF MEXICO: POPULATION AND ECONOMIC ACTIVITIES

Mexico is a country with a federal government system and contains 31 states and a Federal District. In 2005, its population reached 103.3 million people, becoming the eleventh most populated country in the world; its gross national product (GNP) was 375.6 billion dollars (in 1990 constant dollars), the 13th place in the world context. In this way, its GNP per capita was 3638 dollars, representing only 12 per cent of that of the United States in the same year (30 762 dollars).

The central region of the country contains the Federal District (where the head offices of the federal government powers are located and also the central city of the Mexico City Metropolitan Area), and the states of Hidalgo, Mexico, Morelos, Puebla, Querétaro and Tlaxcala. These seven states cover a territory of 98 490 square kilometers (38 027 square miles), which represent 5 per cent of the national territory. In 2005 the region's population was 34.7 million people, representing 33.6 per cent of the national total. Likewise, also for that year, a gross domestic product (GDP) of 148.8 billion dollars was generated in the region, comprising 39.6 per cent of the national wealth. Compared with the state of Pennsylvania, the central region of Mexico has 84 per cent of Pennsylvania's territory, has 2.9 times more population but produces only 42 per cent of the GDP of that state.

This region is characterized by its high level of urbanization. In 2005 it had the Mexico City Metropolitan Area (MCMA) with 19.2 million people, 13 urban and metropolitan areas that together had 7.6 million people, and 46 cities (of 15–99 thousand people), with a total of 1.2 million people. Then, 80.7 per cent of the regional population was concentrated in urban and metropolitan areas; meanwhile the remaining 19.3 per cent was a mixed rural population with dispersed distribution (Figure 6.3).

Between 1980 and 2005 the country saw an important reduction in its rate of population growth, and at the same time an advanced stage of polarization reversal in the model of differential urbanization. The MCMA registered a rate of population growth of 1.2 per cent, which was less than its natural population rate of 2.2 per cent; therefore the net migration balance was negative. On the other hand, the 13 urban and metropolitan areas experienced an annual average rate of 3 per cent and of 2 per cent in the remaining urban areas of the region. Finally, the mixed and rural areas had an average rate of 1.5 per cent and showed a net population emigration (Table 6.1).

The 13 urban and metropolitan areas of the central region, with a population of 100 thousand and more inhabitants in 2005, increased their share in the demographic total of the country from 5.6 per cent in 1980 to 7.4 per cent in 2005. Likewise, their contribution in the total national urban population increased from 9.1 per cent to 10.5 per cent for the same years. In absolute terms, the population of these cities increased by almost four million people, where more than one million and a half were migrants that lived in the MCMA.

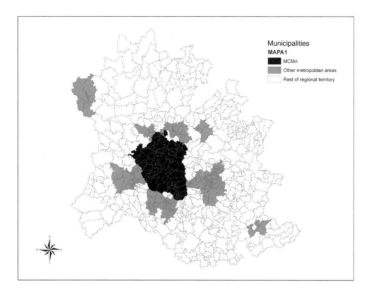

Figure 6.3　Central region of Mexico

From the information in Table 6.1, it can be concluded that between 1980 and 2005 the central region of the country observed a slower growth rate than in the national context, therefore, its concentration level decreased from 35.3 to 33.6 per cent. This fall in the demographic share is mainly explained by the negative net migratory balance of the MCMA, which was of 4.5 million people during those 25 years, but where one-third changed their place of residence to one of the remaining 13 urban areas of the region.

From an economic point of view the following happened: between 1980 and 2005 Mexico's GNP increased from 204 to 376 billion dollars (in 1990 prices), which meant an annual average growth of 2.5 per cent. However, looking at a series of short-term cycles: between 1985 and 1988 the economy was reduced to an annual rate of −0.2 per cent, as a result of the end of the imports substitution model, the decrease in oil prices (the main export good up to that point in the country) and a kind of passive policy in relation to commercial opening (Table 6.2).

From 1988 the economic model of commercial opening was consolidated; it was sustained in the arguments of the Washington Consensus, which favored an annual growth of 4 per cent between that year and 1993. In December 1994 another crisis began which extended until the following year and arose from mistakes in the economic policy, specifically in relation to the exchange rate but also because of the collapse of the financial

Table 6.1 Central region: population, 1980–2005

Entity	Population				Rates of Growth			
	1980	1990	2000	2005	1980–1990	1990–2000	2000–2005	1980–2005
Mexico	66 846 833	81 249 645	97 483 412	103 263 388	1.97	1.84	1.16	1.75
Central Region	23 533 883	27 073 577	32 936 450	34 736 303	1.41	1.98	1.07	1.57
MCMA	14 457 258	15 563 795	18 396 677	19 231 829	0.74	1.69	0.89	1.15
Metropolitan Areas	3 714 193	5 050 981	6 815 957	7 593 246	3.12	3.04	2.18	2.90
Urban Areas	742 427	962 116	1 175 402	1 205 991	2.63	2.02	0.52	1.96
Rest	4 620 005	5 496 685	6 548 414	6 705 237	1.75	1.77	0.47	1.50

Source: National census of population and housing.

Table 6.2   Central region: gross domestic product, 1980–2005

Year	Mexico	Central Region	Share
1980	203 687	88 559	43.5
1985	223 513	89 316	40.0
1988	222 055	91 931	41.4
1993	268 753	113 847	42.4
1995	263 402	108 269	41.1
1998	310 071	127 771	41.2
2003	352 406	141 938	40.3
2005	375 644	148 623	39.6

Source: National Accounts System.

flows and the high level of consumers' debt; this financial crisis required the support of the World Bank, which provided a 60 billion dollars loan, an amount that was used to prop up the banks and financial and other enterprises, but not to support the debtors.

With the beginning of NAFTA (the North American Free Trade Agreement), in 1994, and once the financial problems of large firms were solved, between 1995 and 1998 the GDP of the country increased to an annual average rate of 5.6 per cent. This was mainly as a result of the growth in manufacturing exports, at the same time that the national economic evolution began its close synchronicity with the rhythm of the United States' economy. In this way, between 1998 and 2003 a fall in the GDP growth was observed which was motivated by the crisis in the United States during 2001, and a recovery between 2003 and 2005.

As was mentioned before, between 1980 and 2005 the central region's share in the demographic national total fell from 35.3 to 33.6 per cent. From the economic aspect, there was also a decrease from 43.5 to 39.6 per cent (Table 6.2). However, the main contraction occurred between 1980 and 1985, the years in which the end of the imports substitution model came about with a fall of 3.5 percentage points.

The economic deceleration of the central region in the first years of the 1980s was explained by its concentration of almost 50 per cent of the national manufacturing production, especially intermediate and inheritance goods (automotive, furniture and electrical appliances), the demand for which fell because of the decreasing real income of the population. Another cause was the fall in the state's demand for labor and its decreasing investment in infrastructure (Ariza and Ramírez, 2008).

From 1988 the economy of the central region registered growth rates above those of the country, as a result of the firms' adaptation to export

Table 6.3   Central region: gross domestic product by industry, 1993–2003

Industry	1993	1998	2003
1990 million dollars			
Mexico	268 753	310 071	352 406
Central region	113 847	127 771	141 940
Agriculture	2 536	2 677	3 326
Mining and oil	275	328	373
Manufacturing	24 512	29 808	30 274
Construction	5 805	5 035	5 904
Electricity	987	1 116	1 223
Commerce	23 812	25 776	27 560
Transport	10 817	13 685	17 269
Financial services	15 537	18 577	23 996
Other services	29 565	30 768	32 015
Location quotients			
Agriculture	0.36	0.36	0.41
Mining and oil	0.17	0.19	0.20
Manufacturing	1.15	1.12	1.11
Construction	1.08	0.94	1.03
Electricity	0.55	0.54	0.49
Commerce	0.97	0.99	0.94
Transport	1.04	1.04	1.03
Financial services	1.07	1.15	1.26
Other services	1.15	1.17	1.19

Source: National Accounts System.

initiatives, and also due to the concentration of producer services. However, the financial crisis at the end of 1994 affected the macroeconomic behavior, due to the high concentration of these activities in the region. Finally, from 1998 to 2005 there was a marginal tendency towards a loss of participation in the GDP, caused by the decentralization process of the manufacturing industry in the national territory.

In 1993 the GDP of the region was 114 billion dollars, that is, 42.4 per cent of the national total, while in 2003 it increased to 142 billion dollars but its participation was reduced to 40.3 per cent (Table 6.3). In absolute terms, the most representative industries in the region are other services (producer and consumer services) and manufacturing; these two generated 43.9 per cent of the regional GDP in 2003. Conversely, mining and electricity were less important and provided only 1.1 per cent of the regional GDP.

The location quotients are used to identify the economic activities in which a territory is specialized.[1] According to the results of the quotients from Table 6.3, the central region of Mexico specialized in five industries in 2003: manufacturing, construction, transport, financial services and other services. It is important to mention that the output of the manufacturing and transport quotient fell between 1993 and 2003, which means a lesser relative growth of these activities than that which occurred at the national level, while the financial services and other services registered an increase in the location quotient, showing a tendency towards the strengthening of the superior tertiary sector in the regional economic structure. In 2003 this sector generated a regional GDP of 71 per cent, against the 26.7 per cent of the secondary sector and the 2.3 per cent of the primary sector.

URBAN COMPETITIVENESS AND MANUFACTURING SPECIALIZATION

Urban competitiveness is a controversial concept because there are arguments supporting the idea that competitiveness occurs only among firms, therefore cities do not compete with each other but they operate only as localization spaces for economic activities (Krugman, 1994). Other authors, on the other hand (including myself), support the pertinence of the concept which conceives urban competitiveness as the capacity of cities to attract productive investment (Lever and Turok, 1999); as the change in its economic position inside the national or international urban system (Begg, 1999); or even as the interaction between local economic performance and other social, political and environmental manifestations of urban life (Boddy, 2002; Harding, 2005; Potts, 2002).

A wider definition of urban competitiveness has to do with the degree to which a city, compared with other cities regarding competence, is capable of attracting productive investment that is shown in the generation of employment and increased income, and at the same time increasing and consolidating its cultural amenities, recreational attractions, social cohesion, governance and an adequate environment for its residents (Global Urban Competitiveness Project, 2005).

There are diverse empirical proposals regarding studying the competitive performance of nations (CEPAL, 1995; IMD, 2007; Porter et al., 2000), or cities (Cabrero et al., 2006; Kresl and Singh, 1999; Ni, 2007; Sobrino, 2002). These exercises quantify competitiveness through variables related to moments in the competitive process using diverse statistical techniques.

It is important to mention that in the urban competitiveness concepts and in the methodological proposals used to measure it, a favorable macroeconomic environment in the national and international contexts is considered. However, a global economic crisis, such as the one that began in the second semester of 2008, makes it mandatory to reflect on the concept of urban competitiveness and the processes that are happening in cities. With the contraction of productive investment, the macroeconomic performance of urban areas will be determined by a series of factors, such as: (i) their economic structure and degree of insertion in world consumption networks (Duranton and Puga, 2000); (ii) the strength of their competitive advantages based on quality, which are related to local collaboration among firms, the participation of local governments in the economic promotion of the city and the agreements and interrelations among social agents (Turok, 2005); (iii) the components of local income determination, especially in the marginal propensity of savings (Armstrong and Taylor, 2000), and (iv) the policy actions of central and local governments to stimulate the internal market (Woodford, 1993).

It is clear that a local economic structure mainly oriented to international commerce will make a city more vulnerable in the first instance, therefore the economic and social agents should act to promote a restructuring towards those activities that offer the most competitive advantages.

With the objective of offering empirical observations on the competitive condition of the main cities of Mexico and the urban subsystem of the central region, this chapter describes the results of an exercise using Ni Pengfei's procedure (2007), adapting it to available data for the cities of the country. The empirical measure of urban competitiveness for the main cities of Mexico was made using five variables: (i) logarithm of total GDP in 2003 (GDP); (ii) GDP growth rate between 1998 and 2003 (GDPGR); (iii) logarithm of GDP per capita in 2003 (GDPPC); (iv) employment rate in the period (ER), and (v) quality of life index (QI). The information available in the country makes this exercise possible only for the period 1998–2003.

The variable GDP represents the scale of the urban economy, its participation in the national market, and the potential creation and good use of its competitive advantages related to size. The GDPGR shows the potential performance for the attraction of productive investment. The GDPPC estimates the degree of economic efficiency of the city. The ER represents the impact of the attraction of productive investment on the behavior of the urban labor market. Lastly, the QI measures the access of the local population to public goods.

From these variables a factorial analysis with a principal components method was carried out for the 87 cities of the country with a population of at least 100 thousand inhabitants in 2000. This multivariate technique is used for the reduction and grouping of original variables in a new group of components that are characterized by having a lesser degree of correlation and covariance between them. From the results of the factorial analysis a

Table 6.4   *Competitiveness index for regional urban system, 1998–2003*

Region	Cities	Regional CI average	Standard deviation	Coefficient of variation (%)
North Frontier	24	32	21	66
North	11	44	22	50
West	17	50	30	60
Central	14	43	25	58
South and South-east	21	53	24	45

Source: author's data.

competitiveness index was obtained for the 87 cities of the study (Table 6.4).

The period 1998–2003 was characterized by moderate national economic growth, deceleration of exports, derived from the US crisis of 2001, and the initiation of the cessation of NAFTA. Under these conditions, the 24 urban areas located in the five frontier states with the US had a greater degree of variation. This means that cities with a favorable economic performance and those with depressive symptoms coexisted in that region. There is no evidence about the diffusion of the territorial effects of centripetal forces from the winner cities on their microeconomic context.

The second most successful region was the central, where the variation coefficient was below that of the North Frontier and West regions. This indicates the emergence of diffusion effects of a centripetal kind with their origin in the MCMA. It is important to mention that the urban area with the best CI in the region was precisely this city, which attained third place among the 87 urban areas of the country. Its place is attributed to scale factors and a favorable attraction of investment in financial and producer services. The metropolis also experienced an important economic restructuring that was initiated in the 1980s and consisted of the change of specialized activities from manufacturing towards high-order services. In addition, in the period 1998–2003 the MCMA experienced a deindustrialization phenomenon, which had been seen before in the period 1980–1985.

On the opposite side, the 21 cities of the South and South-East region were those of less than average economic performance. This had been the poorest socioeconomic region for a long time and in this period regional disparities were increased.

The diffusion effects from the MCMA towards cities in its regional area mainly occurred in manufacturing, and not in financial and producer services, and its locational tendency has been towards more concentration.

When disaggregating the manufacturing GDP according to 26 groups and getting location quotients for the MCMA and its 13 cities in the regional area in 2003, it can be observed, first, that the MCMA was the metropolis with the highest degree of manufacturing diversity because it was specialized in 17 of the 26 groups, while on the other hand there was an urban area of few more than 100 thousand inhabitants which specialized in oil refining and had no metallic minerals. Second, there is an association between manufacturing size and diversity, that is, the higher the scale of manufacturing, the higher the number of specialized groups.

Third, the average number of specialized cities in the 17 groups of the MCMA was 4.4, while in the nine non-specialized groups of the MCMA the average of cities fell to 2.7. These data show that there were diffusion effects of a centripetal type from the MCMA towards its cities of influence; these benefited from their proximity to that area and from the conformation of their manufacturing structure.

As a final point, the diffusion effects took place in manufacturing groups of a traditional kind: food, textiles, garments, and others of an intermediate character as well as those such as paper and cardboard, chemical and rubber. The diffusion effects were not present in modern and high-technology manufacturing groups; the MCMA was not specialized in those activities.

A curious aspect is that deindustrialization in the MCMA occurred mainly due to the delocation of the automotive sector, whose dynamism had been strongly related to international commerce. Until 1980, this metropolis was the main location node to that activity and was oriented to the internal market. The commercial opening generated prosperity in this kind of productive investment but also a change in its location pattern and in favor of cities located in the North Frontier and West regions.

BUSINESS ORGANIZATION

The phenomenon of business networks or association formation is studied from diverse disciplines. Maybe the perspective most related to the territorial dimension is the economic geography discipline that analyses clusters or industrial districts of small, innovative and high-tech firms (Boschma and Kloosterman, 2005). The principles orienting the formation of these groups in specific terms are innovation and knowledge to keep competitiveness in this global era. Economic geography privileges the regional scale for the study of innovation systems.

An alternative way to study the business organization phenomenon is through business sociology, which has a systemic perspective and analyzes the formation of business networks and their level of integration and embeddedness with the community, locality or region where they are formed (García, 2002; Lomnitz, 2001). The key variables to explain innovation and knowledge processes are confidence, the social capital accumulated in society and the tacit exchange of knowledge.

When the conditions to promote innovation and knowledge among firms are analyzed the institutional context is pointed out as a central element. It is essential to have institutions that are flexible, responsible and with new schemes of governance, where collaboration among government, firms and civil society is seen through more attractive economic results for firms and substantial improvements in the labor and life conditions of the resident population.

Networks are forms of social integration and social spaces of relationship and connectivity, which are defined by the dynamic exchange between the agents involved. These are constructed as an open and horizontal social participation that makes it possible to increase resources and solve problems. The network nodes need to be connected to communicate with each other. The network's fundamental attribute is the construction of interaction for solving problems and satisfying needs. Its logic has nothing to do with equilibrating social groups but in organizing society within diversity, through the structuring of relationships among individuals with common interests and concerns.

Recent studies on regional economic development emphasize the need to analyze the degree of evolution that organizational and business capacities have reached in regions, because opportunities for economic activity on a local scale and the exploitation of endogenous capacities for growth and competitiveness depend on them to a great degree, they make a territory specific (OECD, 2001; Porter, 1996). The endogenous development makes the elevation of employment levels possible, improving income and life conditions, reducing poverty levels and opening real opportunities for social development.

In a recent study carried out by the Center for Demographic, Urban and Environmental Studies at El Colegio de Mexico, and coordinated by Dr. María Eugenia Negrete, about business organization in the central region of Mexico, the following findings were obtained. According to expectations, the impact of the transformation in the means of producing and exchanging global market goods has been relevant in all the regional economic industries. The effects have been so notorious that it has been mandatory to take diverse types of measures to look for new ways of remaining in the market and finding new improvement opportunities in the competitiveness of the regional products.

From the business organization perspective, the traditional forms of association in chambers are no longer valid because they responded more to production and hierarchical government structures of a corporate kind, and less to the new needs originating from the phase of commercial opening. The new conditions have made governments face these challenges in a different way in relation to attending to social groups, and looking for new forms of collaboration with the diverse social actors, especially with business people.

In addition to the diminishing relevance of the chambers as agents promoting business organization, there is a wide range of formal and informal associations that have emerged from the need to look for solutions to common problems in manufacturing production, but also specifically in activities such as construction, textiles, automotive, software specialization and floriculture. It is about formal groups of business people from the same kind of activity, or informal groups of friends or acquaintances; some of these groups work as networks and meet to express their concerns and exchange ideas to find solutions to the problems of their firms.

In spite of the existence of a wide number of associations, the existence of a lack of confidence among business people and the lack of a business culture are also emphasized. However, some groups, the minority of them, have understood that collaboration is not the enemy of competence. This business culture means, on the one hand, the formation of networks and non-hierarchical groups, and on the other, information flows to advance the adoption of technological innovations.

In relation to the role of government as a promoter of economic development and the formation of networks, it can be said that all the officials interviewed showed a special interest in that but recognized the difficulties in instrumenting actions due to the lack of a culture of association. There was also agreement about the need for more public–private relationships but, in general terms, there was no commitment observed or effective strategies from state governments to promote business networks. Their role, in the best of the cases, consisted of formulating state economic development programs and offering a scarce range of concrete actions: financing micro, small and medium enterprises; organizing fairs and exhibitions; crating databases about providers; installing offices to attend business opening; eliminating steps to initiate a business, and offering employment opportunities.

Lastly, and in relation to the territorial aspect, the conclusion is that territory is a variable recognized neither by business people nor by state government officials. In spite of the economic concentration that exists in the central region, the regions inside each state are a matter of interest but this does not happen among states. Therefore, the logic is working on a minor scale in the topic of business organizations, identifying the territoriality of interest groups and maybe, as an afterthought, exploring the possibilities of collaboration with business people of a similar sector in neighboring states.

There is no clear relationship of collaboration among the governments of the seven states of the central region because they perceived each other as competitors and not as allies in relation to the promotion of the individual states to make them more attractive to foreign investors. Most of the economic development ministers talk about the localization advantages of their state in relation to internal or international markets. Therefore, there is a special interest in improving the communication infrastructure, mainly highways, but not fast transport systems. The challenge is to create a regional culture in order to promote economic growth and territorial integration; it is necessary to change the spatial scale from a narrow vision of the states towards a metropolitan region perspective.

FINAL COMMENTS

The global crisis that began in the second semester of 2008 and originated from the financial system's imbalance has shown a loss of employment and the intention to nationalize banks and important enterprises by some national governments as an initial manifestation. Unemployment has reached unbelievable levels in countries such as Spain, Ireland, France, the United States and Greece, affecting mainly young workers; there have been important social movements in Latvia, Chile, Bulgaria and Ireland, while in Great Britain and France the number of strikes has increased. This global crisis has inspired the economic model to open up commerce and for commercial deregulation to be reformulated towards an increasing participation by the central state in market regulation, public investment and reactivation of the internal market. In the emergent economies, there is fear that the growing unemployment could generate a pro-occidental distant market economy, while in developed countries unemployment could be used to fortify initiatives to protect local industries at the expense of global commerce.

This crisis makes it essential to rethink certain concepts, such as urban competitiveness, and also to plan alternative scenarios for the territorial redistribution of the population. There is no doubt that the urban competitiveness concept should be revised; this was defined as the capacity of cities to attract productive investment based on a series of factors known as competitive advantages, which cover the attributes of the city related to scale (agglomeration economies) and quality (role of local government; software and hardware for transmission flows; adoption of technological innovation; business organization).

Talk about urban competitiveness in this context means taking into account four fundamental elements. First is the economic structure of the city and its level of insertion into world consumption circuits. Urban areas with an economic base supported by real estate, finance, tourism or the automotive industry have been the most affected during the first manifestations of the world crisis. As a result it is imperative to formulate policy lines oriented to sectorial restructuring towards other activities, mainly those focused on local and regional markets.

Second, there are the components for local income determination; factors that determine the income level in a city. Using a Keynesian model, the literature about spatial economy has mentioned that the income level in a city depends, from the expenses point of view, on consumption, investment, government, exports and imports; meanwhile, from the income point of view, on consumption, savings and taxes. In a normal situation, a city with healthy macroeconomic aggregates is one where exports are superior to imports, savings to investment, and taxes to public expenses. In a crisis situation, such as the one we are experiencing, these balances in the financial flows surplus are crucial, because there is a major marginal propensity to saving that could be used for consumption; spend money now and save later could stimulate the urban economy now and help those individuals to face their financial problems in the long term. Spending is crucial at this moment because it prevents the loss of employment and could even promote investment attraction.

Competitive advantages based on quality appear as the third aspect. This is the level of strength that has been reached through business collaboration, the participation of local governments in the economic promotion of cities and the agreements and interrelations among social agents. Competence also means cooperation, and urban areas that have developed a societal sense of development, and not only a forced environment of coexistence, will be more able to face economic problems successfully. In the case of the central region of Mexico this aspect is missing, thus the resident population of that part of the nation will continue to face this challenge.

Finally, the crisis in the global markets makes it necessary to turn to internal consumption, but this could also encourage protectionist policies that would affect the world market behavior even more. Internal consumption may be stimulated by central governments through more public investment, but also schemes for endogenous growth based on theoretical models elaborated on in the 1980s could be revised which emphasize the use of human capital or the adoption of technological innovations. In this way, the central government and the local governments should also intervene in the promotion of the internal market.

In the case of territorial distribution, the experience of Mexico shows that migration movements are still the fundamental factor that explains changes in the distribution patterns of population and the population dynamism of some urban areas. Nowadays, internal migration is characterized by a predominant urban–urban flow, in which the original primary city is no longer the main destination. Economic crises reduce flows in the first instance, but also modify previous trajectories. In Mexico, the crisis of the imports substitution model in the 1980s stopped the rural–urban exodus, but stimulated international migration to the United States as well. In this crisis, the transnational flow will suffer a reduction and internal migration will take a central place again.

Attention should be paid to internal migration and also to the relocation of population that will happen inside the metropolitan regions; for that it will be necessary to extend and consolidate the infrastructure and systems of transport. Public investment should take a central role in this search for maintenance of centrality; otherwise, the public investment executed would have a limited effect on local development in the short term.

In summary, this global crisis has increased the weaknesses of the neoliberal model, such as the insufficient generation of qualified employment or the risk of complete abandonment of the invisible hands markets. But it also represents the opportunity to rethink the approaches and initiate dialogue, discussion, and the formulation and implementation of actions and programs for the promotion of economic activity, their territorial location, the creation and consolidation of networks for the solution of common problems and the provision of improvements in the quality of life of the resident population.

NOTE

1. The location quotient is a simple coefficient for comparing an area's percentage share of a particular activity with its percentage share of some basic aggregate. It therefore shows the extent to which that area departs from the norm. A value of 1.0 means that the activity is represented in the area in exactly the same proportion for the nation; a value over 1.0 shows that the area has more than its fair share (Duranton and Puga, 2000).

REFERENCES

Ariza, M. and J. Ramírez (2008), 'Urbanización, mercados de trabajo y escenarios sociales en el México finisecular', in A. Portes, B. Roberts and A. Grimson (eds), *Ciudades latinoamericanas*, México, Universidad Autónoma de Zacatecas-Miguel Ángel Porrúa.

Armstrong, H. and J. Taylor (2000), *Regional Economics and Policy*, Oxford, Blackwell Publishers.

Balchin, P., D. Isaac and J. Chen (2000), *Urban Economics. A Global Perspective*, New York, Palgrave.

Barbiero, V. (2007), 'Urban Health: An Inevitable International Imperative', in A. Garland, M. Massoumi and B. Ruble (eds), *Global Urban Poverty*, Washington, Woodrow Wilson International Center for Scholars, pp. 189–203.

Begg, I. (1999), 'Cities and Competitiveness', *Urban Studies*, **36** (5–6), 795–809.

Boddy, M. (2002), 'Linking Competitiveness and Cohesion', in I. Begg (ed.), *Urban Competitiveness*, Bristol, The Policy Press, pp. 33–53.

Boschma, R. and R. Kloosterman (2005), *Learning from Clusters. A Critical Assessment from an Economic-Geographic Perspective*, Amsterdam, Springer.

Boyle, P., K. Halfacree and V. Robinson (1998), *Exploring Contemporary Migration*, Harlow, Longman.

Cabrero, E., I. Orihuela and A. Ziccardi (2006), 'Competitividad de ciudades: la nueva agenda de los gobiernos urbanos', in IBERGOP, *Desarrollo regional y competitividad*, México, Centro de Investigación y Docencia Económicas-Porrúa, pp. 31–51.

Champion, A. (2001), 'A Changing Demographic Regime and Evolving Polycentric Urban Regions: Consequences for the Size, Composition and Distribution of City Populations', *Urban Studies*, **38** (4), 657–77.

Clark, W. (1987), 'The Roepke Lecture in Economic Geography: Urban Restructuring from a Demographic Perspective', *Economic Geography*, **63** (1), 103–25.

Cliquet, R. (1991), *The Second Demographic Transition: Fact or Fiction?*, Strasbourg, Council of Europe.

Comisión Económica para América Latina y el Caribe (CEPAL) (1995), *Análisis de la competitividad de las naciones*, Santiago de Chile.

Duranton, G. and D. Puga (2000), 'Diversity and Specialisation in Cities: Why, Where and When Does it Matter?', *Urban Studies*, **37** (3), 533–55.

García, A. (2002), 'Redes sociales y clusters empresariales', *Revista Hispánica para el Análisis de Redes Sociales*, **1** (6), 785–801.

Geyer, H. and T. Kontuly (1993), 'A Theoretical Foundation for the Concept of Differential Urbanization', *International Regional Science Review*, **17** (2), 157–77.

Global Urban Competitiveness Project (2005), *Mission Statement and Activities of the Global Urban Competitiveness Project*, Ottawa (mimeo).

Gordon, I. and I. Turok (2005), 'How Urban Labour Markets Matter', in N. Buck, I. Gordon, A. Harding and I. Turok (eds), *Changing Cities*, New York, Palgrave, pp. 242–64.

Gottmann, J. (1961), *Megalopolis*, New York, The Twentieth Century Fund.

Harding, A. (2005), 'Governance and Socio-Economic Change in Cities', in N. Buck, I. Gordon, A. Harding and I. Turok (eds), *Changing Cities*, Houndmills, Palgrave, pp. 62–77.

Institute for Management Development (IMD) (2007), *World Competitiveness Yearbook*, Lausanne.

Kresl, P. and B. Singh (1999), 'Competitiveness and the Urban Economy: Twenty-Four Large US Metropolitan Areas', *Urban Studies*, **36** (5–6), 1017–27.

Krugman, P. (1994), 'Competitiveness: a Dangerous Obsession', *Foreign Affairs*, **74** (2), 28–44.

Lever, W. and I. Turok (1999), 'Competitive Cities: Introduction to the Review', *Urban Studies*, **36** (5–6), 791–3.

Lomnitz, M. (2001), *Redes sociales, cultura y poder*, México, FLACSO-Miguel Ángel Porrúa.

Malecki, E. (1997), *Technology and Economic Development*, Harlow, Longman.

Meltzer, J. (1984), *Metropolis to Metroplex*, Baltimore, The Johns Hopkins University Press.

Moomaw, R. (1981), 'Productivity and City Size: A Critique of the Evidence', *The Quarterly Journal of Economics*, **96** (4), 675–88.

Ni Pengfei (2007), *Urban Competitiveness in China*, Beijing, Social Science Academic Press.

Organisation for Economic Cooperation and Development (OECD) (2001), *Asociaciones locales para una mayor gobernabilidad*, Paris: OECD.

Polèse, M. (2005), 'Cities and National Economic Growth: A Reappraisal', *Urban Studies*, **42** (8), 1429–51.

Porter, M. (1996), 'Competitive Advantage, Agglomeration Economies, and Regional Policy', *International Regional Science Review*, **19** (1–2), 85–94.

Porter, M., P. Cornelius, J. Sachs, M. Levinson, A. Warner and K. Schwab (2000), *The Global Competitiveness Report*, New York, World Economic Forum–Harvard University Press.

Potts, G. (2002), 'Competitiveness and the Social Fabric: Links and Tensions in Cities', in I. Begg (ed.), *Urban Competitiveness*, Bristol, The Policy Press, pp. 77–98.

Prud'homme, R. and C. Lee (1999), 'Size, Sprawl, Speed and the Efficiency of Cities', *Urban Studies*, **36** (11), 1849–58.

Smith, D. (2000), 'Social Justice Revisited', *Environment and Planning A*, **32** (8), 1149–62.

Sobrino, J. (2002), 'Competitividad y ventajas competitivas: revisión teórica y ejercicio de aplicación a 30 ciudades de México', *Estudios Demográficos y Urbanos*, **17** (2), 311–63.

Turok, I. (2005), 'Cities, Competition and Competitiveness: Identifying New Connections', in N. Buck, I. Gordon, A. Harding and I. Turok (eds), *Changing Cities*, Houndmills, Palgrave, pp. 25–43.

Woodford, M. (1993), 'Self-Fulfilling Expectations and Fluctuations in Aggregate Demand', in N. Mankiw and D. Romer (eds), *New Keynesian Economics. Vol. 1*, Cambridge, The MIT Press, pp. 77–109.

7. Cooperation and competition between cities: urban development strategies in Hong Kong and Shenzhen

Jianfa Shen

INTRODUCTION

Urban competition has been intensified as cities compete against each other to attract TNCs and their regional headquarters, international capital and talents in the age of globalization. Increasing studies have focused on urban strategies to compete against other cities (Begg, 1999). There is growing sense of city rivalry. A city's growth is often considered at the expense of another city resulting in 'destructive interplace competition' (Brenner and Theodore, 2002: 5 and 20). With a few exceptions, intercity competition is considered a negative phenomenon. In the context of the Pearl River Delta (PRD) and Yangtze River Delta (YRD), Chen (2007: 195) argued that 'inter-local or intra-regional competition breeds fragmentation or even disintegration'. But there is inadequate explanation for the emergence of such keen competition or solutions to such a situation.

Indeed, cities may also cooperate to enhance the competitive advantage of both cities by seeking agglomeration effects, facilitating innovation processes, managing externalities, avoiding duplicative capacities, improving efficacy and minimizing risks (Heeg et al., 2003).

While many studies have been done on how cities adopt various strategies to enhance urban competitiveness and the ranking of urban competitiveness of various cities, fewer studies have examined in detail the nature of intercity competition and how the growth of one city actually affects another city (Begg, 1999; Jessop and Sum, 2000; So and Shen, 2004). Furthermore, there are also many studies on intercity cooperation. It has been rare to study intercity competition and cooperation of the same pair of cities at the same time. The changing relations between Hong Kong and Shenzhen provide a good case for a detailed study of intercity competition and cooperation under regionalization and globalization. This chapter attempts to examine this issue based on two case studies: airports and the development of the boundary area in Hong Kong and Shenzhen. The chapter will demonstrate how the two cities have navigated towards cooperation for mutual benefit, starting from different priorities of intercity cooperation. The changing context of urban development in the two cities, adopting intercity cooperation as urban strategies, and the emerging consensus among the public and between two cities are considered as key factors facilitating the progress of cooperation in airports and boundary area development.

CHANGING RELATIONS BETWEEN HONG KONG AND SHENZHEN

Hong Kong had a population of 7 million in 2008. Since 1978, due to economic complementarities and the comparative advantages of Hong Kong and the PRD, a spatial division of labour has been established, generally called 'front shop and back factory model' (Sit, 1998; Shen, 2003). Hong Kong has become a prominent service centre specializing in trading, transport and communication, and financial services.

Hong Kong has enjoyed a long period of economic growth over the past four decades. Hong Kong's economy was affected by the Asian financial crisis in the period 1997–2000. Hong Kong's GDP per capita increased from US$5966 in 1981 to US$27170 in 1997 and then declined to US$26095 in 2005 (CSD, 2001, 2006). Shenzhen city was established in 1979. Its population increased rapidly from 0.31 million in 1979 to 8.48 million in 2006. Its GDP per capita increased from US$829 to US$3097 in 1997 and US$7422 in 2005 (Shenzhen Statistics Bureau, 2007).

Hong Kong plays an important role in the economic growth of Shenzhen. Shenzhen is the major recipient of FDI from Hong Kong. It received 16.5 per cent of Hong Kong's FDI to mainland China in 2005. Shenzhen's export grew from US$9.9 billion in 1991 to US$101.5 billion in 2005. Outward processing related exports accounted for the bulk of exports from Shenzhen, reaching US$75.5 billion in 2005. Shenzhen to Hong Kong exports grew from US$9.3 billion in 1991 to US$45.1 billion in 2005.

In terms of some main economic indicators, Shenzhen has been catching up to Hong Kong quickly. Indeed, Hong Kong and Shenzhen have been ranked as the top and second most competitive cities in China in 2006–2008 (Ni et al., 2008). Shenzhen's exports overtook Hong Kong's domestic exports in 1998. In terms of total exports, Shenzhen's exports in 2006 reached the level of Hong Kong in 1993 and was equivalent to 42.96 per cent of the total exports of Hong Kong in 2006. Shenzhen's GDP in 2006 reached the level of Hong Kong in 1989 (US$69 billion) and was equivalent to 38.48 per cent of Hong Kong's GDP in 2006. Shenzhen's GDP per capita in 2006 reached the level of Hong Kong in 1986 (US$7405) and was equivalent to 31.52 per cent of Hong Kong's GDP per capita in 2006.

Hong Kong and Shenzhen have developed close economic relations since 1980. With the development of high-tech industry and service sectors in Shenzhen, the economic relation between Hong Kong and Shenzhen is in a state of flux. Hong Kong has increasing concerns with the growth of the container port and airport in Shenzhen. In the meantime, both Hong Kong and Shenzhen are actively seeking cooperation from each other.

To stimulate Hong Kong's economy after some years of stagnancy due to the 1997 Asian economic crisis and subsequent social-economic problems, the central government of China has offered several incentive measures to enhance economic integration between Hong Kong and mainland China since July 2003 (Shen, 2008a; Yeung and Shen, 2008). The HKSAR (Hong Kong Special Administrative Region) government and the public are forming a consensus to strengthen cooperation with the mainland especially Shenzhen and the PRD. The Hong Kong and Shenzhen governments have moved on quickly to establish a formal framework for intercity cooperation and develop a joint vision for the two cities.

In 2004, two city governments signed the Memorandum of Enhancing Hong Kong–Shenzhen Cooperation and eight other cooperation agreements on tourism, technology and legal services, and so on. It is called '1 plus 8' in brief. The Hong Kong and Shenzhen governments have formally agreed to embark on deep intercity cooperation aiming to form the Hong Kong–Shenzhen Metropolis (BFRC, 2007). Two Hong Kong–Shenzhen Co-operation Forums were held in 2006 and 2007. Two Hong Kong–Shenzhen Co-operation Meetings were held in 2007 and 2008. Acting Chief Executive of Hong Kong SAR, Henry Tang said in the second Hong Kong–Shenzhen Co-operation Forum held on 13 August 2007: 'The long-term objective of our co-operation is to jointly develop a world-class metropolis comparable with Greater New York and Greater London. This metropolis, covering 3 200 square kilometers and a population of about 20 million, will be one of the top metropolises in respect of economic size, trade volume and investments' (Hong Kong Economic and Trade Office, 2007).

CONCEPTUALIZING INTERCITY COMPETITION: RELATIVE VERSUS ABSOLUTE COMPETITION

Intercity competition is a very popular term but relative competition and absolute competition should be differentiated. First, relative competition refers to the comparison of aggregated indicators and their position. By relative competition, the development of a city will not harm another city.

Cities are often compared using aggregated indicators without considering the particular economic and market processes producing such conditions. Performance in GDP, FDI (foreign direct investment) and exports are often considered key indicators of urban competitiveness or strength. When a less advanced city (city B) is catching up an advanced city (city A), city A perceives competition pressure from city B. Such relative competition often gets attention from the government and the public. But one cannot draw the conclusion that city B is growing at the expense of city A. Thus relative competition should not be the main concern of cities.

Second, absolute competition refers to the situation of win or loss. City B grows at the expense of city A. To determine whether city A and city B are under direct competition, intercity competition at sector or firm level should be considered. In the age of globalization and regional integration, the spatial boundary may be blurred for various firms and consumers. Many firms may operate and consumers may use services in both cities that are perceived to be in competition. To consumers, competition between producers from the same city or from different cities will lead to lower prices and more choices. Thus competition is generally beneficial to consumers in both cities, which is consistent with the principle of market economy.

Various producers, including service providers, can compete with each other within the same city or between different cities. When producers from one city compete against producers from another city, this may be regarded as a kind of intercity competition and a city government may try its best to support its own producers. There are also opportunities for cooperation even in such cases. Hong Kong and Shenzhen airports belong to the case that service providers belong to two different cities. Absolute intercity competition means that two cities will compete for external resources, such as foreign investment, or markets. In the case of airports, there is absolute competition if they compete for passengers and freights. But if two airports mainly serve their own markets and aim to increase efficiency through cooperation, then there is no absolute competition between the two airports.

When producers operate in both cities, they can make the best use of resources in the two cities and there may be no absolute intercity competition. Hong Kong and Shenzhen container ports may belong to such a case. In some cases, two cities may be involved in a joint project such as boundary area development. Then cooperation is the only option.

In the case of Hong Kong and Shenzhen, there are serious concerns over competition between the airports. In the meantime, both city governments have increasingly engaged in intercity cooperation including cooperation between the two airports and the joint development of the boundary area. These cases will be examined in detail in the following two sections. The chapter will demonstrate how the two cities consider airports and boundary area development as strategic projects and how they reconcile their intentions and move towards win–win scenarios that can benefit both cities.

INTERCITY COMPETITION AND COOPERATION: THE CASE OF HONG KONG AND SHENZHEN AIRPORTS

In the Greater Pearl River Delta (GPRD), there are five international airports located within a radius of only 80km, including Hong Kong International Airport, Guangzhou Baiyun International Airport, Shenzhen Baoan International Airport, Macau International Airport and Zhuhai Airport. Airports have become the strategic infrastructure that these cities have attempted to invest in. The five airports have been considered an example of infrastructure duplication as a result of intercity competition (Song, 2002).

Hong Kong airport is the leading international airport in the region with the largest passenger and air cargo throughput. Guangzhou airport is designated as one of the three aviation hubs in mainland China. It has the potential to compete with Hong Kong airport in the long term. Shenzhen airport concentrates on domestic flights to mainland cities, but its expanding air cargo services may also compete with Hong Kong airport over time. There is an intricate relationship between Hong Kong and Shenzhen airports. The competition and cooperation between the two airports is the focus of this section.

Airport Development as City Strategic Projects

The passenger throughput in Hong Kong airport increased from 28.3 million to 47.80 million in the period 1997–2007. Air cargo throughput increased from 1.79 million to 3.70 million tons in the same period. It was ranked number 14 and number 2 in terms of passenger and air cargo throughput respectively in 2007 in the world (Airports Council International, 2008). The airport has direct flights to 40 mainland cities and 115 international cities in 2007.

HKSAR government owns Hong Kong Airport Authority. Making

a profit is not its main objective. But the government does have a keen interest in maintaining the leading position of Hong Kong airport for the general interest of Hong Kong's economy. Given the rapid growth of Guangzhou and Shenzhen airports in the region, seeking cooperation with Shenzhen airport for a regional division of labour between Hong Kong and Shenzhen airport has been a strategy of the Hong Kong Airport Authority for some years. Such a cooperation strategy is considered important to reduce duplication of international flights. But there has not been much progress in the cooperation with Shenzhen airport until recently. HKSAR government and Hong Kong Airport Authority (HKIA) have shown their determination recently to study the feasibility of building a third runway to expand the capacity of Hong Kong airport in their strategic report for development up to 2025, published in 2006.

Shenzhen airport was opened in 1991 (Shenzhen Airport, 2008a). Its passenger throughput increased from 1.66 million in 1992 to 12.06 million in 2007. Air cargo throughput reached 0.62 million tons in 2007. It was ranked number 63 and number 33 in terms of passenger and air cargo throughput respectively in 2007 in the world (Shenzhen Airport, 2008b). By 2007, the airport has direct flights to 68 mainland cities and 34 cities out of mainland China.

The Shenzhen airport is operated by Shenzhen Airport Company Ltd and 54.64 per cent of the company is owned ultimately by the Shenzhen government (Shenzhen Airport, 2008a). Developing a strong airport and container port is a key strategy of the urban development of Shenzhen city. First, 'The strategic planning of medium and long term development of Shenzhen airport' completed in October 2006, proposed to develop the airport as the air cargo gateway to south China. Second, the Shenzhen government regards the growth of its container port and airport as a major achievement of the city. It held a special meeting to celebrate that the two ports reached container and passenger throughputs of 20 million TEUs and 20 million passengers respectively in 2007 (Shenzhen Airport, 2008c). Third, the Shenzhen government introduced '[t]entative measures of managing a support fund for new air cargo service lines in Shenzhen Baoan International Airport' to provide financial incentive to airlines for expanding air cargo service in its airport on 1 January 2007. The total incentives to such airlines were over RMB 20 million in 2007 (Shenzhen Airport, 2008b).

With strong government support, Shenzhen airport is expanding its facilities and services. A second runway and terminal 3 will begin operation by 2011. The total passenger handling capacity for Shenzhen airport will reach 36 million by 2015 (Passengerterminaltoday.com, 2008). A UPS (United Parcel Service of America, Inc.) Asia-Pacific transfer centre will start operation in 2010 with an initial 108 flights per week (Shenzhen Airport, 2008b).

Due to the rapid growth of Shenzhen airport, it seems that there is competition between Hong Kong and Shenzhen airports. As mentioned before, it is important to distinguish relative competition from absolute competition. There is no doubt that relative competition exists as the two airports compare with each other in aggregated indicators such as passenger and cargo throughput. Such relative competition often gets attention from the government and the public. Thus the growing strength of mainland cities such as Shanghai and Shenzhen is often perceived as putting competition pressure on Hong Kong. A famous press commentator, Johnny Y.S. Lau, commented that Shenzhen will bring a greater and greater threat to Hong Kong in the next ten years (*Singtao Daily*, 2008a).

But is there absolute competition? Is Shenzhen airport growing at the expense of Hong Kong airport? Certainly, the passenger and cargo throughput in Hong Kong airport continued to grow until late 2008 when the world financial crisis broke out and the global economy began to shrink, indicating that Hong Kong airport had not been undermined by the rapid growth in Shenzhen airport. The future growth in both Hong Kong and Shenzhen airports depends ultimately on the economic growth and logistics needs of the GPRD region. Hong Kong, Shenzhen and Guangzhou airports have their own immediate hinterland for their services. Local residents usually choose the nearest airport where flight services are offered. Hong Kong and Shenzhen airports duplicate some flight services to mainland cities. But differences in cost, service quality and airport accessibility allow each airport to catch its own passengers.

Views from Public and Airport Users of Hong Kong

This section will focus on the views of public and airport users on the relationship between Hong Kong and Shenzhen airports. A telephone survey of public opinion on cooperation and competition between the airports of Hong Kong and Shenzhen was conducted among Hong Kong residents to find out their perception, needs and views on competition and cooperation between the two airports. Hong Kong residents are both users of airports and the ultimate stakeholder of Hong Kong airport. Their views are very useful for forming development strategies for Hong Kong airport. The survey was conducted from 13 to 15 March 2008 via the Telephone Survey Research Laboratory at The Chinese University of Hong Kong. The survey covered a random sample of 514 respondents aged 18 or above in Hong Kong with a response rate of 51.8 per cent.

According to the survey, Hong Kong residents consider that the airport

*Table 7.1   Public opinion on possible policies to enhance Hong Kong
airport's competitiveness (%)*

Opinion	Government subsidize airport authority and airlines	Build third runway
Strongly disagree	1.9	1.9
Disagree	22.0	27.9
Agree	64.8	56.7
Strongly agree	5.8	6.2
Don't know	5.4	7.2
Number of respondents	514	513

Source: Telephone survey on 13–15 March 2008 by the author.

is very important. Ninety-six per cent of the respondents think that maintaining the leading role of Hong Kong airport in passenger and cargo transportation is important/very important for the Hong Kong economy. Over 62.3 per cent of respondents agree/strongly agree that the development of Shenzhen airport will affect the position of Hong Kong airport. The perception of competition between Hong Kong and Shenzhen airports is strong among the public.

For policies/potential policies to enhance Hong Kong airport's competitiveness, providing financial assistance to the Airport Authority and airlines, and building the third runway are supported by over 56 per cent of respondents (Table 7.1). Thus residents mostly are conscious of competition and are willing to use taxpayers' money to support Hong Kong airport. But the degree of support is weaker than the view on the importance of the airport. Only about 6 per cent of residents strongly supported the above two measures and over 22 per cent of residents did not support these measures.

Nevertheless, some Hong Kong residents are users of both Hong Kong and Shenzhen airports. From the users' point of view, expanding services in both airports is beneficial. Regarding the use of the two airports, 13.8 per cent use both Hong Kong and Shenzhen airports, and 19.1 per cent have never used any airport. Respondents were asked whether they accept that more Hong Kong residents use Shenzhen airport. The answer was very positive over making use of Shenzhen airport, with 72.6 per cent accepting using Shenzhen airport to go to mainland cities and 59.8 per cent accepting using Shenzhen airport to go to overseas cities. Thus Hong Kong residents consider Shenzhen airport another choice for their travel to mainland cities and even international cities. They have no concerns about competition between the two airports. On the other hand, the competition for passengers is not keen between the two airports. The majority of the respondents, 65.5 per cent, only use Hong Kong airport for travel while 1.6 per cent of the respondents only use Shenzhen airport. It is clear that Hong Kong airport does not lose too many passengers to Shenzhen airport as Hong Kong residents prefer to use Hong Kong airport.

It is clear that the public in Hong Kong, and perhaps HKSAR government and the airport authority, have a strong sense of 'relative' competition. Hong Kong airport has strong local support. Currently, Hong Kong residents mainly use Hong Kong airport thus there is little overlap in the passenger market of Hong Kong and Shenzhen airports. Hong Kong residents are actually also willing to use Shenzhen airport to travel to mainland and overseas destinations, thus absolute competition between the two airports is not serious at this time.

Nevertheless, the main origin and destination of the air cargo services of Hong Kong airport are in the Pearl River Delta, thus its hinterland overlaps with Shenzhen airport. Both airports may compete in the market of air cargo services. Hong Kong airport currently dominates the market due to its dense international flight routes. Further expansion of international flight services in Shenzhen can pose serious competition to Hong Kong airport. But any such expansion in Shenzhen or Guangzhou airports should be based on sound cost–benefit analysis. It is not advisable to use government revenue to support flight services for a long period of time just for the sake of increasing air cargo volume. Otherwise, duplication of service and surplus airport capacity may be the result, just like the situation of Zhuhai airport. For Hong Kong airport and airlines, they should offer air cargo services at a competitive price to remain attractive to their clients. Cooperation for mutual benefit is a possible solution to such competition and this has been pursued by HKSAR government and Hong Kong airport from the very beginning.

Cooperation Between Hong Kong and Shenzhen Airports

Generally, Shenzhen government has been more active than Hong Kong government regarding cooperation between the two cities even before the return of Hong Kong to China in 1997. Airport cooperation is an exception. Hong Kong has been very active while Shenzhen has been less responsive until recently. Hong Kong Airport Authority actively sought to get certain shares of Shenzhen airport through share exchange. But Shenzhen airport did not accept such a kind of cooperation. There is certain tension between the two airports although it does not necessarily mean that they compete directly.

Indeed, the two cities have ample opportunities to cooperate. For example, Hong Kong airport may benefit from frequent domestic flights from Shenzhen airport so that it can concentrate on international flights due to its limited landing capacity. Shenzhen airport helps bring mainland tourists to Hong Kong. Of the 13.60 million tourists from the mainland to Hong Kong, 3 million used Shenzhen airport in 2006 (Shenzhen Airport, 2007). One initial step towards cooperation was the sea link between Shenzhen and Hong Kong airports which was opened in September 2003 to serve transfer passengers. It reduced travel time from 2 hours by land to 45 minutes by sea. The transfer procedure and boarding pass can be processed in both airports and direct cross-boundary bus services are offered every half-hour (*Singtao Daily*, 2008b).

As mentioned before, intercity cooperation between Hong Kong and Shenzhen has become a major urban strategy of both Hong Kong and Shenzhen. Both governments are seeking ways to move on the cooperation. Among the two cases discussed in the chapter, Hong Kong was previously more active than Shenzhen in airport cooperation while Shenzhen was more active than Hong Kong in the boundary area development. Thus the two cooperation projects have moved ahead as both cities can benefit from cooperation. This can be considered a result of reconciling and consensus building by seeking common ground for cooperation.

A Hong Kong/Shenzhen co-operation meeting was held in Hong Kong on 18 December 2007. The meeting was co-chaired by the Chief Secretary for Administration of HKSAR, Henry Tang, and the Mayor of Shenzhen Municipal Government, Xu Zongheng. The meeting decided to set up two joint task forces, namely the 'Task Force on Airport Co-operation between Hong Kong and Shenzhen' and the 'Hong Kong–Shenzhen Joint Task Force on Boundary District Development' to accelerate collaboration between the airports of the two cities and studies on the planning and development of the boundary district (Information Services Department, 2007). The Task Force on Airport Co-operation would study the feasibility and economic benefits of connecting the two airports with a rail link and pursuing airport business cooperation respectively.

The proposed direct rail link between the two airports is 30 km long. The idea is that the two airports will be linked by rail link in 23 minutes so that passengers can transfer between Hong Kong and Shenzhen airports conveniently (*Ming Pao*, 2008a, 2008b). A middle stop has been added as the volume of transfer passengers may not be large enough to sustain the railway operation.

The public also supports the cooperation between the two airports. According to the public survey mentioned above, 53.9 per cent of respondents agree that Hong Kong will face more competition if Hong Kong and Shenzhen airports do not cooperate. Regarding policies or potential

Table 7.2   Public opinion on possible policies on airport cooperation (%)

Opinion	Improve ground transport to Shenzhen airport	Build railway to link two airports	Establish joint cooperation of two airports
Strongly disagree	1.0	2.3	1.8
Disagree	9.9	28.8	25.1
Agree	71.8	58.2	63.8
Strongly agree	13.2	6.4	3.7
Don't know	4.1	4.3	5.6
Number of respondents	514	514	514

Source: Telephone survey on 13–15 March 2008 by the author.

policies for the cooperation of the two airports, a majority of the respondents support three policies/potential policies: improving ground transportation to Shenzhen airport, building a railway to link the two airports and establishing a joint cooperation for the two airports (Table 7.2).

From the point of view of airport users, improving accessibility to both airports is very important if both airports are going to be used by residents in Hong Kong and Shenzhen conveniently. The number of transfer passengers is much smaller than the local passengers from the two cities. Thus the policy direction should focus on improving ground transportation from the two cities to the two airports. Such improvement should be made taking into consideration the existing and planned transport rail and MTR networks in the two cities. Currently, it is not convenient for Shenzhen residents to go to Hong Kong airport and for Hong Kong residents to go to Shenzhen airport. It is suggested that the airport rail link mentioned above should have one to two stops in Hong Kong that are connected with the existing railway network such as *West Rail* so that Hong Kong passengers can also make use of the rail link to reach Shenzhen and Hong Kong airports conveniently.

INTERCITY COOPERATION: THE CASE OF BOUNDARY AREA DEVELOPMENT

Urban Development in the Boundary Area

Hong Kong and Shenzhen are divided by the Shenzhen River as their boundary which is 35 km long. The Hong Kong side of the boundary is not developed while the Shenzhen side is well developed. Indeed, Shenzhen city is built east–westwards along the Shenzhen River. Some housing estates are built next to the Shenzhen River so that their residents can view Hong Kong clearly from their flats. Shenzhen likes to take full advantage of being close to Hong Kong to benefit from the economic impact of Hong Kong as the leading business centre.

On the other hand, urban development in Hong Kong has been concentrated in Hong Kong Island and Kowloon Peninsula for many years. The population has begun to diffuse to the New Territories only since 1973 when large-scale new town and public housing programmes were introduced to house the increasing population. The population share of the New Territories increased from 26.3 per cent in 1981 to 46.8 per cent in 1996 and 52.1 per cent in 2006 (CSD, 2007a: 16). Hong Kong maintains a Frontier Closed Area (FCA) as a buffer zone between Hong Kong and Shenzhen. It was set up on 15 May 1951 to enforce boundary control as well as to deal with illegal migration and smuggling. The FCA was extended to its current area of 2800 hectares in 1962 which extends 0.5–2km from the Hong Kong–Shenzhen boundary. There are over 20 villages with a total population over 10000 (DAB et al., 2004: 1) in FCA. No development is allowed in the area and people need to apply for special FCA entry permit to go to various sites in the area.

One outstanding case of boundary area development is the Lok Ma Chau river loop area (RLA or Lok Ma Chau Loop). This area was originally within the Shenzhen side of the Hong Kong–Shenzhen boundary. In the early 1990s, the Hong Kong and Shenzhen governments reached agreement to implement an improvement project in Shenzhen River to reduce the risk of frequent flooding. The Phase 1 project was completed from May 1995 to April 1997 and straightened the river channel. As a result, the RLA, about 1 km^2, falls within the Hong Kong side of the Hong Kong–Shenzhen boundary after the project. The RLA is owned by Shenzhen city but is under the jurisdiction of Hong Kong. It lies to the south of the Shenzhen Futian commercial area and is surrounded by fishponds and wetlands of high ecological value. During the river training of Shenzhen River, it was used as a dumping ground for contaminated and uncontaminated mud dredged from the river (Planning Department of HKSAR and Shenzhen Municipal Planning Bureau, 2009).

From the Shenzhen point of view, the RLA located in Hong Kong is valuable to Shenzhen. If feasible, a small part of Shenzhen would locate within Hong Kong and operate under the law of Hong Kong. Thus Shenzhen has a great interest in developing the RLA as a strategic project. Nevertheless, the boundary area and RLA are backyard gardens of Hong Kong. They contain many ecologically important areas such as Mai Po

Nature Reserve for conservation. The RLA is just one piece of undeveloped land and has no clear priority for development especially when there is not much intercity cooperation between Hong Kong and Shenzhen (Yeung and Shen, 2008). Hong Kong had no plan to implement any substantial land development there until 2008. Thus the intercity cooperation on boundary area development has not made significant progress even after 1997.

However, social and economic relations between Hong Kong and Shenzhen have been enhanced greatly since the early 1980s, shown by the large volumes of goods, passengers and traffic flows between the Hong Kong and Shenzhen boundary (Shen, 2008b). For example, the number of tourists from mainland China increased from 2.4 million in 1997 to 13.6 million in 2006. Although mainland China was already the largest source of tourists in 1997, its share in total tourists increased further from 18.4 per cent in 1997 to 53.8 per cent in 2006. As a result, the total number of tourists coming to Hong Kong increased from 13.0 million in 1997 to 25.3 million in 2006 (CSD, 2001: 184; 2007b: 126). It is expected that the number of tourists will further increase in the future. The boundary area would be an ideal place to offer shopping and various financial and professional services to residents from Shenzhen. It is also a place to offer education or R&D for convenient cooperation of researchers and experts from both cities.

Establishing a development zone such as the RLA in the boundary area will significantly reduce the physical distance between the core urban areas of Hong Kong and Shenzhen (Shen, 2008a). Many businesses and professional and shopping services for mainland clients can be done in the boundary area. This can not only help to save time for mainland clients but also reduce the traffic flow from the boundary area to the urban area of Hong Kong, making it possible for Hong Kong to serve an even greater number of mainland tourists. It will also make it convenient for Hong Kong residents living and working on the mainland to acquire essential social services from the government.

As mentioned before, along with airport cooperation, the Hong Kong and Shenzhen governments agreed to jointly develop the RLA as an experimental project of intercity cooperation in 2007. The RLA is an intercity cooperation project which does not involve intercity competition, but the changing attitude of HKSAR government from being indifferent to the project to becoming an active partner does reflect the dynamism of intercity relations. The two cities also have to reconcile and reach consensus on the development direction of RLA.

Although consensus has been built up in Hong Kong to develop the RLA area as a strategic project of intercity cooperation between Hong

Kong and Shenzhen, there has been a great debate on the development direction of the RLA. The progress of the RLA project has not been very satisfactory, as was revealed by a public survey in Hong Kong.

Views from the Public on Boundary Area Development

A telephone survey of public opinion on the boundary area development and the RLA of Hong Kong and Shenzhen was conducted among Hong Kong residents to find out their perception and views. The survey was conducted from 18 to 23 April 2008 via the Telephone Survey Research Laboratory at The Chinese University of Hong Kong. The survey covered a random sample of 504 respondents aged 18 or above in Hong Kong with a response rate of 51.7 per cent.

According to the survey, the majority of the respondents (76.3 per cent) support developing the boundary area, as they think that developing the boundary area is important for Hong Kong's development and will generate positive impacts on the living and life of residents in the boundary area. Generally speaking, compared with residents not living in the boundary area and respondents with a middle income level, residents living in the boundary area and respondents with high and low income levels showed more support for developing the boundary area.

However, regarding the impacts of developing the boundary area on the life of residents living in the boundary area, the attitudes of residents not living in the boundary area (66.8 per cent) is more positive than that of residents living in the boundary area (56.1 per cent). The reason is that residents living in the boundary area are a direct interest group in developing the boundary area, and they take a cautious stance towards developing the area.

Some 77 per cent of the respondents support Hong Kong and Shenzhen governments jointly developing the RLA (Table 7.3). For the development direction of the RLA, eco-tourism (32.5 per cent) receive the highest support. Commerce and trading (24.4 per cent), manufacturing (23.8 per cent), logistics (23.8 per cent) and R&D (23.4 per cent) are also preferred by the respondents. Real estate, higher education and convention/exhibition also receive over 11–16 per cent of support (Table 7.4). Clearly, there are diverse views by the Hong Kong residents on the development direction of the RLA. A strategic and professional evaluation of various development scenarios should be undertaken to make the best use of the land in the boundary area.

For some potential policy options that may be considered in developing the RLA, Hong Kong residents' views are divided without clear consensus. Fifty-four percent of the respondents agree that the government

Table 7.3   Do you agree that Hong Kong–Shenzhen governments jointly develop the river loop area of Lok Ma Chau?

Opinion	Percentage (%)
Strongly disagree	1.4
Disagree	14.5
Agree	73.6
Strongly agree	3.4
Don't know/Hard to say	7.1
Number of respondents	504

Source: Telephone survey on 18–23 April 2008 by the author.

Table 7.4   Which function do you think should be developed in the river loop area? (multiple answers allowed)

Direction of development	Number of respondents	Percentage (%)
1. Commerce and trading	123	24.4
2. Manufacturing	120	23.8
3. R&D	118	23.4
4. Convention/exhibition	57	11.3
5. Logistics industry	120	23.8
6. Eco-tourism	164	32.5
7. Higher education	66	13.1
8. Real estate	82	16.3
9. Other	4	0.8
No development should take place	2	0.4
Don't know/Hard to say	83	16.5
Total	504	100

Source: Telephone survey on 18–23 April 2008 by the author.

should introduce a special boundary-crossing policy to allow free entry for both Hong Kong and Shenzhen residents. However, 41.3 per cent of the respondents are against this policy (Table 7.5). The respondents are even more conservative in responding to the possible migration policy of allowing mainland workers to work in the RLA. Only 33.5 per cent of respondents support such a policy while 60.5 per cent are against such a policy. It is understandable that Hong Kong residents would like to protect the job opportunities in the RLA. Without the support of the

Table 7.5   Do you agree that the government should introduce the following special policies in the river loop area? (%)

Opinion	Allow both Hong Kong and mainland residents to enter the river-loop area freely	Allow mainland workers to enter the area to work
Strongly disagree	4.4	7.3
Disagree	36.9	53.2
Agree	50.4	32.3
Strongly agree	3.6	1.2
Don't know/Hard to say	4.8	6.0
Number of respondents	504	504

Source: Telephone survey on 18–23 April 2008 by the author.

residents on importing workers from Shenzhen, manufacturing may not be a viable option in the RLA as Shenzhen may be more attractive with low labour costs.

On the other hand, most respondents agree that the government should introduce special development measures in the development of the boundary area. As many as 84.9 per cent and 79.4 per cent agree that the government should build infrastructure in advance and offer tax incentives respectively (Table 7.6). When asked who should play the leading role, government or enterprises, in the development of boundary area, the majority of the respondents (60.4 per cent) think that the government should play the leading role in developing the boundary area (Table 7.7). Only 14.7 per cent think that enterprises should play the leading role. But only 35.2 per cent are satisfied with the performance of the government in developing the boundary area and only 38.2 per cent are satisfied with the progress of the development of the boundary area (Table 7.8). Therefore, the government should take a more pragmatic approach in developing the boundary area. Public support for developing the RLA and high expectations of a leading role by the HKSAR government are certainly important to push the progress of intercity cooperation.

Cooperation in Boundary Area Development Between Hong Kong and Shenzhen

Cooperation in boundary area development between Hong Kong and Shenzhen has not been smooth in the past. It involves two key questions.

Table 7.6　Do you agree that the government should introduce the following special development measures? (%)

Opinion	Build infrastructure in advance	Offer tax incentives
Strongly disagree	0.8	1.0
Disagree	9.5	15.5
Agree	77.5	72.8
Strongly agree	7.4	6.6
Don't know/Hard to say	4.8	4.2
Number of respondents	503	503

Source: Telephone survey on 18–23 April 2008 by the author.

Table 7.7　Who should play the leading role, government or enterprises, in the development of the boundary area? (%)

Player	Percentage
Government should play the leading role	60.4
Enterprises should play the leading role	14.7
Government and enterprises are equally important	20.9
Don't know/Hard to say	4.0
Number of respondents	503

Source: Telephone survey on 18–23 April 2008 by the author.

Should the boundary area be developed? What kind of development should take place in the boundary area? The ideas on developing the boundary area have been initiated both in Shenzhen and Hong Kong. Various development options for the RLA have also been proposed over the years. Generally, the Shenzhen side has been very active in the RLA while the HKSAR government has been indifferent to the RLA until 2002. Great progress has been made in recent years in the joint development of the RLA. The process towards cooperation can be divided into three stages.

The first stage was the Shenzhen preparation stage, 1996–1998. In this stage, various scholars and institutions in Shenzhen made various suggestions leading to the official suggestion by the Office of High-tech Industry of the Shenzhen government in 1998. Scholars and research institutions in Shenzhen were the earliest to advocate the development of the boundary

Table 7.8   *Are you satisfied with the progress and the performance of the government in the development of the boundary area? (%)*

Opinion	Progress of the development of boundary area	Performance of the government in the development of boundary area
Very unsatisfied	2.6	2.0
Unsatisfied	34.5	37.0
Satisfied	37.6	34.6
Very satisfied	0.6	0.6
Don't know/Hard to say	24.7	25.8
Number of respondents	503	503

Source: Telephone survey on 18–23 April 2008 by the author.

area. Their ideas may have also affected the views of business groups and organizations in Hong Kong. In June 1996, the Shenzhen-based China Development Institute (1996) completed a study on Shenzhen–Hong Kong integration. It proposed the establishment of a Shenzhen–Hong Kong Joint Cooperation and Development Zone. The scope of the zone in four scenarios ranged from the boundary area to the whole Shenzhen and Hong Kong territories. In April 1996, the Shenzhen–Hong Kong Economic Development Foundation of the Shenzhen Special Economic Zone released a research report on Futian–RLA development. It suggested setting up a residential zone, a commerce and trade zone and a science/communication/service zone in the area, adopting the policies of a free trade zone.

In early 1998, the Office of High-tech Industry of the Shenzhen government proposed setting up a 'Hong Kong–Shenzhen high-tech industrial zone' in the boundary area, 3.5 km^2 from Shenzhen and 4.24 km^2 from Hong Kong (Shiu and Yang, 2000: 30–31). The Shenzhen side was very active during that period as it was expected that intercity cooperation would proceed quickly after the return of Hong Kong to China in 1997.

The second stage was the Hong Kong preparation stage, 2000–2006. In Hong Kong, as early as 1985, some industrialists suggested the Hong Kong government should set up an industrial zone in the boundary area to overcome the rising production costs in Hong Kong (DAB et al., 2004). In the period 1996–2000, Hong Kong was indifferent to the various proposals made by the Shenzhen side. Various organizations in Hong Kong began to make suggestions on boundary development in 2000 when China was about to join the World Trade Organization (WTO). This stage ended in 2006 just before the Hong Kong and Shenzhen governments agreed to jointly develop the RLA as an experimental project of intercity cooperation in 2007.

Shiu and Yang (2000) suggested setting up a boundary development zone of 7.5 km^2 with seven sub-zones such as a high-tech industrial zone, export processing zone, tourism zone, Chinese medicine development zone, trade, exhibition and convention zone, higher education and R&D zone, and residential zone. The study sponsored by DAB et al. (2004) proposed developing a comprehensive economic development zone in the RLA and a high-tech industry development zone in the boundary area. To benefit Hong Kong's economy and make use of labour from the mainland, it was proposed that firms in the industrial development zone could employ three workers from the mainland for every Hong Kong worker employed.

As mentioned before, the HKSAR government had no particular interest in developing the RLA at the very beginning. According to a conversation with a senior urban planner, Hong Kong has many development sites to meet its land needs. Furthermore, the RLA is close to ecologically sensitive areas and it has much contaminated mud. It is in an isolated area without any urban infrastructure. The RLA development would involve significant investment in infrastructure, while the land is owned by Shenzhen.

Following many suggestions from politicians and businessmen, one senior official of the HKSAR government responded for the first time in July 2002 that the possibility of opening the FCA and setting up a manufacturing zone or convention centre in the RLA would be studied. But the proposal of setting up a tax-free special industrial zone proposed by the leading industrialist, Li Ka-shing, in 2003 was declined by the HKSAR government on the grounds of disagreement on labour importation between business and labour sectors. In June 2004, the Mayor of Shenzhen and Chief Executive of HKSAR declared to include the RLA development in the agenda of cooperation.

Overall, the following suggestions had been proposed by the time the two city governments formally began considering the RLA development: a boundary industrial zone, financial industry zone, commerce/residential/tourism zone, convention and exhibition industry, university park, integrated development of the Shenzhen river and Shenzhen bay. Generally, the RLA is considered for development as a special zone within a special zone that can make use of abundant talents and labour from the mainland and get access to customers and markets on the mainland.

The third stage was the cooperation stage from 2007. A significant breakthrough came only in 2007 along with the advancement of intercity cooperation. The RLA was chosen as an experimental project of the inter-city cooperation strategy of Hong Kong. In his 2007–08 Policy Address, the Chief Executive of HKSAR announced a partnership with Shenzhen to explore the feasibility of developing the RLA for the mutual benefit of both sides. Hong Kong 2030 proposed a Northern Development Axis located in the northern New Territories close to the boundary with Shenzhen. There will be non-intensive technology and business zones and other land uses to capitalize the strategic advantage of the boundary location (HKSAR Government, 2007: 125).

With increasing convenience for the mainland Chinese to visit Hong Kong, the need to use the FCA to control illegal migration and smuggling has declined since 2003. Three major political parties in Hong Kong – DAB, Liberal Party and Democratic Party – as well as most business groups support the reduction of the FCA and the setting up of a boundary development zone (DAB et al., 2004: 5). Thus the HKSAR government (2008) recently announced a reduction in the coverage of FCA from 2800 hectares to about 400 hectares. After the completion of the planning study on the conservation and development of the land based on the principle of sustainable development, some land may be released for development.

The Hong Kong/Shenzhen cooperation meeting was held in Hong Kong on 18 December 2007 and decided to set up the 'Hong Kong–Shenzhen Joint Task Force on Boundary District Development' to accelerate collaboration on the planning and development of the boundary area (Information Services Department, 2007). The first meeting of the Hong Kong–Shenzhen Joint Task Force on Boundary District Development took place on 10 March 2008 in Shenzhen. The Joint Task Force would meet every six months and would co-ordinate, liaise and steer work on the studies in relation to the planning and development of land in the boundary area. The recent focus is on the development of the RLA and the new control point at Liantang/Heung Yuen Wai. The meeting decided that three working groups should be formed including a Working Group on the Mode of Development of RLA, a Working Group on Environment, Planning and Works of the RLA, and a Working Group on Preliminary Planning of the Control Point at Liantang/Heung Yuen Wai. Both cities would collect views on the future development of the RLA from the general public and experts to provide a basis for the comprehensive study (Development Bureau, 2008).

A Public Engagement Exercise was undertaken in June and July 2008 to collect community views and aspirations in Hong Kong on the possible future land uses for the RLA from the general public, experts and stake-holders in Hong Kong, via four Focus Group discussion sessions, a Public Forum as well as a briefing to the Greater Pearl River Delta Business

Council. The Shenzhen Municipal Planning Bureau (2008) also carried out a similar public engagement exercise in the same period.

There is a general consensus from the two cities on the RLA project. It should be beneficial to both cities. It should make best use of its boundary location. It should be a strategic project with significant contributions from both cities. It should leverage on Hong Kong and Shenzhen's competitive advantages. It should consider the planned development in nearby areas in Shenzhen and Hong Kong. The development should be sustainable and environmentally acceptable. Close cooperation between the governments of both cities is essential for the success of the project. In the future operation of the RLA, special immigration control measures such as free access to mainland residents is needed and the support from central government needs to be sought.

Among the proposed land uses, higher education, the research and development of new and high technology, and cultural and creative industries received wide support on both sides. The financial industry was supported in Shenzhen but had a strong objection from Hong Kong. The bio-medical complex supported in Hong Kong is close to the health services/research on Chinese medicine supported in Shenzhen (Planning Department et al., 2008; Shenzhen Municipal Planning Bureau, 2008; Planning Department of HKSAR and Shenzhen Municipal Planning Bureau, 2009).

After the completion of the above public consultation, a Hong Kong/ Shenzhen cooperation meeting was held in Shenzhen on 13 November 2008. Both sides initially considered that higher education might be developed as the leading land use in the RLA with high-tech R&D facilities and creative industries incorporated (Information Services Department, 2008). The meeting signed a cooperation agreement on a joint comprehensive study of the RLA. The study would be funded jointly by the two governments. Hong Kong and Shenzhen would lead the study in the areas within their own territory to undertake the planning and engineering feasibility study.

The Hong Kong and Shenzhen governments reached agreement on the above development direction of the RLA finally in 2009 (*Ming Pao*, 2009). The two cities would jointly plan the RLA development zone. The zone would contribute to human resources development in South China, enhance the competitiveness of the Pearl River Delta, and benefit the long-term economic development of Hong Kong and Shenzhen (Information Services Department, 2007).

The final positioning of the RLA reflects the negotiation and concessions of the two city governments to move towards a win–win situation for both cities. According to Table 7.9, the development options adopted are supported by both Hong Kong and Shenzhen that may facilitate cooperation. From the Hong Kong point of view, general commercial and

Table 7.9   Public views on the development direction of the RLA

Views from	Development supported	Development proposed with strong objection	Development not supported
Hong Kong	Higher education; R&D of new high technology; Cultural and creative industries; Bio-medical complex.	Financial industry; Convention and exhibition industry; Logistics industry; Information technology industry; Trade; Manufacturing; Conservation uses.	
Shenzhen	Higher education; R&D of new high technology; Cultural and creative industries; Financial industry; Health services/ Research on Chinese medicine.		High-tech manufacturing; Logistics industry; Housing development; Trade and convention industry; Large hospital.

Source: extracted from Planning Department et al. (2008), Shenzhen Municipal Planning Bureau (2008).

real estate development in the RLA are not necessary as there is an alternative to the RLA even near the boundary area. Hong Kong would bear the cost of infrastructure but the land value would belong to Shenzhen. On the other hand, Hong Kong has a clear advantage in higher education and has a great interest in R&D and creative industries to upgrade its economic structure. Higher education in the RLA would also be convenient for students resident in Shenzhen.

The above development option also benefits Shenzhen equally, although it is different from the original ideas of a free trade zone or a high-tech industrial zone. Of course, it is still debatable whether the proposed option is the best development option or the best land use for the RLA. R&D and creative industries may benefit from its boundary location to make use of talents from both Hong Kong and Shenzhen. It is not certain if higher education would benefit from its boundary location. Full-time students are generally expected to live in university campuses, thus other land sites can equally be used to develop higher education. On the other hand, it may be not convenient for faculty members from Hong Kong to teach in the RLA which is generally remote from the major urban areas of Hong Kong, and no housing close to the RLA is available.

The proposed development option is for public use generally and will cause the least debate in Hong Kong as any commercial or trade facility development may seem to benefit the business sector only. This is another constraint that the HKSAR government faces in its decision making. It is a big challenge for Hong Kong to develop significant public–private partnership projects due to strong pressure from the public and legislators. Indeed, my public survey among Hong Kong residents shows that many respondents support the option of developing eco-tourism, commerce and trading, and manufacturing in RLA. These options are excluded considering the need for significant contributions to the urban economy, the business interest in central Hong Kong and land use compatibility with CBD in Futian. It is clear that the selection of development option depends on the reconciliation of the two city governments as well as the particular context of public policy-making in Hong Kong.

CONCLUSION

In the age of globalization, intercity competition has been intensified. It is generally assumed that cities are in competition in a zero-sum game and there is a growing sense of city rivalry. Cities may also cooperate to enhance the competitive advantage of both cities. While many studies have been done on how cities adopt various strategies to enhance urban competitiveness, much fewer studies have examined in detail the nature of intercity competition and how the growth of one city actually affects another city (Begg, 1999; Jessop and Sum, 2000; So and Shen, 2004). There are also many studies on intercity cooperation, but it has been rare to study intercity competition and cooperation between the same pair of cities at the same time.

Hong Kong and Shenzhen have developed close economic relations since 1980. Due to economic growth and restructuring in Shenzhen, Hong Kong–Shenzhen economic relations have changed dramatically in the last three decades. Hong Kong is facing increasing 'competition' pressure from Shenzhen especially in the logistics sector. This chapter shows that city governments and the public have a strong sense of 'competition'.

The chapter argues that relative competition should be distinguished from absolute competition. Both city governments of Hong Kong and Shenzhen engage in relative competition. But absolute competition between the two cities is not serious. On the other hand, both cities seek intercity cooperation actively. The HKSAR government and the public have been forming a consensus to strengthen cooperation with the mainland, especially Shenzhen and PRD, since 2003. In 2004, the two city governments signed the Memorandum of Enhancing Hong Kong–Shenzhen Cooperation. In 2007, the Hong Kong and Shenzhen governments formally agreed to embark on deep intercity cooperation aiming to form the Hong Kong–Shenzhen Metropolis.

The chapter has examined intercity competition and cooperation simultaneously based on two case studies: airports and the development of the boundary area in Hong Kong and Shenzhen. In the case of the two airports, both city governments and the public have a strong sense of relative competition. For example, the HKSAR government would like to support Hong Kong airport by considering the building of a third runway at very high cost. Hong Kong residents would like to support Hong Kong airport and airlines using taxpayers' money. Interestingly, Shenzhen airport was not interested in cooperating with Hong Kong airport initially, wanting to keep its independent status for growth and competition.

But the competition between the two airports is not serious since Hong Kong airport has not been undermined even with the rapid growth of Shenzhen airport. The future growth of Hong Kong airport as well as Shenzhen airport depends ultimately on the economic growth and logistics needs of the GPRD region. Hong Kong and Shenzhen airports have their own immediate hinterland for their services. Local residents usually choose the nearest airport where flight services are offered. On the other hand, Shenzhen airport offers another alternative service for Hong Kong residents who can accept using Shenzhen airport for mainland and international destinations.

This chapter demonstrates how the two cities have navigated towards cooperation for mutual benefit, starting from different priorities for intercity cooperation. In the case of the RLA development, the HKSAR government showed no interest before 2002. But considering the tremendous opportunities for joint development, both cities have considered intercity cooperation as a major urban development strategy. The two city governments have chosen airports and the boundary area development as two experimental projects. To some extent, they have reconciled their cooperation objectives. The HKSAR government has shown great interest in moving forward the RLA project while the Shenzhen government has also become active in promoting airport cooperation. Clearly, the changing context of urban development in the two cities, adopting intercity cooperation as urban strategies, and the emerging consensus among the public and between the two cities are key factors facilitating the progress of cooperation in the airports and the boundary area development.

With steady progress in intercity cooperation driven by the two city governments, detailed cost and benefit analysis of specific projects is still needed. This is especially important when Hong Kong and Shenzhen have a different political status. Hong Kong is a special administrative region in China with strong support from central government. Shenzhen is a city with a special economic zone under the administration of both Guangdong and central governments. Shenzhen has the special obligation to support and serve Hong Kong for its prosperity. Thus it is necessary to make sure that Shenzhen also benefits from any kind of cooperation.

Hong Kong should also avoid the mistake of seeking cooperation just for the growth of its own airport while ignoring the needs of Hong Kong residents and the economic cost. For example, the most important need for airport cooperation is to improve the ground transport to the two airports for residents of both cities. The proposed rail link between the two airports emphasizes the needs of transfer passengers and Shenzhen residents to some extent. But the rail link has little direct benefit to Hong Kong residents. It is suggested that 1–2 stops inside Hong Kong should be set up to connect with the existing railway network so that Hong Kong residents can also make use of the rail link to go to two airports.

The proposed RLA development option focuses on public land use such as higher education and R&D. It is still debatable whether the proposed development option is the best for the RLA. It is not certain whether higher education would benefit from its boundary location. Full-time students are generally expected to live in a university campus thus another land site can equally be used to develop higher education. On the other hand, it may not be convenient for faculty members from Hong Kong to teach in the RLA which is generally remote from the major urban areas of Hong Kong. According to the public survey in this research, Hong Kong residents also support the option of developing eco-tourism, commerce and trading, and manufacturing in the RLA. Commerce and trading development or a free trade zone in the RLA is also favoured by the Shenzhen side. Is this option excluded to protect the business interest in the central urban area of Hong Kong or to avoid accusations of business favouritism by the HKSAR government? Is the government choosing a public land use oriented development option with the least objection and resistance from society? Will this undermine the overall and long-term interests of Hong Kong and Shenzhen? These issues need further investigation and consideration.

ACKNOWLEDGMENT

The work described in this chapter was supported by a Public Policy Research Grant from the Research Grants Council of HKSAR (RGC Project No. CUHK4005-PPR-4).

REFERENCES

Airports Council International (2008), Statistics: Top 30 world airports by passengers/cargo, *Information Brief*, July, http://www.aci.aero/aci/aci/file/Press%20Releases/2008/TOP30_Passengers_2007.pdf, accessed on 26 September 2008.

Begg, I. (1999), Cities and competitiveness, *Urban Studies*, **36**(5/6), 795–809.

BFRC (Bauhinia Foundation Research Centre) (2007), *Building a Hong Kong–Shenzhen Metropolis*, Hong Kong: Bauhinia Foundation Research Centre.

Brenner, N. and Theodore, N. (2002), Cities and geographies of 'actually existing neoliberalism', in N. Brenner and N. Theodore (eds), *Spaces of Neoliberalism: Urban Restructuring in North America and Western Europe*, Malden and Oxford: Blackwell Publishing, pp. 2–32.

Chen, X. (2007), A tale of two regions in China: rapid economic development and slow industrial upgrading in the Pearl River and the Yangtze River Deltas, *International Journal of Comparative Sociology*, **48**, 167–201.

China Development Institute (1996), *Shenzhen–Hong Kong Integration for Joint Prosperity*, Tianjin: Nankai University Press.

CSD (Census and Statistics Department) (2001), *Hong Kong Annual Digest of Statistics 2001*, Hong Kong: Hong Kong Government Printer.

CSD (2006), *Hong Kong Annual Digest of Statistics 2006*, Hong Kong: Hong Kong Government Printer.

CSD (2007a), *2006 By-census Main Report: Volume I*, Hong Kong: Hong Kong Government Printer.

CSD (2007b), *Monthly Digest of Statistics*, February, Hong Kong: Hong Kong Government Printer.

DAB, China Development Institute and The Hong Kong Construction Association (2004), *Prosperous Border and Prosperous Hong Kong: Scenarios and Appraisal of the Development of Border Regions between Hong Kong and Shenzhen*, Hong Kong: DAB (Democratic Alliance for the Betterment and Progress of Hong Kong).

Development Bureau, HKSAR Government (2008), Hong Kong–Shenzhen Joint Task Force on Boundary District Development meets, Press Release, 10 March, http://www.devb-plb.gov.hk/eng/press/2008/200803100189.htm, accessed on 8 March 2009.

Heeg, S. Klagge, B. and Ossenbrugge, J. (2003), Metropolitan cooperation in Europe: theoretical issues and perspectives for urban networking, *European Planning Studies*, **11**(2), 139–53.

HKSAR Government (2007), *Hong Kong 2030: Planning Vision and Strategy*, Hong Kong: The Development Bureau and The Planning Department.

HKSAR Government (2008), Plan finalised for reducing coverage of Frontier

Closed Area, Press Release, http://www.info.gov.hk/gia/general/200801/11/P200801110129.htm, accessed on 14 January 2008.

Hong Kong Economic and Trade Office (2007), Hong Kong–Shenzhen Cooperation Forum Held in Hong Kong, News Release, http://www.hketowashington.gov.hk/usa/press/2007/aug07/081307_2.htm, accessed on 7 April 2008.

Information Services Department, HKSAR Government (2007), Hong Kong/Shenzhen co-operation achieves a milestone, Press Release, 18 December.

Information Services Department, HKSAR Government (2008), CS attends HK/Shenzhen co-operation meeting, Press Release, 13 November.

Jessop, B. and Sum, N. (2000), An entrepreneurial city in action: Hong Kong's emerging strategies for (inter-) urban competition, *Urban Studies*, **37**(12), 2287–313.

Ming Pao (2008a), Hong Kong Shenzhen airport railway plan to add middle stop at Qianhai, 5 July.

Ming Pao (2008b), Hong Kong Shenzhen airport railway planning started with transfer time of 20 minutes, 18 January.

Ming Pao (2009), Hong Kong and Guangdong cooperation measures are implemented and 2.2 million Shenzhen residents can visit Shenzhen unlimitedly, 4 March.

Ni, P., Hou, Q., Wang, Y., Liu, Y. Shen, J., Lin, Z. and Yang, Y. (eds) (2008), *Blue Book of City Competitiveness: Annual Report on Urban Competitiveness No. 6*, Beijing: Social Sciences Academic Press.

Passengerterminaltoday.com (2008), Shenzhen chooses Fukas for T3 design, http://www.passengerterminaltoday.com/news.php?NewsID=4747, accessed on 26 September 2008.

Planning Department of HKSAR and Shenzhen Municipal Planning Bureau (2009), Possible future land uses for Lok Ma Chau loop, http://www.pland.gov.hk/lmc_loop/e_index.htm, accessed on 8 March 2009.

Planning Department, Public Policy Research Institute of the Hong Kong Polytechnic University and Dudley Surveyors Ltd (2008), *Community Views and Aspirations on Possible Future Land Uses for the Lok Ma Chau Loop: a Public Engagement Exercise, Final Report*, http://www.pland.gov.hk/lmc_loop/en/e_05a_consult_report.htm, accessed on 8 March 2009.

Shen, J. (2003), Cross-border connection between Hong Kong and mainland China under 'two systems' before and beyond 1997, *Geografiska Annaler Series B, Human Geography*, **85B**(1), 1–17.

Shen, J. (2008a), Inter-city relations between Hong Kong and Shenzhen: implications for urban planning and governance, *Planning and Development*, **23**(1), 2–14.

Shen, J. (2008b), Hong Kong under Chinese sovereignty: economic relations with mainland China 1978–2007, *Eurasian Geography and Economics*, **49**(3), 326–40.

Shenzhen Airport (2007), Check-in service of Shenzhen airport opened in Hong Kong, http://www.szairport.com/Catalog_183.aspx?t=5045, accessed on 2 December 2007.

Shenzhen Airport (2008a), Airport introduction, http://www.szairport.com/Catalog_198.aspx?t=2354, accessed on 26 September 2008.

Shenzhen Airport (2008b), Shenzhen airport's rank in the world rose steadily, http://www.szairport.com/Catalog_183.aspx?t=5946, accessed on 26 September 2008.

Shenzhen Airport (2008c), City government held meeting to celebrate that container port and airport reached container and passenger throughputs of 20 million TEUs and 20 million passengers respectively, http://www.szairport.com/Catalog_183.aspx?t=5344, accessed on 22 March 2008.

Shenzhen Municipal Planning Bureau (2008), *Public Consultation Report of Future Land Uses for the Lok Ma Chau Loop*, http://www.szplan.gov.cn/main/lmzht/index.htm, accessed on 8 March 2009.

Shenzhen Statistics Bureau (2007), *Shenzhen Statistical Yearbook 2007*, Beijing: China Statistical Press.

Shiu, Sin-por and Yang, Chun (2000), *Strategic Study on the Development Zone in Hong Kong-Shenzhen Boundary*, Hong Kong: One Country Two Systems Research Institute.

Singtao Daily (2008a), Hong Kong's competitiveness ranked the top in China in the 6th year, 29 March, p. A08.

Singtao Daily (2008b), Hong Kong and Shenzhen airport transfer services open today, 9 October, p. A15.

Sit, V.F.S., (1998), Hong Kong's 'transferred' industrialization and industrial geography, *Asian Survey*, **38**(9), 880–904.

So, M. and Shen, J. (2004), Measuring urban competitiveness in China, *Asian Geographer*, **23**, 71–91.

Song, D.W. (2002), Regional container port competition and co-operation: the case of Hong Kong and South China, *Journal of Transport Geography*, **10**, 99–110.

Yeung, Y.M. and Shen, J. (2008), Hong Kong, in Y.M. Yeung and J. Shen (eds), *The Pan-Pearl River Delta: An Emerging Regional Economy in a Globalizing China*, Hong Kong: Chinese University Press, pp. 207–39.

8. A city loses its major industry – what does it do? The case of Turin

Daniele Ietri

In this contribution the relationship between a city (Turin) and its major industry (the automobile) is discussed, summarizing both sides of the coin: the firm and its dynamics, and the urban policies of the city. The first section presents a brief account of how the automotive industry evolved and influenced the city according to a Fordist paradigm and how the emergence of an articulated productive system limited the impact of the economic crises. At the same time, the town faced the consequences of the rise and the fall of its 'one company': in a first stage apparently just adapting to the needs of the industrial system; in a second stage starting interventions which have reshaped the urban form and eventually the economic base of the city from the 1990s. This will be presented in the second section, reorganizing the main recent policies for the city in three distinct agendas, whose positive or negative effects are discussed where possible.

The most recent economic highlights report on the renewed strategy of Fiat, approaching markets and competitors in both the USA and Germany; this is probably the starting point of a new phase which is still at too early a stage for any discussion on its effects on the city. In the final section two weaknesses of the policymaking process are pointed out in the form of proposals for the ongoing debate and eventually as a caveat for planning interventions in similar contexts.

ONE COMPANY, ONE TOWN[1]

The origin of manufacture in Turin can be traced back to the end of the nineteenth century, when the automobile manufacturer company Fiat (founded in 1899 in Turin) started its rapid growth. Fiat's ascent in the twentieth century drove the development of the whole Italian car industry. In Turin, the presence of Fiat led to the establishment of a Fordist productive paradigm that profoundly influenced the urban economy and society. This paradigm was based on the presence of a few big plants vertically integrated, mass production in automotive and metal-mechanic technologies, and the formation of a localized supply system of small and medium suppliers. As a consequence, a local concentration of competencies in the processing of metal components and industrial machinery arose in Piedmont and in Turin in particular, which still represents one of the most evident traits of the local economy. In the area of Turin a very strong economic, social and cultural relationship between the city and the firm emerged, heavily influencing the city's landscape and its image as well. For a very long period, Turin has thus been described by media and foreigners, as well as by its citizens, as a 'one-company town'.

In this section we will briefly analyze the changes in automotive production in the last decades and the extent to which the rise and crisis of the industry affected the city. Several distinct phases could be pointed out, from the first post-war period to the very uncertain conjuncture of the last few years.

Postwar 'Absolutism'[2]

Immediately after WWII, the internal Italian market for cars rapidly expanded and Fiat concentrated production in a few large factories, vertically integrated, localized in and around Turin. The rapid ascent of Fiat affected the economic, social, cultural and political development of Turin so deeply that the city started to be known as the Automobile Capital of Italy, eventually comparable to Detroit, but dominated by a single corporation (Amari, 1980; Conti, 1983; Conti and Enrietti, 1995). This had many effects on the city itself, which suddenly grew as a consequence of migration flows from the countryside and from eastern and southern Italy. From its historical headquarters in Lingotto, the company built a huge facility in the city (the 'Mirafiori' area) and in two towns close to Turin – Chivasso and Rivalta. In the 1960s, Turin attracted waves of immigration, largely from the southern regions of Italy, and its population reached 1 million and peaked at 1.5 million in 1975: several residential districts were set up for workers in peripheral areas.

In its efforts towards vertical integration – also with the acquisition of several suppliers and the localization of some multinational suppliers in Piedmont – the firm was dependent on a network of at least 1.2 thousand suppliers. Fiat provided design, machinery, materials and credit, with suppliers – many of them being former Fiat workers – asked only to guarantee delivery times. It is evident how these suppliers were essentially dependent on the corporation.

Table 8.1   Vertical integration levels of Fiat Auto (%)

Year	1982	1987	1992	1996	1998	1999	2000
External production	50	52	65	70	70	73	72
External design	30	30	45	59	70	73	72

Source: Whitford and Enrietti (2005, p. 783).

Rationalization

After the oil crisis in the 1970s, Fiat began a reorganization aimed at improving productivity and diversification, with an effort at modernizing the factory through automation, and finally proposing massive layoffs. The company's employees were reduced from 135 000 in 1980 to 78 000 in 1986; in the meanwhile, as a consequence of central government's policies, employment shifted towards the south of the country – although strategic functions remained in Turin. Fiat still relied on a large network of suppliers, most of them technologically underdeveloped: in 1980–81 the suppliers were reduced by almost one third. With the remaining suppliers, Fiat signed contracts providing investments in the development of new products in exchange for the property rights to designs: thus this period started a general trend of reduction in the vertical integration of the company (Table 8.1).

The Last Decade: Responses to Crisis

In 1990, more than 60 per cent of Fiat's production was in three plants in or near Turin. Two of them (in Chivasso and Rivalta) were shut down respectively in 1992 and 2002. Mirafiori, in the city, went from 60 000 employed workers in the 1980s to almost 11 500 in 2004.

As figures confirm (Table 8.2), this impressive loss in Fiat production did not actually destroy the automobile-centered regional economy or – at least – did not affect the manufacturing employment in the province of Turin. The negative consequences for automotive-related industries have been avoided mainly thanks to the market diversification of many of the local suppliers who were progressively active in international markets,[3] especially after the reorganizations in the 1980s (see above).

The relationship between the city and the firm evolved in a system consisting of small and large suppliers, design and niche producers, technology-transfer and training organizations, and also university programs. This was a system of enterprises that became progressively independent and self-sufficient, explaining at least in part how the city could

Table 8.2 Auto production and manufacturing employment in the province of Turin

	1993	1997	2001	2002	2003	% Change 2003/1993
Auto production, Turin	571472	568368	374379	306000	250000	−56.25
Auto production, rest of Italy	593128	1059232	897384	819769	776454	30.91
Percentage Piedmont/ Italy	49.07	34.92	29.44	27.18	24.35	−50.38
Workers, Mirafiori & Rivalta	40061	31399	25285	21909	15695	−60.82
All workers in province of Turin (000s)	880	879	916	912	924	5.0
Mfg workers, province of Turin (000s)	309	306	292	297	288	−6.8
Italian industrial employment (000s)	5431.5	5294.9	5339.6	5375.1	5380	−0.96

Source: Whitford and Enrietti (2005, p. 778).

bear the effect of the fall of its major industry, but still having the corporation in a central and directive role, which keeps it at the center of the political debate.

Questions for Policymaking

This brief account, still missing many details, shows that the crisis the industry (and the city) faced in the last decade is not the first in its history. As a consequence of shocks and reorganizations, the system evolved from Fiat's hierarchical domination to de-integration, but with an unvarying role of the corporation as a 'coordinator'. 'Although this articulated system was born very much of an interaction between Fiat, its suppliers and other regional actors, it has always had Fiat at its center in a directive role, as the sole actor with both the interest and the ability to provide key collective goods' (Whitford and Enrietti, 2005, p. 771) (for example through the ongoing activity of its research center, the 'Centro Ricerche Fiat'). The first question for policymaking is then not how to face the possible event of a definitive shut-down of the automotive firm, but more importantly who/what is going to take the place of Fiat in producing coordination in the local manufacturing productive system.

The second question for policymaking is related to the co-evolution of Fiat, the city of Turin and the Italian industrial policy. In this field, most of the intervention to support the automotive sector was in the form of bail-outs, which will not apply nowadays because of EU prohibition of all direct subsidies. Moreover, from a political perspective, Fiat is no longer recognized as Italy's most important large company. But at the same time as investments might have flown from the country to Turin, an inverse flow can be unveiled. The automotive industry in Turin has in fact been affected by the state incentives for investments in Southern Italy – with eleven factories built in the Italian Mezzogiorno between the late 1960s and 1970s, employing some 35000 workers in the 1980s. According to Calafati (2003), the city was conditioned by the demands of national economic development, inducing Fiat to invest outside Turin. The issue is whether the growth process of the company (so highly tied to the city, as we have seen) could have been different if not conditioned by state policies. 'One easily forgets that Turin paid a price higher than that of any other Italian city as a result of this long term policy (. . .). No other Italian city was asked to use so much of its evolutionary potential outside its boundaries' (Calafati, 2003, p. 3). From this point of view, the country still owes some support to the automotive corporation and, to an extent, to the city of Turin. In 2009, once again facing a rapid slowdown in car demand, the national government issued demand-side incentives. Criticism on these interventions is consistent – short-term policies hoping for a brief recovery of the economy. But what if this does not happen? And what if the automotive industry is going to progressively lose its economic and occupational relevance? What if new technological paradigms will definitively get rid of the few survivors of the Fordist era? These kind of questions have been 'in the air' in the city of Turin at least for the last two decades. An interpretation of what the city did is presented in the next section.

THE STRATEGIES: ONE PLAN FOR THREE CITIES

As the effects of the crisis in the automotive industry became more and more evident, in the urban elites there emerged the need for a reflection on the future of the city – and more pragmatically, the urgency of massive interventions in the local economy and the urban form. The joint efforts of some relevant urban players allowed the constitution of the 'Associazione Torino Internazionale' ('International Turin Association') that promoted a new urban vision and two strategic plans, the first in 2000 and the second in 2006.[4] Instead of presenting the details of the two stages of strategic planning for the city, the initiatives promoted for the city will be grouped in three Turin(s), following an original proposal by Belligni (2008).[5] Each Turin will refer to a policy agenda, concerning different aspects of the city, and promoted and sustained by specific urban coalitions (or 'regimes'). The focus on the urban elites supporting each of the three policy agendas refers to the local political debate, and will not be presented here. We just highlight here that it seems unrealistic to think in separate interest groups – rather, urban elites in contemporary Turin are frequently over-lapping, many of the key players being very hard to refer to a single group. Moreover, the image outlined at least disputes a diffused idea of a city 'ruled' by very few actors, all belonging to the same elite or regime.

Metamorphic Turin

The city is 'built around – and in part *by* – Fiat and the auto industry' (Whitford and Enrietti, 2005, p. 771). Probably the most notable effect of de-industrialization of the city (or, in other words, the decline of its Fordist urban form) has been the proliferation of unused industrial areas. In the 1990s, the urban planning elaborated well before the first Strategic Plan, faced some 1 million square meters of brownfield areas (the total unused land for the whole metropolitan area is four times bigger). After real-izing the need for an active role by the municipality in those huge urban transformations, the last Plan in 1995 (PRG, in Italian, 'piano regolatore generale') and the Strategic Plans issued in 2000 and 2006, approach the restoration issue as a challenge and an opportunity to widely reshape many central areas of the city[6]. Housing and infrastructural transformations have been set up, benefiting from land made available by former industrial areas and putting the railway underground. With its two stations in the city center, the city has been 'wounded' by railway lines crossing down-town from north to south and from west to east. This project (which has still to be completed) has already made large areas available, and trans-formed them into a boulevard, green areas and newly built residential districts. At the same time, some industrial buildings have been restored and are now used by the universities or as seats for research centers. Other areas are now residential and commercial districts. Notably, the plans for restoring many areas of the city largely benefited from the funds allocated for the Winter Olympic Games:[7] some neighborhoods have been regener-ated to be used for example as a 'media village' during the Games, and are

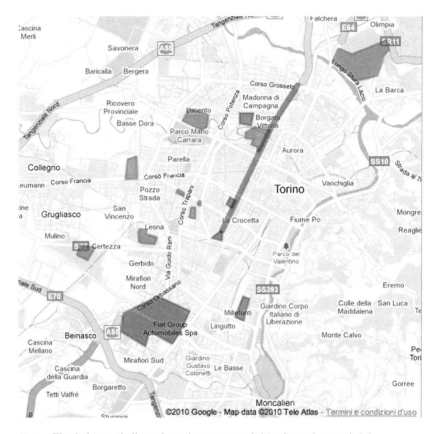

Note: The dark areas indicate the main areas occupied (or formerly occupied) by automotive-related factories; the solid line from the center to the upper right represents the main 'corridor' made available from railway tracks moved underground.

Source: own elaboration from http://maps.google.com.

Figure 8.1   A map of the transformation in Turin

now available to the housing market. In many peripheral areas, restoration has been possible thanks to funds from the national government and the European Union ('programmi di riqualificazione urbana' – 'urban regeneration programs' at the national level; Urban II[8] from EU funds). Finally, confirming the concern for Fiat's health, there is a growing debate on what should be done with the large 'Mirafiori'[9] plant (see Figure 8.1) that could eventually be shut down if the firm stops its production lines in Turin (Berta et al., 2006).

At the same time, the city benefited from several infrastructural projects.

Internal to the city is a new (the first, actually) subway line connecting the western areas with downtown and with southern districts (the line will be completed by 2011). External to the city are infrastructural investments related to: the Olympic Games, with a new speedway to the Alpine valleys; strategic infrastructural improvements at the national level, with the restoration of speedways and a new high-speed railway to Milan; infrastructural projects at the European level, with Turin being involved in a Trans-European Network[10] connecting Italy with France and the Iberian peninsula. From the 'metamorphic Turin' point of view, the city (and the interest groups) has benefited from an unprecedented flow of projects and funds. By the way, as many of the workshops are still running, the positive effects of infrastructure-oriented projects are still to be verified.

Polytechnic Turin

The need to overcome the crisis of the automotive industry put the economic and industrial issues at the center of the debate on the future of the city. Standing on the role of the two academic institutions of the city (Università di Torino and Politecnico di Torino) and on the generalized emphasis on the service economy and ICT, the Strategic Plan and several initiatives by local actors committed to restoring the local fabric towards knowledge-based sectors. Both the academic institutions started radical reorganization, enlarged or restored their seats, and set up initiatives such as business incubators and research centers for specific subjects. Through the support of the region, two science parks were set up in the city, specializing in environment-related industries and the multimedia industry. The Chamber of Commerce supported several internationalization projects, such as 'From concept to car'[11] for the promotion abroad of automotive-related industries or 'Think-up'[12] for ICT-related industries, with a good return on investment for their first years of activity.[13] Here the influence of the theories of regional development is clear, focusing on knowledge-intensive sectors and the idea of an innovative process emerging from a virtuous interaction among enterprises, governmental agencies and universities (Leydesdorff and Etzkowitz 1996, 1998; Morgan, 1997). This is confirmed in the Second Strategic Plan (2006), which commits to the project of transforming the local fabric into a knowledge-based economy, provided that 'the metropolitan area of Turin owns the assets necessary for a knowledge based development' (Associazione Torino Internazionale, 2005, p. 10). The academic structures are undoubtedly an asset for the city – with some 3050 academic staff in 2007[14] and 82 502 students – not considering the many seats in other towns of the region.

The existence of an innovative vocation and a solid ICT district is instead hard to verify – and statistics are controversial. According to the Regional Innovation Scoreboard,[15] Piedmont region ranks 73rd at the European level; it is the third Italian region, far from Lazio (44th) and a bit lower than Lombardia (71st); if compared with other regions geographically close to Piedmont, the region ranks approximately the same as Provence-Alpes-Cote d'Azur in France (75th), but far from Rhone-Alpes (the region of Lyon, 33rd). Also according to data on patents or investments in research and development, the regional ranking is comparable with other Italian regions, but very far from the European competitive arena in which the city pretends to act as a protagonist.[16]

Nevertheless, the Piedmont region ranks as the second Italian region for expenditure in research and development vs GDP (1.75 per cent; the first is Lazio, with 1.81 per cent); 80 per cent of the expenditure is made by the private and non-profit sector, the highest figure in Italy (L'Eau Vive, Comitato Giorgio Rota, 2008). The attitude of businesses in an investment in research higher than that of the public sector is comparable with the most innovative regions in Europe: nevertheless, the current economic situation may induce a fall in profit and a consequent restriction of private funds allocated to research.

Recent surveys (CCIAA Torino, 2006; L'Eau Vive, Comitato Giorgio Rota, 2007), identified 1593 'innovative firms' in the Turin metropolitan area, estimated as 0.7 per cent of the total number of businesses in the area, most of them in the advanced services, metal-mechanic, electricity and electronic appliances sectors; a smaller number belonging to the chemical, rubber, plastic and automotive sectors. Another research (CCIAA Torino and Unimatica Torino, 2006), surveyed 6500 businesses in the Province of Turin,[17] 57 per cent of them in the metropolitan area, pointing out the (well known) weaknesses of the sector: small size (only 2.7 per cent of businesses have more than 50 employees); family-owned and run (80 per cent); low turnover and produced mainly within the region (71 per cent). The Torino Wireless Fundation[18] has been supported by the region since 2003 in order to overcome the cited structural problems and create a technological district in the city: the first results were expected for 2010 – now this deadline has been shifted to 2012.

An examination of actors and initiatives in the Piedmont region and in the city of Turin shows an impressive number of institutional actors (region, municipalities, chambers of commerce, industrial associations, financial institutions and bank foundations) engaged in fostering innovation through the activity of a comparable number of agencies (science parks, university labs, business incubators, research centers, and so on). A certain fragmentation of the system emerges (far from being a 'regional innovation system') and scarce relationships with firms (except those localized in some of the science parks) – that should be instead the key players of innovation.

A regional innovation system is thus missing, 'with many initiatives intended to support innovation without coordination in a robust and defined governance framework, resulting in initiatives not always coherent, sometimes overlapping and with no homogeneous quality levels' (Boffo et al., 2005, p. 149). Recently, more initiatives have been promoted to reduce fragmentation in the 'regional innovation system', such as the cited 'Think-up' (for ICT), 'From concept to car' (for automotive) and 'Torino Piemonte Aerospace'[19] (to support a traditional aerospace specialization, tied to Alenia or Fiat Avio). The results are still preliminary, but data confirm more cooperation among firms and research centers (businesses initiating collaboration programs with research centers are 14.4 per cent in ICT industries and 25 per cent in automotive; L'Eau Vive, Comitato Rota, 2008).

Finally, the tendency of a shift towards a service (or immaterial?) economy should not be taken for granted as a necessary and preferred evolutionary trajectory for the urban economy. This may be true for many cities – the case of Turin seems different. Research by Russo (2006) based on an input–output table of the province of Turin diminishes the role of the service industry, even if its occupational effect counts as 63 per cent of total employment, with manufacturing being 34 per cent and agriculture a little residual. If one considers the demand, only 42.5 per cent is directed to services, while 52.8 per cent is to manufacturing – this share rises to more than 80 per cent for the demand originated outside the province. In this view, the occupational relevance of services is not due to their being required by the economy; rather, it is more their 'classical' role as support to the manufacturing sectors, that turn out as the most demand-led, especially for export.

Pyrotechnic Turin

This agenda groups projects for the city centered on two sets of initiatives:

1. the city as a seat for events and mega events, following the 'wave' of the Winter Olympic Games in 2006;
2. the city as a 'cultural district', standing on the relevant museums and cultural institutions in the city and a recent re-investment in the movie-making industry.

The effects of a mega-event such as the Winter Olympic Games on the economy of a metropolitan area are hard to determine – and results are uncertain for most of the cases. The task is harder in the case of Turin, as the games were organized in a relatively vast area, involving the city but also some Alpine valleys.

In Turin, the event undoubtedly had the effect of attracting huge investments in the city, which pushed the transformation and some important infrastructural projects (see 'Metamorphic Turin' above). The Olympic Games, during the years before the event, had a positive effect evaluated as an increase in GDP of +0.3–0.4 per cent and a reduction in unemployment by 0.3–0.47 per cent. The most evident effects were seen in the building sector, due to the infrastructural investments (Regione Piemonte, 2005). In 2006, tourism in the area rose, according to the number of visitors and number of businesses, by 3.7 per cent (L'Eau Vive, Comitato Giorgio Rota, 2007) although this rise was limited in time to the period of the Games.

Turin had its leading event in the 'Salone dell'auto' (automobile fair), with large attention from the media and four times more attendants than the actual major event, the book fair ('Salone del libro'). According to attendance, another leading fair was 'Salone del gusto', a wine and food exhibition related to the 'Slow food' movement, based in Piedmont. Both the book and the 'Slow food' fair succeeded in attracting visitors and are comparable to concurrent events in Italy and Europe (such as the 'Buchmesse' in Frankfurt). A very similar positive trend is reported for arts and music events: in this case an experiment of a joint music festival with Milan resulted in the MiTo festival.[20]

Local authorities put great emphasis on the movie industry and on the local 25-year-old film festival. The city has a long tradition, being the first seat for the movie industry in Italy. Actually, the Torino Film Festival does not succeed in competition with the popular Venice festival and the recently inaugurated film festival in Rome, attracting three and two times the attendance of Turin, respectively. The specialization in the movie industry has been supported by huge investment also in new technologies, with a 'Virtual Reality and Multimedia' science park built in a brownfield area in the north of the city.

Events in general and the movies in particular may have a large impact on the image of a region or a city. In the last years, in almost all Italian regions, several 'film commissions' have proliferated, aimed at promoting certain areas as sets for movies – and thus promoting indirect territorial marketing through the diffusion of a suggestive image of the region. If we consider the image of Turin represented by movies, even now we see how the city is still used as a typical background for various social diseases – poverty and immigration (*Così ridevano*, Gianni Amelio, 1998; *La seconda volta*, Mimmo Calopresti, 1995), political struggles and terrorism (*La meglio gioventù*, Marco Tullio Giordana, 2003; *Mio fratello è figlio unico*, Daniele Lucchetti, 2007) and lack of prospects for the younger genera-tion, especially for the second generation of immigrants (*Santa Maradona*, Marco Ponti, 2001; *Tutti giù per terra*, Davide Ferrario, 1997).[21] The pro-motion of the city as a set for movies is part of the objectives stated in the Strategic Plan; a generous investment has been allocated to the local Film Commission, aimed at supporting the city as a set for movies. Curiously, almost none of the movies produced are supporting a strongly positive image of the city, in a 'territorial marketing' approach followed by other regions – for example the superb image of Tuscany in *Stealing Beauty* (Bernardo Bertolucci, 1996). Moreover, the diffusion of the image of the city is limited by the fact that few productions are actually distributed internationally.

Similar weaknesses have been pointed out for the exploitation of the Olympic image of the city. The adoption of the 'Torino 2006' logo is almost unused by firms, universities and other actors promoting at the global scale. Generally speaking, 'the city proposes to press on an inter-national audience an image of tradition, food, culture, art [...]. A quite generic image, good for anywhere in Italy, without destination-specific icons' (Bottero, 2007, p. 171). Thus, in 2008 Turin was the World Design Capital and hosted an international design fair; in 2009 the city hosted the European Science Foundation conference; and sports events have included the Paralympic Games, 'Universiadi', and a world chess tournament.

Turin is now entering the preparatory phase for a new event, with at least national relevance. In 2011 the city will host the 'Italia 150' event, the celebration of 150 years of unification of the Italian country (Turin was the first capital city of Italy, from 1861 to 1865). The organizing committee has prepared a budget of 600 million Euros – the national government has agreed 98 million (L'Eau Vive, Comitato Giorgio Rota, 2008) – with the target of attracting at least 8 million visitors (as in the previous celebra-tions, in 1911 and 1961).

Polytechnic + Pyrotechnic = Creative?

In the First Strategic Plan, much emphasis was given to the promotion of Turin as a city of culture, tourism, commerce and sport. The Second Strategic Plan focuses instead on the knowledge economy, aiming at a valorization of the cultural assets (material and immaterial) towards a competitive ranking of the city as a center for cultural production and innovation – a *locus* for a 'creative class'. This seems to be the new chal-lenge that city (and region) leaders are proposing for public discussion – to foster Torino as a capital city for knowledge at the European and national scale. A joint effort by the region, municipality and the two local universities was launched in a Forum and in several press conferences by the Mayor of Turin and the President of Piedmont Region (Trabucco, 2009).

This is a great challenge, considering the actual ranking of the city, at least according to the presence of individuals belonging to the 'creative class'. A study by Tinagli and Florida (2005) ranks Turin 53rd among the 103 Italian provinces – and last among Italian metropolitan areas – for the presence of the creative class. This is due, above all, to the relevance of medium-skilled technical employment in the manufacturing industries – a strong industrial heritage still characterizing the urban economic base. The overall creativity index, considering Florida's three Ts (Talent, Technology, Tolerance), ranks Torino 7th for its very good performance in Technology. Technology and innovation-oriented infrastructures are thus a crucial asset for the city, while its attractiveness and 'openness' could be fostered by good coordination of the policy agendas.

DISCUSSION

In this final section we will examine a couple of the lessons from the experience of Turin with the loss of a major industrial activity; lessons that should have some relevance for cities and towns in the industrial regions of Pennsylvania.

Focusing on Shared Targets: from Elite to Grassroots Policymaking

From the interaction of the three policy agendas (metamorphic, polytechnic, pyrotechnic) emerges an unprecedented process of modernization (material and immaterial) of the city. This process – fostered by the concurrent inflow of funds from various government levels – has had the positive effect of changing the built form in vast areas of the city dramatically and initiating a process of restoration of its economic base. On one side, as cited above, the crisis of the automobile industry did not have such a dramatic impact, thanks to the presence of largely independent subcontractors and to the national government's interventions. Nevertheless, it is probably too early to propose a sound forecast on what is going to happen in the next years – especially considering the actual economic slowdown.

As the metamorphic agenda is soon going to finish its cycle, our focus should now be directed at the perspectives for the polytechnic and pyrotechnic agendas. Most of the uncertainties of those agendas could be determined by an excessive fragmentation of the targets. If this is unavoidable (and eventually may prove to be opportune) in the first 'diagnostic' phase, it is now time for the city to focus on more specific medium-term targets and also the availability of funds, which are likely to be much lower in the future. This selective process will be very complicated in practice, but policymakers will probably be forced to more structural choices by the effects of economic crisis. In only a few Italian cities and regions have the local authorities been so deeply engaged in the attempt to lead and govern the effects of economic transition. In Turin, the transition has been led by public institutions, and by urban elites rooted in the 'old, traditional' institutions of the city: Fiat, the universities, and so on. Nowadays, the city 'is still missing an adequate capacity to produce an elite representative of the new social composition' (Bonomi, 2008, p. 85). The transition from Fordism to the forthcoming economic paradigm has thus been smooth and 'non-violent', but with 'old powers being diluted in a governance renewed in contents and widened in memberships' (Bonomi, 2008, p. 86).

Maybe this could be the opportunity for promoting the participation of citizens in policymaking. The city has an administrative organization appropriate for enhancing participation at the level of local neighborhoods. The urban leaders, formally elected and being part of an urban elite, could now open up the circle of the 'happy few' to include informal participants in 'grassroots' decision-making processes, who could share the benefits and the responsibilities of leading the city through the next turning points.

The City, the Region and the Global Scale

If one considers the strategic plans of Turin, it is clear how the city aimed at becoming a protagonist on the international/global scale. The name of the association promoting the two Strategic Plans reveals this general target for the evolution of the city – 'Torino internazionale' (International Turin). An internationalization of the city, a wider scale of action for players localized in the urban area, is desirable and in some sectors realistic. Nevertheless, this policy target might bring serious downturns.

From the 1990s, the city has continued to think of its geo-economic relationships and image at the national, European and global scales, almost ignoring the importance of the relationships with its region – especially in economic terms. This could be acceptable in those regions characterized by an industrially developed city surrounded by a generally underdeveloped region, in which lower order towns establish dominance/dependence relationships. But most of the provinces of Piedmont are not at all areas with a low industrial profile. Wine and food products sold globally are produced in several areas of the region, especially the south. An SME from Fubine, on the way to Alessandria, provided the lighting for the downtown Manhattan landscape, from the World Trade Center area. Many towns in the eastern part of the region are strongly industrialized, even in highly innovative industries, and are progressively more related with the (spatially and functionally) closer Milan. These are only a few examples among many. While Turin was elaborating strategies for its internationalization, all the other provinces reshaped their relationships – eventually on a trans-regional and global scale – bypassing the capital city of the region. The most recent documents in regional planning are fostering a general recall and a new role for Turin as a protagonist for the region, a role apparently hard to recover after a substantial loss of economic centrality.

NOTES

1. This section is based on: Enrietti (1987, 1995); Enrietti and Lanzetti (2003); Whitford and Enrietti (2005); Conti and Enrietti (1995); Conti and Giaccaria (2001).
2. The definition of the historical phases is given by Whitford and Enrietti (2005).
3. Between 1990 and 1997, local firms more than doubled their share of exports (Whitford and Enrietti, 2005).
4. http://www.torino-internazionale.org/.
5. In what follows, the taxonomy proposed by Belligni (2008) is adopted with several changes in names and contents. Anyway, the original idea by the author of three ongoing policy agendas is acknowledged.
6. One should always keep in mind that, in most European cities, the urban form is relatively 'fixed' by the presence of huge historical (sometimes, archeological) districts, especially in the city center. Thus, the availability of huge portions of land in downtown is very unlikely to happen as an opportunity for urban policymakers – at least after the bombings during WWII.
7. Turin was the host city for the 2006 Winter Olympic Games; see discussion later.
8. 'The program covers the southern suburbs of Torino, with 24843 inhabitants and a surface area of 2135 km^2, next to the FIAT industrial area "Mirafiori Nord". The area is struggling with severe social and economic problems: unemployment, crime, poverty, low levels of education and training, decaying buildings and public spaces, a deteriorating high level of social housing and environmental damage. Main roads with a high level of air and noise pollution cross the area' (http://ec.europa.eu/regional_policy/urban2/towns_prog_it.htm).
9. See Figure 8.1 – the 'mirafiori' area is on the bottom left corner of the map.
10. Trans-European Networks (TENs) are European-wide priority infrastructural projects promoted and (partially) financed by the European Union.
11. http://www.fromconcepttocar.com/home.html.
12. http://www.thinkupict.org/.
13. In terms of the value of contracts signed by the local firms involved vs. the investment allocated by local authorities on the initiative.
14. This figure (source: http://statistica.miur.it) refers only to those faculties holding tenure.
15. http://www.proinno-europe.eu/ScoreBoards/Scoreboard2006/
16. It should be remarked that data in this field are mostly at the regional level; the hypothesis that most of the innovation-related activity in the Piedmont region is concentrated in Turin is far from being verified.

17. The Italian administrative system is organized in regions, provinces and municipalities (and some intermediate levels, actually aggregations of municipalities). From the demographic point of view, the Piedmont region has more than 4402 thousand inhabitants, the Province of Turin has 2278 thousand, the Municipality of Turin has 908 thousand (survey on 1/1/2008, source http://demo.istat.it).
18. http://www.torinowireless.it/
19. http://www.torinopiemonteaerospace.com/
20. http://www.mitosettembremusica.it/en/
21. See Vanolo (2008) for an informed discussion of the image of Turin.

REFERENCES

Amari, Giancarlo (1980), *Torino come Detroit: capitale. dell'automobile, 1895–1940*, Cappelli, Bologna.

Associazione Torino Internazionale (2005), *Verso il Secondo Piano Strategico. Materiali di discussione sul futuro dell'area metropolitana di Torino*, http://www.torino-internazionale.org.

Belligni, Silvano (2008), 'Torino polimorfa. Modello di sviluppo e elite civica di governo', *Nuvole*, 32, http://www.nuvole.it.

Berta, Giuseppe, Aldo Bonomi, Chiara Casalino and Salvatore Cominu (2006), *Mirafiori e le altre*, http://images.torino-internazionale.org/f/Eventi/Ri/Ricerca_Mirafiori.pdf.

Boffo, S., M. Calderini and F. Gagliardi (2005), 'Risorse e dinamiche del settore conoscenza scientifica e tecnologica', in Torino Internazionale, *Scenari per il sistema locale. Valutazioni sul Piano Strategico di Torino e sulle prospettive di sviluppo dell'area metropolitana*, Torino: Torino Internazionale.

Bonomi, Aldo (2008), *Il rancore. Alle radici del malessere del Nord*, Feltrinelli, Milano.

Bottero, Marta (ed.) (2007), *L'eredità di un grande evento. Monitoraggio territoriale ex post delle Olimpiadi di Torino 2006*, Celid, Torino.

Calafati, Antonio (2003), 'Socialised development trajectories: the case of Turin', *Italian Journal of Regional Science*, 1.

CCIAA Torino (2006), 'Osservatorio sull'innovazione 2006. Repertorio delle imprese innovative della provincia di Torino', Camera di Commercio Industria Artigianato e Agricoltura di Torino, Torino http://images.to.camcom.it/f/Studi/Re/Relaz_Imprese2006_V02.pdf.

CCIAA Torino – Camera di Commercio di Torino, Unimatica Torino (2006), *L'ICT in provincia di Torino. La sfida dell'innovazione nel mercato globale. Innovazione e reti per crescere e competere*, Torino: Camera di Commercio di Torino.

Conti, Sergio (1983), *Dopo la città industriale: Detroit tra crisi urbana e crisi dell'automobile*, Angeli, Milano.

Conti Sergio and Aldo Enrietti (1995), 'The Italian automobile industry and the case of Fiat: one country, one company, one market?' in R. Hudson and E. Schamp (eds), *Towards a New Map of Automobile Manufacturing in Europe: New Production Concepts and Spatial Restructuring*, Springer, Berlin.

Conti, Sergio and Paolo Giaccaria (2001), *Local Development and Competitiveness*, Kluwer University Press, Dordrecht.

Enrietti Aldo (1987), 'La dinamica dell'integrazione verticale della Fiat Auto Spa', *Economia e politica industriale*, **55**, 113–45.

Enrietti Aldo (1995), 'Il settore dei componenti auto: struttura e dinamica', *Economia e politica industriale*, **88**, 131–51.

Enrietti Aldo and Renato Lanzetti (2003), 'La crisi Fiat Auto e la politica industriale locale: il caso del Piemonte', *Stato e Mercato*, **68**, 241–64.

L'Eau Vive, Comitato Giorgio Rota (2007), *Senza rate. Ottava Rapporto Annuale su Torino*, Milano: Guerini e Associati.

L'Eau Vive, Comitato Giorgio Rota (2008), *Solista e solitaria. Nono Rapporto Annuale su Torino*, Milano: Guerini e Associati.

Leydesdorff, Loet and Henry Etzkowitz (1996), 'Emergence of a triple helix of university–industry–government relations', *Science and Public Policy*, **23**, 279–86.

Leydesdorff, Loet and Henry Etzkowitz (1998), 'The triple helix as a model for innovation studies', *Science and Public Policy*, **25**, 195–203.

Morgan, K. (1997), 'The learning region: institutions, innovation and regional renewal', *Regional Studies*, **31**(5), 491–503.

Regione Piemonte (2005), *Torino 2006. Le Olimpiadi del Territorio Piemotese*, Savigliano: L'artistica editrice.

Russo, Giuseppe (2006), 'Merlino a Torino: un'applicazione dinamica di tabelle input–output', in Giuseppe Russo and Pietro Terna (eds), *Produrre a Torino*, Otto, Torino, pp. 53–69.

Tinagli, Irene and Richard Florida (2005), *L'Italia nell'era creativa*, Creativity Group Europe.

Trabucco, Marco (2009), 'Città della conoscenza. La nuova sfida di Torino', *La Repubblica Torino*, 12/3/2009.

Vanolo, Alberto (2008), 'The image of the creative city: some reflections on urban branding in Turin', *Cities*, **25**, 370–82.

Whitford, John and Henry Enrietti (2005), 'Surviving the fall of a king: the regional institutional implications of crisis at Fiat Auto', *International Journal of Urban and Regional Research*, **29**(4), 771–95.

9. Northeastern US cities and global urban competitiveness

Ni Pengfei

CONCEPTUAL FRAMEWORK AND METHOD OF ANALYSIS

Today, with half of the world population living in cities, we are stepping into the era of urbanization, and the cities are becoming the main location for working and living. Since the 1990s, information technology and economic globalization have thoroughly altered the concepts of time and space, as well as decisions and arrangements concerning the global economy, technology and social activities. Global cities have become more and more important, and the international competition of the cities is also becoming more intensified. Improving the environment of cities, attracting more talent, industry, technology and investment to benefit the people, and promoting the global urban competitiveness have become the focus of mayors of all the cities in the world, the enterprise and all people.

The Marketplace of Global Urban Competitiveness

The global urban system is uneven in different regions. Not only do values differ in different cities, the value within a city declines from the center down to the suburban areas. In the urban industry system under global integration, the industry system and industries are hierarchical. There are changes and relocation. In the context of global integration, the operating factor systems differ from each other. They change continuously.

Cities compete against each other and cooperate through the interaction among the factors of the environment system, industry system, and value system. A city fosters its functional structure system and derivative function system by attracting external factors and maintaining local factors. These determine its position in the global urban value system.

Conceptual Framework

The urban sustainable competitiveness implies a city's ability in relation to other cities in the world to attract and translate resources, control and occupy markets, accumulate wealth as fast as possible and offer urban residents material benefits, which is determined by the combination of its enterprise operating factors and industrial systems.

UC1 = f (the size of GDP, number of international patent applications, the distribution of multinational corporations, price advantages, economic growth rate, GDP per capita, GDP per square kilometer, employment rate and labor productivity).

UC2 = f (E, T, I, L, H, S, G). UC2 means the input or structure of the city's competitiveness, E means the quality of enterprise, T means human resources, I means industry structure, L means the living environment, H means the business soft environment, S means the business hard environment, G means the global connectivity.

UC1 = UC2

Index System

Output components of urban competitiveness
Based on the above analysis, the output index system of global urban competitiveness is listed in Figure 9.1.

Input components of urban competitiveness
The three-level index system of input competitiveness used in the analysis was designed in accordance with the above theoretical analysis. The index system consists of 7 level 1 indices, 40 level 2 indices and 105 level 3 indices. For full explanation of this index system and its interpretation, please refer to Figure 9.2 which shows the first level index system.

City Samples

Five hundred cities were studied for general urban competitiveness measurement universality: cities from 130 countries and regions in five

Figure 9.1   Output index system of global urban competitiveness

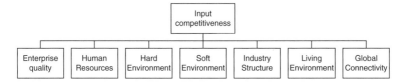

Figure 9.2   Input index system of global urban competitiveness

continents were selected, representing different areas and levels of development. The numbers were determined according to national population and income per capita; and then filtered by the scale, status and the accessibility, accuracy and standardization of the statistical data. There are eight cities from Northeastern US in the 500 cities.

One hundred and fifty cities were studied for detailed analysis representativeness: cities from 47 countries and regions in five continents were selected, with a focus on the key cities of North America, Europe, Asia and Oceania and some pivotal cities located in South America and Africa. The selection criteria were: global influence, the social and economic position in its area, the typicalness of its kind, special research value and accessibility of the data, as well as some consideration of previous research. There are eight cities from Northeastern US in the 150 cities.

Data Sources and Statistical Methods

Data for statistical index
The global urban competitiveness index system has 114 indexes, and the acquirement of the data is complicated. Every sample city has the original statistics related to the indexes, such as urban population and area, but the scopes of statistics are different nationally. The majority of the sample cities have related original statistics, and some are living indexes published by consultancy services. There is no related international or national statistical agency yet, or any subjective survey data, such as industrial index, city function index or enterprise quality.

Data collection channel
International organizations' publications and official statistical publications were studied and processed for consistency (mainly using statistics for 2005, with time series data only from 2001 to 2005). The Internet provided index-related statistics, quantified according to certain criteria (mainly using statistics for 2007, with time series data from 2004 to 2007).

Processing of collected index-related data

Data integration   In order to solve the difference between statistical scopes and criteria, a study was undertaken on the statistical items and criteria of international organizations, such as statistical distributions from the United Nations Statistics Division, World Development Indicators from the World Bank, the database of the Organisation for Economic Co-operation and Development and so on. Then data transformation relations were established among statistical items from different countries. Therefore, using this most reasonable, comparable and complete statistical standard set to process the collected data, we generated a unified database covering 500 cities around the globe.

Missing data   If a city had a deficiency in certain indexes, estimation was made according to the given national statistics, its domestic position and corresponding performance.

Solution for index-related data which cannot be collected

Grading method to replace index   In the light of a unified standard, such an index was replaced by another related index which was the most identical and typical, grading by indirect factors. For example, the distribution of a transnational financial company was used to indicate the urban financing development status.

Typical sample comparative method   According to the standard, typical samples were selected and compared within a sample city, to represent, indicate and standardize certain aspects of this city. For example, enterprises were represented by an example of a typical industry.

Grading method using related information   According to the aspect of the index, find the key point and class standard, then collect related data which can be used to indicate such index.

Method of Quantitative Analysis

Global urban competitiveness index (GUCI) of 500 cities in the world
A non-linear weighted integration method was chosen to deal with data, and a clustering analysis method for comparative research.

Global urban component competitiveness index (GUCCI) of 150 cities in the world
The explanatory component competitiveness sub-indices were divided into three levels, where the third level indices could be integrated into secondary level indices and the secondary level indices into primary level indices using equal weighting.

RESEARCH RESULT 1: OUTPUT OF URBAN COMPETITIVENESS

Global Urban Competitiveness: Cities in Northeastern US make up the Most Competitive City Group

This report measures the competitiveness of 500 cities in the world with nine indexes, namely GDP, GDP per capita, GDP per square kilometer, labor productivity, number of multinational corporation headquarters, number of international patent applications, price advantage, economic growth rate and employment rate.

The regions with the strongest urban competitiveness are North America, Europe and Asia. Table 9.1 shows the top ten competitive cities are New York, London, Tokyo, Paris, Washington, Los Angeles, Stockholm, Singapore, San Francisco and Chicago. The top ten cities are the strongest ones in terms of economy size, development level, technological innovation and economic control. Among the top ten cities, six are located in North America, two in Europe and two in Asia.

Compared to city groups in other sub-regions, cities in Northeastern US are the most competitive. Among the eight sample cities from this region, two are top ten cities, in which New York ranks No. 1 and Washington ranks No. 5; two more are included in the top 20 cities, with Boston ranking No. 13 and Philadelphia ranking No. 19; another three cities are among the top 100 and the lowest-ranking in this region is Pittsburgh, ranking No. 108. There is not another sub-region in the world which has so many cities with such high rankings in urban competitiveness. However, in this aspect, cities in Pennsylvania are comparatively less competitive.

GDP Size: Although Mostly Above Average, Northeastern US Cities Vary Substantially in Size

Market share is also an important index of competitiveness. For cities with both internal and external demands, GDP would be a good alternative to

Table 9.1   Top ten cities and Northeastern US cities among the 500 cities in terms of GUCI

City	Country or Region	Continent	Index	Rank
New York	**Northeastern US**	**North America**	**1**	**1**
London	UK	Western Europe	0.944185	2
Tokyo	Japan	East Asia	0.790169	3
Paris	France	Western Europe	0.759375	4
Washington	**Northeastern US**	**North America**	**0.696406**	**5**
Los Angeles	US	North America	0.668836	6
Stockholm	Sweden	Northern Europe	0.647921	7
Singapore	Singapore	Southeast Asia	0.645897	8
San Francisco	US	North America	0.642095	9
Chicago	US	North America	0.629848	10
Boston	**Northeastern US**	**North America**	**0.596854**	**13**
Philadelphia	**Northeastern US**	**North America**	**0.564911**	**19**
Baltimore	**Northeastern US**	**North America**	**0.482026**	**50**
Portland	**Northeastern US**	**North America**	**0.475558**	**52**
Wilmington	**Northeastern US**	**North America**	**0.427641**	**80**
Pittsburgh	**Northeastern US**	**North America**	**0.388232**	**108**

market share. Through the comparison of their GDPs, we could identify the market features of the competitiveness of individual cities.

The highest ranking ten cities are scattered in different regions, with East Asia's Tokyo, Hong Kong and Seoul ranking No. 1, No. 7 and No. 8, North America's New York and Los Angeles ranking No. 3 and No. 6, Western Europe's Paris and London ranking No. 2 and No. 4, Mexico City ranking No. 5, and Australia's Sydney and Melbourne ranking No. 9 and No. 10 respectively (Table 9.2).

In general, Northeastern US cities have comparatively larger GDP sizes, with most above average. However, they also differ greatly from each other, with New York ranking as high as No. 3 worldwide; Philadelphia No. 28; Washington, Boston and Baltimore ranking No. 74, No. 80 and No. 89 respectively; and Portland, Wilmington and Pittsburgh ranking comparatively lower at No. 130, No. 239 and No. 243.

Economic Growth Rate: Northeastern US Cities are all Below Average and Vary Substantially

Economic growth, particularly the long-term economic growth, is an important index of the sustainable competitiveness of a city. The GDP growth rate is an important indicator of the development growth rate.

Table 9.2   Top ten cities and Northeastern US cities among 500 cities in terms of GDP (unit: US$ billion)

City	Country or region	Continent	GDP	Rank
Tokyo	Japan	East Asia	584.95	1
Paris	France	Western Europe	525.05	2
New York	**Northeastern US**	**North America**	**502.51**	**3**
London	UK	Western Europe	446.20	4
Mexico City	Mexico	Latin America	220.08	5
Los Angeles	US	North America	180.08	6
Hong Kong	China	East Asia	179.78	7
Seoul	South Korea	East Asia	176.60	8
Sydney	Australia	Oceania	171.69	9
Melbourne	Australia	Oceania	134.76	10
Philadelphia	**Northeastern US**	**North America**	**69.48**	**28**
Washington	**Northeastern US**	**North America**	**34.08**	**74**
Boston	**Northeastern US**	**North America**	**31.89**	**80**
Baltimore	**Northeastern US**	**North America**	**29.9**	**89**
Portland	**Northeastern US**	**North America**	**22.63**	**130**
Wilmington	**Northeastern US**	**North America**	**11.12**	**239**
Pittsburgh	**Northeastern US**	**North America**	**10.82**	**243**

Worldwide, growth rates of cities vary substantially, and Chinese cities have shown the highest speed. Among the highest ranking ten cities in terms of economic growth rate, eight are Chinese cities (Table 9.3). West European and North American cities have maintained slow growth; some Asian cities are emerging as new growth centers; and some African cities continue to deteriorate. In developed countries, cities have maintained slow growth, while in emerging countries undergoing industrialization and transformation, fast economic growth has been achieved.

The economic growth rates for Northeastern US cities are all below average, and also vary substantially. The fastest growing Washington and Portland are only ranked No. 293 and No. 300; Philadelphia and New York are ranked No. 394 and No. 410 respectively; while Pittsburgh, Boston and Wilmington are among the lowest growing cities worldwide, ranking only No. 435, No. 443 and No. 453. Of course, the ranking in economic growth rate is closely related to the developing stages these cities are currently undergoing. The last 50 cities in the 500 sample cities are mostly located in regions suffering political upheavals.

Table 9.3   Top ten cities and Northeastern US cities in the 500 sample cities in terms of GDP growth rate (unit: percent)

City	Country or region	Continent	GDP growth rate	Rank
Baotou	China	East Asia	20.00	1
Huhehaote	China	East Asia	20.00	2
Yantai	China	East Asia	19.57	3
Dongguan	China	East Asia	19.25	4
Baku	Azerbaijan	West Asia	19.00	5
Zhongshan	China	East Asia	18.44	6
Huizhou	China	East Asia	18.11	7
Weifang	China	East Asia	17.98	8
Wuhu	China	East Asia	17.97	9
Manaus	Brazil	Latin America	17.96	10
Washington	**Northeastern US**	**North America**	**0.037**	**293**
Portland	**Northeastern US**	**North America**	**0.036**	**300**
Baltimore	**Northeastern US**	**North America**	**0.0211**	**386**
Philadelphia	**Northeastern US**	**North America**	**0.0203**	**394**
New York	**Northeastern US**	**North America**	**0.0168**	**410**
Pittsburgh	**Northeastern US**	**North America**	**0.0117**	**435**
Boston	**Northeastern US**	**North America**	**0.0104**	**443**
Wilmington	**Northeastern US**	**North America**	**0.006863**	**453**

Development Level: Like Central European cities, Northeastern US cities are at the Top Level Worldwide

Economic development level is the foundation for the competitiveness and development of a city. GDP per capita is an important index of the development level of a city or a region.

Worldwide, substantial gaps exist among regions. In spite of the substantial gaps, GDP per capita of cities shows a normal distribution. Geneva is the city with the highest income per capita, which is $62676.92 (2005), and Kinshasa has the lowest, which is $206.77. Twenty-two cities have reported GDP per capita higher than $50000; 162 higher than $30000; 235 higher than $10000; 299 higher than $5000; and 47 lower than $1000.

Northeastern US cities and European cities have the highest levels of development. There are smaller intra-regional gaps, with New York and Washington ranking No. 2 and No. 5, Philadelphia ranking No. 31, 18 positions lower than Boston, and Pittsburgh ranking the lowest at No. 130 (Table 9.4).

Table 9.4   *Top ten cities and Northeastern US cities among the 500 sample cities in terms of GDP per capita (unit: US$)*

City	Country or region	Continent	GDP per capita	Rank
Geneva	Switzerland	Central Europe	62 676.92	1
New York	**Northeastern US**	**North America**	**61 178.19**	**2**
Oakland (US)	United States	North America	60 638.41	3
Edinburgh	United Kingdom	Western Europe	59 540.23	4
Washington	**Northeastern US**	**North America**	**58 548.98**	**5**
London	UK	Western Europe	57 948.69	6
Oslo	Norway	Northern Europe	57 931.4	7
Belfast	UK	Western Europe	56 105.86	8
Basel	Switzerland	Central Europe	55 247.85	9
Zurich	Switzerland	Central Europe	54 056	10
Boston	**Northeastern US**	**North America**	**53 456.08**	**13**
Philadelphia	**Northeastern US**	**North America**	**47 707.4**	**31**
Baltimore	**Northeastern US**	**North America**	**46 985.03**	**34**
Portland	**Northeastern US**	**North America**	**42 427.78**	**71**
Wilmington	**Northeastern US**	**North America**	**35 272.11**	**125**
Pittsburgh	**Northeastern US**	**North America**	**34 194.6**	**130**

Note: the data for London covers the Greater London Region.

Economic Concentration: Northeastern US Cities have Generally Top Rankings, with New York as the World No. 1

Economic concentration enables economies to benefit from external economies and improve their efficiency. GDP per square kilometer is an important index of output concentration resulting from the concentration of production factors. Substantial spatial gaps exist, while both large and small cities have entries in the top ranking list. Continental highs are largely close, while substantial gaps exist between continental averages. North American and Oceanian cities have generally high rankings.

Northeastern US cities have generally top rankings, with New York as the world No. 1 and far ahead of others. Philadelphia ranks No. 28 and Pittsburgh ranks the lowest at No. 134. Comparatively speaking, cities in Pennsylvania are less competitive in this respect (Table 9.5).

Table 9.5   Top ten cities and Northeastern US cities in the 500 sample cities in terms of GDP per square kilometer (unit: $ thousand)

City	Country or region	Continent	GDP per square kilometer	Rank
New York	**Northeastern US**	**North America**	**643 498.2**	**1**
Geneva	Switzerland	Central Europe	633 715.1	2
Victoria (CA)	Canada	North America	565 083.3	3
Macao	China	East Asia	482 636.2	4
Lyon	France	Western Europe	337 620.8	5
San Francisco	US	North America	326 156.5	6
Manchester	UK	Western Europe	309 761.2	7
San Juan	Puerto Rico	Latin America	302 016.4	8
Nottingham	UK	Western Europe	300 355.8	9
Kawasaki	Japan	East Asia	296 998.8	10
Boston	**Northeastern US**	**North America**	**260 997.8**	**16**
Wilmington	**Northeastern US**	**North America**	**252 058.8**	**18**
Washington	**Northeastern US**	**North America**	**209 842.2**	**27**
Philadelphia	**Northeastern US**	**North America**	**197 270.5**	**28**
Baltimore	**Northeastern US**	**North America**	**143 750.9**	**56**
Portland	**Northeastern US**	**North America**	**76 724.82**	**130**
Pittsburgh	**Northeastern US**	**North America**	**75 740.33**	**134**

Employment: Northeastern US Cities are Mostly Below Average, with Wilmington being the Exception

The employment rate of urban residents is closely connected with the macro-economic situation of a nation. In general, countries undergoing transition and industrialization, for example, China, Russia and Mexico, have higher employment rates. Table 9.6 shows the employment rates of selected cities. Cities in countries under transformation and industrialization have the highest rankings, followed by those in developed countries, while cities in less developed regions have relatively low rankings.

Except for Wilmington ranking No. 144 worldwide, other Northeastern US cities have comparatively lower employment rates, with Philadelphia ranking the lowest at No. 411. This indicates the great pressure these cities are facing in their development. The last 50 cities in the 500 sample cities worldwide are mostly located in regions undergoing political upheavals.

Table 9.6   Top ten cities and Northeastern US cities in the 500 sample
cities in terms of employment rate (unit: percent)

City	Country or region	Continent	Employment rate	Rank
Moscow	Russia	East Europe	99.20	1
Tijuana	Mexico	Latin America	99.10	2
Baku	Azerbaijan	West Asia	99.02	3
Acapulco	Mexico	Latin America	99.00	4
Quanzhou	China	East Asia	98.83	5
Oakland (US)	United States	North America	98.67	6
Al Kuwayt	KUWAIT	West Asia	98.51	7
Minsk	Belarus	East Europe	98.50	8
Shenzhen	China	East Asia	98.40	9
Huizhou	China	East Asia	98.20	10
Wilmington	**Northeastern US**	**North America**	**95.2**	**144**
Washington	**Northeastern US**	**North America**	**92.8**	**269**
Portland	**Northeastern US**	**North America**	**92.1**	**300**
New York	**Northeastern US**	**North America**	**91.6**	**321**
Boston	**Northeastern US**	**North America**	**90.9**	**347**
Pittsburgh	**Northeastern US**	**North America**	**89.5**	**382**
Baltimore	**Northeastern US**	**North America**	**88.6**	**400**
Philadelphia	**Northeastern US**	**North America**	**87.6**	**411**

Productivity: Northeastern US Cities Maintain an Absolute Leadership

Worldwide, substantial productivity gaps exist between cities. At the
top of this list is London with $161 120.66, which is 317.6 times that of
Dushanbe's $507.26, the bottom city. North American, European and
East Asian cities have higher productivity levels than African and Latin
American cities. US cities maintain an absolute leadership. In the top
ten cities, four out of the eight Northeastern US cities are listed, and the
lowest-ranking Wilmington is at No. 157 (Table 9.7).

Technological Innovation: Northeastern US Cities Perform Best as a Whole

Technological innovation is the core part of a city's competitiveness. The
results of technical innovation are important reflections of the competitiveness. The number of patent applications is one of the key indexes of
urban competitiveness. The top ten cities in terms of patent application are
Tokyo, Osaka, Paris, London, New York, Seoul, Stuttgart, San Diego,
San Jose and Stockholm.

*Table 9.7   Top ten cities and Northeastern US cities in the 500 sample
cities in terms of productivity (unit: US$)*

City	Country or region	Continent	Productivity	Rank
London	United Kingdom	Western Europe	161 120.7	1
New York	**Northeastern US**	**North America**	**141 880.7**	**2**
Detroit	United States	North America	141 259.2	3
New Orleans	United States	North America	126 097.1	4
Philadelphia	**Northeastern US**	**North America**	**124 986.8**	**5**
Boston	**Northeastern US**	**North America**	**121 893.5**	**6**
Cleveland	United States	North America	119 658.1	7
Oslo	Norway	Northern Europe	118 069.9	8
San Jose	United States	North America	116 237.8	9
Baltimore	**Northeastern US**	**North America**	**113 666.5**	**10**
Washington	**Northeastern US**	**North America**	**101 474.5**	**29**
Portland	**Northeastern US**	**North America**	**85 941.87**	**64**
Pittsburgh	**Northeastern US**	**North America**	**82 313.91**	**76**
Wilmington	**Northeastern US**	**North America**	**59 783.24**	**157**

Note: the data for London covers the Greater London Region.

Most of the world's innovation centers are in global cities and central hi-tech cities. North American, European and East Asian cities dominate the list. US and Japanese cities have the strongest power of technological innovation, while many central cities in South Korea, China and India are catching up fast. Although New York is the only one included in the top ten, Northeastern US cities perform best as a whole and all the eight sample cities from this region are ranked within the top 100, with Wilmington, Washington and Boston ranking No. 11, No. 14 and No. 23, and Philadelphia ranking No. 39 worldwide (Table 9.8).

Economic Control Center: New York is Far Ahead of Others, and the Northeastern US Cities as a Whole Maintain a Comparatively High Level

Economic decision making power is the ability of a city to control the global economy resulting from global competition within the context of globalization. The ability is a reflection of the competitiveness of a city. One of the most important indexes of economic control is the distribution or the number of multinational companies.

A trend of reshuffling of the world economic centers is emerging. World economic centers have been located in Europe, the United States and Japan exclusively. Yet in addition to Tokyo, Beijing and Shanghai have

Table 9.8   *Top ten cities and Northeastern US cities in the 500 sample cities by number of international patent applications*

City	Country or region	Continent	Number of international patent applications	Rank
Tokyo	Japan	East Asia	89 445	1
Osaka	Japan	East Asia	39 718	2
Paris	France	Western Europe	20 364	3
London	United Kingdom	Western Europe	17 968	4
New York	**Northeastern US**	**North America**	**16 915**	**5**
Seoul	Korea	East Asia	16 651	6
Stuttgart	Germany	Central Europe	15 277	7
San Diego	United States	North America	14 338	8
San Jose	United States	North America	12 309	9
Stockholm	Norway	Northern Europe	11 785	10
Wilmington	**Northeastern US**	**North America**	**11 565**	**11**
Washington	**Northeastern US**	**North America**	**10 175**	**14**
Boston	**Northeastern US**	**North America**	**7 309**	**23**
Philadelphia	**Northeastern US**	**North America**	**3 913**	**39**
Portland	**Northeastern US**	**North America**	**2 833**	**60**
Pittsburgh	**Northeastern US**	**North America**	**2 508**	**69**
Baltimore	**Northeastern US**	**North America**	**2 404**	**71**

entered the top ten cities in terms of the presence of multinational companies. It indicates that many Asian cities outside Japan are rising in terms of economic control power and might become new world economic centers.

New York is still the global economic control center. Other Northeastern US cities just have comparatively high scores, with Philadelphia ranking No. 99 and Wilmington ranking No. 298 worldwide (Table 9.9).

Price Advantage: Cities in Developing Countries have Distinct Advantages

Price and cost are important aspects of a city's competitiveness and the ratio of nominal exchange rate to PPP exchange rate shows price and cost advantages. The ratio of nominal exchange rate to PPP exchange rate could reflect the actual price level of a country. If the ratio is smaller than 1, it indicates that the actual price level is higher than the nominal price level; if it is larger than 1, the actual price level is lower than the nominal price level. However, the ratio of nominal exchange rate to PPP exchange rate is not calculated on the basis of cities, but on the basis of countries.

Table 9.9   Top ten cities and Northeastern US cities in the 500 cities in terms of the presence of multinational companies (unit: score)

City	Country or Region	Continent	Numerical Value	Rank
New York	**Northeastern US**	**North America**	**522**	**1**
London	UK	Western Europe	501	2
Hong Kong	China	East Asia	378	3
Paris	France	Western Europe	342	4
Tokyo	Japan	East Asia	332	5
Singapore	Singapore	Southeast Asia	317	6
Beijing	China	East Asia	311	7
Shanghai	China	East Asia	295	8
Moscow	Russia	East Europe	289	9
Sydney	Australia	Oceania	289	9
Washington	**Northeastern US**	**North America**	**234**	**19**
Boston	**Northeastern US**	**North America**	**134**	**57**
Philadelphia	**Northeastern US**	**North America**	**82**	**99**
Portland	**Northeastern US**	**North America**	**71**	**119**
Pittsburgh	**Northeastern US**	**North America**	**59**	**143**
Baltimore	**Northeastern US**	**North America**	**53**	**163**
Wilmington	**Northeastern US**	**North America**	**24**	**298**

That is, in each country, there is only one ratio of nominal exchange rate to PPP exchange rate. With regard to the 500 sample cities, the ratios of Northern Europe, Central Europe, Western Europe, Japan, Kuwait and the United States are smaller than 1, indicating that actual price levels in these countries are higher than nominal price levels, which poses a disadvantage. Notably, Switzerland, Kuwait, Iceland, Norway and Sweden have the most disadvantages and Myanmar, Zimbabwe, Ethiopia, Cambodia and Zaire have the most advantages in actual price level. Among the four BRIC countries, China and India have more advantages than Russia and Brazil.

Northeastern US cities are ranked No. 356, near the bottom of the list, indicating that Northeastern US cities are at a disadvantage in their price levels (Table 9.10).

Table 9.10   Top ten cities and Northeastern US cities in the 500 cities in terms of ratio of nominal exchange rate to real exchange rate (unit: score)

City	Ratio of nominal exchange rate to real exchange rate	Rank
Yangon	11.111111	1
Harare	8.333333	2
Addis Ababa	6.25	3
Phnom Penh	5.555556	4
Pyongyang	5.263158	4
Accra	5.263158	4
Kinshasa	5.263158	4
Ho Chi Minh City	5	8
Hanoi	5	8
Kampala	5	8
New York	**0.943396**	**356**
Washington	**0.943396**	**356**
Boston	**0.943396**	**356**
Philadelphia	**0.943396**	**356**
Portland	**0.943396**	**356**
Pittsburgh	**0.943396**	**356**
Baltimore	**0.943396**	**356**
Wilmington	**0.943396**	**356**

RESEARCH RESULT 2: INPUT OF URBAN COMPETITIVENESS

Enterprise Quality Competitiveness in World's 150 Cities: Seattle Ranks No. 1, Washington Ranks No. 2

The wealth and value of any city are created by enterprises. How much wealth is created depends on the environment that the city provides, as well as the quality of the enterprises. The quality or competitiveness of enterprises can be seen from a number of aspects, namely the foundation, operation and management of businesses. It includes six sub-indices, including corporate culture, corporate system, corporate governance, business operation, branding and business performance. Table 9.11 shows the top ten cities worldwide in terms of enterprise quality. Most of the high-ranking cities are in developed countries in North America, Western Europe, Northern Europe and Australia. In addition, Japanese enterprises

Table 9.11   Enterprise quality: world's top ten cities and Northeastern US cities in 150 cities

City	Enterprise quality	Ranking
Seattle	1	1
Washington	**0.962**	**2**
Zurich	0.94	3
SanFrancisco	0.94	4
Berlin	0.939	5
Philadelphia	**0.929**	**6**
Dallas	0.927	7
TheHague	0.925	8
Boston	**0.923**	**9**
SanJose	0.923	9
NewYork	**0.877**	**27**
Baltimore	**0.844**	**37**
Pittsburgh	**0.797**	**50**
Portland	**0.764**	**65**
Wilmington	**0.631**	**99**

are highly competitive, too. In Eastern Europe, Asia (other than Japan) and Latin America, respectively, a few cities in China, India and Brazil have competitive enterprises, while most others have low ranks. In Africa, most cities have low ranks. Specifically, on the top ten list, Seattle, Washington and Zurich rank the top 3, followed by San Francisco, Berlin, Philadelphia, Dallas, The Hague, Boston and San Jose, which rank from No. 4 to No. 10.

In the 150 sample cities, Washington ranks No. 2, Philadelphia No. 6, Boston No. 9, New York No. 27 and the other four Northeastern US sample cities are also in the top 100. This indicates that Northeastern US cities are generally performing well in enterprise quality competitiveness.

Industrial Structure Competitiveness: Tokyo Ranks No. 1, New York Ranks No. 2

Industrial structure competitiveness is the overall development level of a city's industries and the standard and professional level of the development. A city's main industries are the manufacturing and service industries. Since the financial and high-tech industries are also very important in the development of the city, we separate them out from the two main industries and then form four second-class indices of manufacturing, services, finance and high-tech.

Table 9.12   Industrial structure: world's top ten cities and Northeastern US cities in 150 cities

City	Industry structure	Ranking
Tokyo	1	1
New York	**0.971**	**2**
London	0.958	3
Paris	0.809	4
Hong Kong	0.777	5
Chicago	0.736	6
Toronto	0.707	7
Taipei	0.703	8
Zurich	0.698	9
Singapore	0.694	10
Washington	**0.663**	**14**
Boston	**0.622**	**26**
Pittsburgh	**0.59**	**40**
Philadelphia	**0.529**	**63**
Portland	**0.505**	**78**
Baltimore	**0.494**	**86**
Wilmington	**0.48**	**94**

Substantial gaps exist among performance of Northeastern US cities. Although New York is ranked No. 2, other cities in the region fail to be listed in the top ten. Such is also suggested by the index, in which Philadelphia ranks No. 63 and Wilmington ranks only No. 94, with an index value of 0.48 lower than the average 0.5 (Table 9.12).

Human Resources Competitiveness: Paris Ranks No. 1, Washington Ranks No. 8

Human resources are a valuable resource hotly pursued in the time of the knowledge economy. In the Cobb–Douglas regional economic development model, human resources and physical capital are two major independent production factors. In this study, the human resources of a city include four aspects: the health condition of the citizens, education of the citizens, availability of the workforce and professionals in the city. Table 9.13 shows the top ten among 150 cities worldwide. In this aspect, high-ranking cities are seen both in developed regions, including North America, Europe and Australia and in developing regions, such as Mexico and Brazil in Latin America, China and India in Asia.

It is worth mentioning that the study mainly shows human resource

Table 9.13   Human resources: world's top ten cities and Northeastern US cities in 150 cities

City	Human resources	Ranking
Paris	1	1
Tokyo	0.954	2
Sao Paulo	0.885	3
Singapore	0.881	4
Prague	0.87	5
Bogota	0.856	6
Mexico City	0.855	7
Washington	**0.843**	**8**
Seoul	0.837	9
The Hague	0.835	10
Boston	**0.789**	**34**
Wilmington	**0.782**	**37**
New York	**0.775**	**44**
Philadelphia	**0.773**	**45**
Portland	**0.765**	**56**
Pittsburgh	**0.717**	**99**
Baltimore	**0.71**	**109**

competitiveness. Since large cities in developing countries are usually abundant with human resources, they tend to perform well in the study. Among Northeastern US cities, Washington ranks No. 8.

Hard Environment Competitiveness: Tokyo Ranks No. 1, New York Ranks No. 2

Hard environment competitiveness mainly means the cities' basic factors, financial markets, science and technology innovation facilities and achievements, as well as the support to the development of the city by market scale. Basic factors are essential for the existence and development of a city. A developed finance market can provide rich and steady financial support to the development of the city. Innovation is the spirit of a city and the city's competitiveness. Only innovation can bring the city high value and benefit. The utilization of the science and technology resources, science and technology facilities, science and technology servicing system, innovation environment, innovation promoting policies and the environmental quality comprise a city's innovation environment system. While providing businesses with a sound technical base, the hard environment of a city turns out to be a powerful magnetic field to external production factors and hi-tech enterprises.

Table 9.14   Hard environment: world's top ten cities and Northeastern US cities in 150 cities

City	Hard environment	Ranking
Tokyo	1	1
New York	**0.968**	**2**
Boston	**0.878**	**3**
San Francisco	0.873	4
London	0.862	5
Chicago	0.862	6
Washington	**0.834**	**7**
Philadelphia	**0.823**	**8**
San Jose	0.819	9
Seattle	0.814	10
Portland	**0.758**	**25**
Baltimore	**0.757**	**26**
Pittsburgh	**0.752**	**29**
Wilmington	**0.628**	**90**

Except for Wilmington, Northeastern US cities perform generally well in hard environment competitiveness, with four listed in world's top ten, namely New York, Boston, Washington and Philadelphia ranking No. 2, No. 3, No. 7 and No. 8 respectively. Meanwhile Portland, Baltimore and Pittsburgh ranks No. 25, No. 26 and No. 29 (Table 9.14).

Soft Environment Competitiveness: Singapore Ranks No. 1, Boston Ranks No. 4

The soft environment of cities refers to the urban environment for enterprise operation and industrial development. The soft environment competitiveness of a city is an integral part of urban environment competitiveness, and is generally measured in terms of market environment, social management environment and public policy environment. Table 9.15 shows the top ten cities in terms of soft environment competitiveness, among which Singapore ranks first, followed by Chicago and Hong Kong. So it is clear that these cities enjoy great advantages in terms of soft environment. This can be accredited to their free economy, strong protection of the intellectual property, a competitive and regulated market, and efficient social management.

Northeastern US cities perform less well in soft environment competitiveness, with only Boston listed in the top ten, ranking No. 4. New York is ranked No. 12, Philadelphia No. 25 and the lowest-ranking Portland is at No. 63.

Table 9.15   Soft environment: world's top ten cities and Northeastern US cities in 150 cities

City	Soft environment	Ranking
Singapore	1	1
Chicago	0.945	2
Hong Kong	0.943	3
Boston	**0.926**	**4**
San Francisco	0.924	5
Los Angeles	0.922	6
Wellington	0.912	7
Geneva	0.91	8
Seattle	0.909	9
Phoenix	0.908	10
New York	**0.906**	**12**
Philadelphia	**0.871**	**25**
Washington	**0.869**	**26**
Baltimore	**0.842**	**37**
Pittsburgh	**0.82**	**49**
Portland	**0.783**	**63**

Living Environment Competitiveness: Paris Ranks No. 1, Wilmington Ranks No. 14

The quality of the urban living environment contributes to a city's competitiveness by attracting and cultivating talented individuals. A high quality of living environment plays an important role in attracting and cultivating high-quality talent as well as the maximum application of their abilities. Living environment competitiveness is generally divided into natural environment, housing environment, shopping and dining environment, environment for leisure and entertainment, as well as security environment. From Table 9.16, we can see that, among the world's top ten, Paris ranks No. 1, followed by Sydney, Lisbon, Melbourne, Brisbane, Rome and Vienna. Most of the high-ranking cities are those with a proud cultural, historical or artistic traditions and such cities as Paris, Vienna, Rome, Athens and Budapest tend to focus on the improvement of the local living environment.

Northeastern US cities are performing poorly in this aspect, with the highest-ranking Wilmington only at No. 14. In the 150 sample cities, Philadelphia, Pittsburgh, New York and Boston are all out of the top 100, ranking only No. 109, No. 111, No. 121 and No. 122.

Table 9.16   *Living environment: world's top ten cities and Northeastern US cities in 150 cities*

City	Living environment	Ranking
Paris	1	1
Sydney	0.975	2
Lisbon	0.966	3
Melbourne	0.958	4
Brisbane	0.951	5
Rome	0.948	6
Vienna	0.941	7
Milan	0.931	8
Athens	0.929	9
Auckland	0.918	10
Wilmington	**0.892**	**14**
Washington	**0.864**	**24**
Portland	**0.817**	**79**
Baltimore	**0.804**	**93**
Philadelphia	**0.791**	**109**
Pittsburgh	**0.788**	**111**
New York	**0.774**	**121**
Boston	**0.773**	**122**

Competitiveness in Terms of Global Connectivity: New York Ranks No. 1, Boston Ranks No. 10

Against the background of globalization, cities have become the subjects in global competition and the urban network has gradually formed worldwide. A city's economic, social and cultural development is gradually linked to, and merged with, the international economic, social and cultural development, and has become a crucial part of the integrated international development system. On the other hand, cities in the global community contribute to the further development of economic globalization by the diffusion and spread effect of their economies. The global connectivity index is used to measure a city's participation in the global competition as well as its position among all cities worldwide, including location capacity, transportation connectivity, resident connectivity, information linkage and enterprise connectivity. Among the top ten cities, both New York and London are conveniently situated, enjoying a high level of diversity, with advanced information-based infrastructures. The headquarters of many renowned multinational companies are based in the two cities. They rank among the top in global connectivity. Los Angeles,

Table 9.17   Global connectivity: world's top ten cities and Northeastern US cities in 150 cities

City	Global connectivity	Ranking
New York	**1**	**1**
London	0.973	2
Los Angeles	0.838	3
Paris	0.804	4
Singapore	0.798	5
Amsterdam	0.771	6
Rotterdam	0.757	7
Tokyo	0.741	8
Chicago	0.723	9
Boston	**0.713**	**10**
Philadelphia	**0.684**	**16**
Baltimore	**0.655**	**21**
Washington	**0.63**	**26**
Wilmington	**0.55**	**40**
Portland	**0.539**	**48**
Pittsburgh	**0.45**	**90**

Paris, Singapore and Amsterdam follow down the line. Tokyo ranks the eighth next to Rotterdam ranking seventh. Most cities among the top ten are port cities. In addition, Northeastern US cities are performing the best in global connectivity, with New York ranked No. 1 and Pittsburgh the lowest at No. 90. Other sample cities in the region are performing well, among which Boston ranks No. 10 and Philadelphia No. 16. Baltimore, Washington, Wilmington and Portland are ranking No. 21, No. 26, No. 40 and No. 48 respectively (Table 9.17).

POLICY SUGGESTIONS FOR PROMOTING URBAN COMPETITIVENESS

Currently, technology, information and economic globalization are changing the concepts and decision-making processes of economic, technological and social activities worldwide. While enhancing the role of cities in global affairs, they have further intensified the competition among them. For every city including Northeastern US cities, anything is possible in the fierce global competition.

In order to maintain their central and leading positions, to avoid being marginalized or to decline, local governments in Northeastern US cities, as well as relevant government agencies worldwide, should properly handle the following general issues in addition to specific problems.

Central Governments vs. Local Governments: Decentralization

The division of public power, particularly the power of taxation between central and local governments has a significant impact on the development of countries and sub-regions. Therefore, city governments should assume more responsibilities and play more important roles. Central governments should grant more decision-making power to city governments to enable active and flexible handling of issues encountered in the competition and development of cities. In the meantime, governments should review their fiscal and taxation systems, and build sound systems allowing a proper division of power to enable city governments to better fulfill their duties and support the development of local enterprises and the improvement of public welfare.

Government vs. Market: Mutual Infiltration

City governments should take an active part in market competition, create a sound business environment, build a strong brand and increase their appeal to more valuable enterprises. On the other hand, with innovative systems and extensive applicable technologies, enterprises and non-government organizations are now able to provide more public services and quasi-public services and to improve the efficiency and quality of their service. It is necessary to encourage more enterprises, non-government organizations and private businesses to participate in city management and to build an extensive city governance mechanism.

Industrial Upgrading and Employment: National Lifelong Education

Industrial upgrading is a permanent theme of development, as well as the momentum of sustainable development for a city. However, industrial upgrading, or the development of high-end industries, would result in a higher demand for talent, and the conflict of the human resource supply–demand structures. In other words, while a large number of high-end professionals are needed, many low-end workers would lose their jobs. This has been a challenge for many international cities. The key to solving this challenge is to promote lifelong education for every citizen. By building and improving a sound education system, cities would be able to improve the quality and skill structure of their populations, and eventually solve the conflict between employment and industrial upgrading.

Economic Development vs. Social Security: a Proper Balance Needed

It is necessary to ensure the complementation and mutual support of social security and economic development. In view of the fierce competition in the global market, city governments need to provide their citizens with good education, job opportunities and housing, as well as necessary life facilities and public services. In the meantime, they should also try to create a sound business environment, support competitive industries and assume responsibilities for economic development.

Specialization vs. Diversification: Refocusing Strategy

To leverage the advantages and avoid the disadvantages, it is necessary for cities to adopt the strategy of refocusing for functional positioning and industrial structure development. That means that they should select neither just one industry, nor numerous industries. Instead, they should select a number of interrelated industries as their pillar industries. This approach could ensure the economic benefits of the specialization model and the stability of the diversification model, and avoid the disadvantages of both.

Business Environment vs. Living Environment: Both are Important

Ensuring a good living environment should be regarded as the ultimate objective of industrial development. In the meantime, maximum efforts should be made in industrial development to ensure the protection of the living environment. The principle of mutual support between the living environment and the business environment should be adopted to build a new mechanism for the sustainable and harmonious development of ecological, cultural and social elements in both the living environment and the business environment.

Competition vs. Cooperation: Both are Essential for Development

Competition and cooperation between cities are natural phenomena. A wise city government should employ both competition and cooperation strategies. It should not sacrifice competition for cooperation, or vice versa. Appropriate competition and cooperation strategies would enable the sharing of the benefits and the taking of opportunities to avoid zero sum or negative sum games and to achieve win–win or success for both.

10. Industrial tourism: opportunities for city and enterprise

Leo van den Berg, Alexander Otgaar, Christian Berger and Rachel Xiang Feng

10.1 INTRODUCTION

This chapter summarizes the findings of a large international compara-tive study carried out by the European Institute for Comparative Urban Research (Euricur) into the development of industrial tourism in cities. Industrial tourism is a type of tourism which involves visits to operational or non-operational firms with a core business that is non-tourism related; industrial tourism offers visitors an experience with regard to the product, the production process, the applications and historical backgrounds. The aim of this research has been to promote knowledge development in the field of industrial tourism, resulting in concrete recommendations for municipalities, firms and other stakeholders.

The international research is based on the assumption that industrial tourism offers opportunities for both city and enterprise. Particularly for cities with a considerable industrial base, industrial tourism comprises interesting possibilities to strengthen the economic structure (direct and indirect employment) and to increase the supply of tourist products. For such cities, industrial tourism is a potential growth sector that matches with their identity: the sector offers opportunities to strengthen their dis-tinctiveness and image, notably by building on their existing assets.

Many cities have the assets to develop industrial tourism, but fail to capitalise on them. In most cases industrial tourism is only restricted to low-profile company visits, without any clear vision of the municipality or firm on the strategic value of it, not to mention coordinated product development. For that reason, our study targets cities and firms that have given or intend to give industrial tourism a prominent place in their vision and strategy.

The development of industrial tourism largely depends on the ability of firms to cooperate. On the one hand, we observe that many firms consider company tours an obligation with more costs than revenues. Many companies are afraid of leaking confidential business information, and also security often constitutes a problem. On the other hand, more and more companies also recognise the opportunities of industrial tourism: industrial tourism can help to market their product, to secure their license to operate (reputation), and to remain attractive as employer.

From the observation that industrial tourism offers opportunities for city and enterprise, and the fact that in many cities these potentials are not utilised to the full, we come to the following central question:

Under what circumstances can industrial tourism make a strategic contribution to the competitiveness of city and enterprise?

To answer the research question formulated above, Euricur has carried out an international comparative study. In this study six case studies have been carried out. For the case studies, information has been collected by means of desk research and interviews with representatives of (potential) stakeholders in industrial tourism.

Case Studies

Wolfsburg – Germany

In this case study we provide a description and analysis of industrial tourism in the German city of Wolfsburg, with a particular focus on the most dominant local actor in the realm, the Volkswagen Group, which has its global headquarters in Wolfsburg. Volkswagen's industrial tourism activities are commonly seen as best practices, and various authors – among them Mader (2003) – acknowledge them as such. The Wolfsburg case is particularly interesting because it is already in a very mature stage of development. Moreover, cars are an extremely attractive consumer product, which is why the interest in car manufacturers has been high since the early days. Car manufacturers were 'naturally driven' to develop company tours and this is probably also the reason why the car industry today is a forerunner when it comes to the quality of company visits. The industry has a long history and ample experience with it. In Wolfsburg, traditional company visits have been complemented by the theme park-like *Autostadt* ('car-city') in 2000, which is a subsidiary of the Volkswagen Group.

Cologne – Germany

In this case study we provide a description and analysis of industrial tourism in the German city of Cologne – or Köln, as the city is called in German. We selected the case of Cologne, because of the wide offer of industry tours in different sectors. Moreover the wider Cologne region still possesses a substantial base of manufacturing companies. Many of these companies do not manufacture consumer products – with a natural appeal to visitors – but semi-final products for other firms in the industrial value chain. Other reasons to include Cologne are the city's approach to include surrounding municipalities (most notably the cities of Leverkusen and Hürth) in its efforts to promote industrial tourism, and the fact that the city has made efforts to open up public companies and organisations. Interesting examples are a.o. Bayer and a chemical business park.

Pays de la Loire region – France
In this case study we discuss the development of industrial tourism in the French Pays de la Loire region, one of the most active European regions in the field of 'economic discoveries' as the French prefer to call it. In contrast with other chapters we focus on the region rather than on one city. The reason is because one of the most interesting initiatives is taken on a regional level: the association 'Visit Our Companies in the Pays de la Loire Region' (Visitez nos entreprises en la Pays de la Loire), hereafter abbreviated as Visit Our Companies. This association is playing a key role in assisting companies with opening their doors, taking away barriers, improving quality and promoting industrial tourism in general. Interestingly, the companies that open their doors are active in different sectors, including sectors that are not consumer-oriented (business-to-business). Nantes is the largest city in this region, but our analysis mainly focuses on companies in two neighbouring towns: the city of Angers (which hosted the first European conference on company visits in 2006, and invented the Made in Angers event in 2000) and St Nazaire (a port city with two major companies that opened their doors: Airbus and Aker Yards).

Turin – Italy
In this case study we analyse the development of industrial tourism in Turin and the Piedmont region. The case of Turin was selected because the tourism organisation – Turismo Torino e Provincia – and the Chamber of Commerce have jointly developed a special industrial tourism programme (Made in Torino; Tour the Excellent) which targets visitors and residents. Moreover, Turin is a typical industrial city that is trying to convert itself into a modern European city with a more diversified economic structure. It is interesting to see how Turin is coping with the challenge of improving its image without neglecting its industrial base. Not surprisingly, the Winter Olympic Games in 2006 have played a key role in the development of tourism in general, and industrial tourism in particular. Industrial tourism in Turin includes several segments such as cars, design and personal aerospace. For car designers such as Pininfarina only display sites can be visited.

Shanghai – China

This case study comprises a description and analysis of industrial tourism in the Chinese metropolis of Shanghai. There are several reasons why we selected Shanghai for this comparative research. Firstly, Shanghai is the largest economic, financial, trade and logistic centre of China and is also commonly known as the 'factory of the world': the city possesses substantial amounts of industries in many different sectors. Secondly, the public influence is a lot stronger in China, when compared to European countries, and thus we can expect that the public programmes for support are also rather mature in Shanghai. And indeed, public initiatives to promote industrial tourism in Shanghai had already started in 1997: The Industrial Tourism Promotion Center delivers comprehensive programmes with visits to factories (for example Baosteel and Yakult), creative business parks, museums and industrial landmarks.

Rotterdam – the Netherlands

Rotterdam was one of the first cities on the European continent that discovered industrial tourism as a niche market in urban tourism: already in 1997 the local tourism organisation had started to offer visits to operational firms. In 2003, however, political and financial support for the development of industrial tourism declined, and subsidies to industrial tourism development were cancelled. Today several organisations are somehow involved in supplying company visits, but the general impression is that Rotterdam is not fully utilising its potential, with one of the largest ports of the world as a unique asset.

The six cases have been analysed according to four categories of conditions that, according to previous research (for example Mader, 2003, and Van den Berg et al., 2003) are relevant in the development of industrial tourism: adequate target group selection (Section 10.4), an attractive product (Section 10.5), benefits in terms of image and identity for city and enterprises (Section 10.6) and the organisational set-up (Section 10.7). First, however, we address two fundamental questions; what is industrial tourism (Section 10.2) and is there a demand for industrial tourism (Section 10.3).

10.2   WHAT IS INDUSTRIAL TOURISM?

Our research concentrates on visits to operational firms, regardless of the visitor's motive, the sector in which a company is active, and a company's ownership structure. The term industrial tourism is a bit misleading as it is often associated with industry (as in manufacturing industry) and tourism (as in leisure tourism).

The confusion of tongues concerning industrial tourism also manifests itself in the six foreign case studies.

Wolfsburg

In the case of Wolfsburg we must conclude that Autostadt is actually an industrial theme park, or brands park (for all brands of the Volkswagen Audi Group), often seen as a good example of industrial tourism, but not exactly an example of a visit to an operational firm. The visit to the operational Volkswagen factory is officially not an integrated part of Autostadt although many people visit both. The theme park and the factory meet each other in the power plant which is partly operational (for the factory) and partly used by Autostadt for events (as industrial heritage).

Cologne

In Cologne both the tourist board and the chamber of commerce prefer to use the more general term 'company visits' (Firmenbesichtigungen) or the more specific term 'technical visits', but not 'industrial tourism' which is most associated with industrial heritage tourism; company visits have also been integrated in the event 'Expedition Colonia' which provides opportunities to discover the city. Apart from several company visits (to UPS, Rheinenergie, Magic Media Company, and so on) we also found an example of a brand park: BayKomm, the communication centre of Bayer. Interestingly, a visit to a waterfront redevelopment project (Rheinauhafen) is also in the list of technical visits.

Pays de la Loire

In Pays de la Loire regional tourism policy makers talk about 'economic discoveries' (découvertes économiques) as a group name for visits to (1) companies; (2) industrial heritage; and (3) science museums. The regional association Visit Our Companies (Visitez nos entreprises en Pays de la Loire) wants to contribute to the regional policy to develop this sector, mainly by promoting the development of the first sub-group, also referred to as 'industrial tourism' (tourisme industriel) and 'company visits' (visites d'entreprises). The association can only be joined by active companies; but it does not matter in what sector they are active (manufacturing, agricultural, services, and so on). Interestingly, visits to so-called display sites (sites vitrines) are also seen as company visits, suggesting that corporate communication centres, company museums, factory outlets and company theme parks could also be promoted by Visit Our Companies. Our sample of examples in this region not only includes visits to factories (Airbus, Aker Yards, Cointreau) but also to the Port of St Nazaire, the salt marshes of Guérande and several research centres in the field of horticulture.

Turin

In Turin they developed a programme called 'Made in Torino; Tour the Excellent' which comprehends visits to active companies only, although not necessarily to their production sites. Near their production sites which cannot be visited, car design companies such as Pininfarina and Giugiaro have set up display sites and museums which can be visited. Among the production sites that can be visited are the factories of Fiat, Aurora (pens) and Gufram (design objects and furniture). On a regional level, industrial tourism is mostly associated with industrial heritage (such as Lingotto, the old Fiat site in Turin) and agricultural tourism (for example visits to vineyards).

Shanghai

Shanghai's Industrial Tourism Promotion Center promotes the development of six categories of industrial tourism – they use this term in English – including individual factories, business parks, museums and exhibition centres, and even industrial landmarks such as the Maglev high-speed train line. The Center clearly uses a rather broad definition of industrial tourism, not only approaching manufacturing firms, but also service companies: participation of service companies is considered to be crucial, as Shanghai wants to be perceived not only as a place where manufacturing takes place, but also as a creative place. In this case study we analysed visits to individual factories of companies such as Baosteel, Shanghai Volkswagen and Yakult, but also visits to one creative business park (M50).

Rotterdam

Many scholars and policy makers refer to Rotterdam as one of the places where industrial tourism was first developed and promoted. From the very beginning, however, industrial tourism has been mainly restricted to visiting the port and its related industry, taking the activities of the foundation Industrial Tourism, the Educational Information Centre and the World Port Days into consideration. Also the companies in our sample – Broekman, Happy Shrimp Farm, Schmidt Zeevis, Verstegen – belong to the port and industrial complex. Only very recently has the Chamber of Commerce put 'technical visits' on the agenda, suggesting that also companies from other strong sectors in Rotterdam (creative industries, medical industry, services, and so on) could open their doors for visitors, though with a clear emphasis on visitors with an educational and business motive.

We conclude that the six cities/regions that we investigated use different definitions of industrial tourism and different names for industrial tourism. Definitions of industrial tourism range from very narrow (Rotterdam) to very broad (Shanghai), which makes it difficult to compare activities and their results, for instance in terms of visitor numbers. No matter what definition is used, it is important to understand the position of company visits in relation to other types of 'economic discoveries' and other tourist attractions. For policy makers, it seems wise to take a somewhat broader view, approaching company visits as a sub-group of economic discoveries or industrial tourism in the broadest sense of the word, paying attention to potential synergies with other sub-groups such as industrial heritage, science museums and company theme parks.

10.3   IS THERE A DEMAND FOR INDUSTRIAL TOURISM?

Several studies indicate that there is a growing demand for industrial tourism. When we started our research we expected the demand for industrial tourism to grow, notably in view of the increasing demand for 'purposeful visits', combining pleasure with education. But what can we learn from the case studies?

Wolfsburg

In the exceptional case of company town Wolfsburg, visits to Volkswagen generate the majority of the overnight stays, while 90 per cent of the package trips to the city include a visit to Autostadt. The park attracts 2 million visitors a year, while the factory of Volkswagen receives almost 200 000 people a year and even more requests (the capacity is limited).

Cologne

In Cologne the Tourist Board considers industrial tourism a 'niche segment' of the tourism industry. Nevertheless, the companies we analysed report substantial visitor numbers: 6200 for Rheinenergie, 10 000 for the

Magic Media Company and almost 120 000 for Bayer's communication centre (average per year).

Pays de la Loire

In Pays de la Loire the growing demand for economic discoveries was one of the occasions for the region of Pays de la Loire to set up the association Visit Our Companies: the initiators expected that people are increasingly interested in their roots, in the working life of their fathers and forefathers, and in the economic identity of the region they live in or visit. In 2004, company visits took a share of 11 per cent in the total number of visits to regional tourism attractions, corresponding with 1 million visitors a year. The Port of St Nazaire and Terre de Sel both report increasing visitor numbers (attracting 10 000 and 55 000 visitors respectively), while Cointreau and Aker Yards experienced a decline recently (to 30 000 and 22 000 respectively), but this has to do with very specific reasons (an increase in the entrance fee at Cointreau and the fact that the number of visits to Aker Yards very much depends on the cruise ships under construction).

Turin

For Turin and the Piedmont region industrial tourism is a small segment of the tourism industry, at least according to the policy makers. There is, however, considerable demand for company visits. Fiat receives on average 23 000 visitors, while Aurora registers more than 2000 visitors a year. Moreover, we observed that the supply generated by the Made in Torino Tour is insufficient to meet the demand not only from inhabitants but tourists as well.

Shanghai

In Shanghai industrial tourism has been recognised as one of the ten key segments of the tourism industry, with 6 million visitors in 2006 (a share of 6.4 per cent of all visits to attractions), compared to an estimated 2 million in 2004. It has to be said, however, that the usefulness of these data is questionable, also in view of the broad interpretation of industrial tourism. Nevertheless, it can be said that the demand for industrial tourism has increased for sure, notably because domestic tourism in China experienced an impressive increase of more than 100 per cent in the last four years. Individual companies are successful in attracting large numbers of visitors, with 80 000 visits to Baosteel, 100 000 to Shanghai Volkswagen, about 12 000 to M50 and almost 70 000 to Yakult.

Rotterdam

In Rotterdam the foundation Industrial Tourism and the Educational Information Centre together arrange tours for about 35 000 customers a year. The company tours during the World Port Days generate another 25 000 company visits, and expectations are that the Rotterdam Port Experience, not exactly a company visit but rather a brand park for the port, will attract up to 300 000 visitors a year. In addition, individual companies also attract substantial numbers of technical visitors, ranging from about 1000 for the Happy Shrimp Farm and Verstegen to 20 000 for the Port Authority (annually). During the year the demand for company tours from individual visitors (citizens and tourists) seems considerably lower and less stable, at least if we take into consideration that the foundation Industrial Tourism decided to focus on business visitors when it became independent from the municipality in 2003.

The general conclusion is that there is a substantial demand for industrial tourism. There are many indications that the demand for industrial tourism is growing, supported by the fact that several actors invest in industrial tourism because they expect the market to grow. Obviously, for cities the demand for 'economic discoveries' very much depends on the kind of attractions within their borders. Big companies with well-known names such as Volkswagen, Airbus, Baosteel and Fiat are able to attract more visitors than the smaller firms. Furthermore we emphasise that the size of the industrial tourism market very much depends on the definition of industrial tourism, since industrial museums and industrial theme parks can attract many more visitors than factories can. Another factor of importance is the size of the local market, partly explaining the impressive visitor numbers in Shanghai.

Visitor numbers give some idea about the demand for industrial tourism, but more information is needed to get the full picture. Aggregated data on industrial tourism is not available in all cities/regions, making it hard to draw any conclusions and to make comparisons between the case studies. Therefore, it has not been the aim of our study to actually prove that the demand for industrial tourism is growing, because to answer such a question, a more in-depth quantitative analysis would have been needed. Moreover, we emphasise that visitor numbers are restricted by the capacity of companies to receive visitors: in our view the actual demand for company tours can only be measured by means of market research. And finally, not only quantitative but also qualitative information concerning the demand is needed: what groups in society are actually interested in visiting firms? As we will see in the next sections, the quality of the demand is often more important than the quantity.

10.4   WHAT GROUPS SHOULD BE TARGETED? AND WHAT GROUPS ARE REACHED?

Industrial tourism may target several groups, ranging from leisure tourists to students, professionals, journalists and researchers. The case studies provide us with insights on what groups are targeted by the actors involved, but also on what groups are actually reached. What are the main observations and conclusions?

Wolfsburg

The experiences of Volkswagen (Wolfsburg) make it clear that for companies it makes sense to target specific groups, without excluding groups. Because the factory tour is offered to people who pick up their car, they automatically reach one of the most important target groups: customers. Another effective strategy to reach particular target groups is to offer special (VIP) tours for them. However, as a consumer-oriented company Volkswagen is happy with any visitor, for the simple reason that every visitor is a potential car buyer or at least involved in the decision of a car buyer (for example children). The share of international visitors to Autostadt is 9 per cent, and an additional 51 per cent travel more than 100 km, illustrating the large catchment area of an industrial theme park.

Cologne

In the Cologne region, Bayer (Leverkusen) targets specific groups of visitors, trying to reach opinion makers with considerable influence on other actors. Other companies focus on one specific stakeholder group, such as customers (Rheinenergie) or universities and schools (Knapsack). The Chamber of Commerce and Industry has identified foreign investors and business visitors (participants of conferences and trade fairs) as potential target groups of company visits. Leisure tourists appear to be less interesting as a target group: many tourists (not only from Germany but also Austria, where German TV shows are broadcasted) are interested in the media sector, but media companies such as Magic Media seem to adopt a defensive approach (visitors will come anyway, there is no need for active promotion). Energy company Rheinenergie found a very simple solution for allowing individuals to participate in tours: they can join groups (which is possible because they all participate for free).

Pays de la Loire

The Pays de la Loire case shows that companies, in general, are more interested in attracting primary stakeholders (customers, suppliers, shareholders, employees) than the general public (secondary stakeholders, including citizens and tourists). Particularly young people are targeted, in some cases because they are potential employees (for example Terre de Sciences), in other cases because young people are desired as consumers (Cointreau). Visit Our Companies has decided not to define target groups on a regional level, leaving this task to companies and travel agencies. The association does assist, however, by providing visitor statistics and promoting the product nationally and internationally, in cooperation with the regional tourism bureau. The average share of international visitors is high, with 25 per cent. Particularly British tourists appear to visit industrial sites relatively often, probably because they are used to this kind of tourism. Visitor statistics of the event 'Made in Angers' demonstrate that older people (50+) are overrepresented in visitor figures, which is a general conclusion we also found in the other cities.

Turin

In Turin also we found that company visits under the umbrella of Made in Torino are particularly popular among senior citizens and visitors. Remarkably, young people with an age up to 16 cannot participate because of safety restrictions, although companies are generally very much interested in reaching this target group. More in general we conclude that Made in Torino attracts many visitors that are not targeted by the companies. With the programme, the tourism organisation Turismo Torino deliberately also targets tourists (people who stay in the city for a long weekend), but because the capacity is limited many tourists cannot participate. The companies we analysed are generally more selective in the acquisition of visitors than the tourism office, although pen producer Aurora is clearly an example of a firm that has adopted the philosophy that any contact with the outside world can be valuable.

Shanghai

In Shanghai we observed that the Shanghai Industrial Tourism Promotion Center targets a very broad audience, but with a specific focus on business groups (excursions, business trips) and the Japanese market (apart from the Chinese market of course). Also groups of leisure tourists (of all ages) are targeted; individual tourists are less relevant because most Chinese tend to travel in groups. Travel agencies take care of organising visits to the firms, and the impression is that they are not very selective. What we *have* seen, however, is that a firm like Shanghai Volkswagen takes care of organising visits for groups that are more important for the firm's business, just like the big companies in St Nazaire (Pays de la Loire) do.

Rotterdam

In Rotterdam industrial tourism mainly targets business visitors and educational visitors; only during the World Port Days can individual citizens and tourists also visit the firms. We found, however, that notably companies in the port and industrial complex are increasingly concerned about shortages on the labour market, implying that students, but also families with children (all potential future employees) gain importance as target groups. While some companies open their doors to primary stakeholders only (for example Verstegen and Smit Internationale), other firms such as the Happy Shrimp Farm and Schmidt Zeevis seem to have adopted a more proactive approach, arguing that secondary stakeholders (the general public, citizens, the media, politicians, and so on) are important as well for the long-term continuity (also in view of corporate citizenship).

Overall, we conclude that many groups *can* be targeted and reached with industrial tourism. In general, public bodies define target groups broader than companies do. For instance, tourism organisations that aim to increase the number of bed nights are more interested in visitor numbers and maybe not that much in what kind of visitors arrive. Firms tend to focus on primary stakeholders (customers, suppliers, students, and so on) and in many cases exclude secondary stakeholders (citizens, tourists, and so on) from visiting their site. In other cases, they do receive secondary stakeholders, but emphasise that they are not their target group. Many companies that open their doors to visitors without a business or educational motive report high shares of seniors (50+), in most cases not exactly the most relevant group, particularly not in view of attracting future employees.

Companies that are willing to receive citizens and tourists are mostly consumer-oriented firms, but in that case these groups can be considered (potential) primary stakeholders (buyers of their product). Also firms that are (partly) owned by the government – such as port and transport authorities in Rotterdam, Cologne and St Nazaire, and several companies in Shanghai – open their doors to the general public which is not only the result of an economic weigh-off but presumably also the result of giving account to the taxpayers who are indirectly shareholders of these firms.

More and more companies without government involvement, however, also realise that it is in their interest to build sustainable relations with all actors that give them a license to operate. In this 'open door' policy these firms still target specific groups, but without closing the door for any group.

Looking at the geographic reach of industrial tourism (scale), we conclude that regional target groups are most relevant, particularly if the ambition is to change the image of the (manufacturing) industry as employer and responsible citizen. Particularly open door events such as the World Port Days, Made in Angers and Expedition Colonia seem to target a regional or national audience. Made in Torino, which is in fact also an event, is an interesting exception because the initiators want to use company visits as a tool to enrich Turin's image abroad, demonstrating that the city is more than Fiat. If the ambition is to attract many foreign tourists we would recommend focusing on specific countries where people are used to visiting companies: Great Britain, the US, China and Japan would probably meet that condition.

10.5   HOW CAN INDUSTRIAL TOURISM BE MADE ATTRACTIVE AND ACCESSIBLE?

The attractiveness of an industrial tourism product depends on the company and its products: firms that produce goods with a symbolic character for the region, branded goods, consumer goods, goods of everyday life, luxurious goods, technologically demanding goods, special interest goods and/or handicraft goods are probably in a better starting position than companies that produce other kinds of goods. Taking this into account, however, company visits can be made more attractive by improving the quality of visitor services (for example through investments in facilities and professional guides) and making them more accessible. The case studies give several suggestions on how to do this.

Wolfsburg

The most important conclusion in Wolfsburg is that the combination of a theme park and a factory visit make industrial tourism very attractive, as it combines leisure and learning (with a museum, interactive games and exhibitions) with 'the real thing'. For the factory visits, Volkswagen only uses professionally trained guides with workfloor experience, and only allows visitors to visit their sites if machines are running, for the sake of authenticity. The five-star Ritz Carlton hotel, with an outdoor swimming pool in front of the factory and the power plant, is a spectacular element of Autostadt. Another strong feature is the landscape which demonstrates that an industrial site can be made very appealing. The accessibility of the theme park and the factory has been secured through the construction of a bridge that connects the site with the high-speed train station.

Cologne

In Cologne we learned that Bayer's communication centre benefits from its location: an attractive park landscape with a beautiful Japanese garden, easily accessible by public transport. The Rheinauhafen, currently redeveloped by the port and transport authority, partly owes its popularity as a destination to its favourable location near the city centre. In general, we conclude that companies with a less favourable location (outside the city centre, difficult to access by public transport) find it difficult to attract visitors. Furthermore we observed that companies aim to secure the quality of tours by handling a maximum group size in order to enable sufficient interaction between the guide and the participants. The Cologne case study also shows that company tours can be made attractive by arranging tours with prominent guides (Expedition Colonia) or organising tours at night (UPS). Another method is to invite students to come up with innovative ideas to improve the accessibility and attractiveness of the industrial tourism product, as in the case of industrial park Knapsack.

Pays de la Loire

The association Visit Our Companies (Pays de la Loire) plays a key role in making sure that company visits meet certain quality standards, concerning the availability of visitor facilities, the provision of information on the website and the skills of guides. Several obligations apply to members, acting as an incentive for other companies to meet the conditions too. In addition, members can attend workshops and courses on how to make their product more attractive. In St Nazaire the tourism office of Escal'Atlantique has invested in visitor facilities such as an elevated walkway, information displays and signing to make tours more attractive and accessible. Cointreau (Angers) is a good example of a company that succeeded in turning a company visit into an experience by building a museum and a trendy bar right next to the distillery.

Turin

The case of Turin shows how companies make a tour attractive by small changes in their production schedule to show the audience some action, as design company Gufram reported (although admittedly, these tours only take place two or three times a year). Pen producer Aurora made its product more appealing by placing art objects and information displays in the workshops, and turning one room into a photo gallery with famous people who visited the site too. For the Made in Torino tour several quality standards apply: a maximum group size, professional guides and a maximum distance between the city centre (where tourists are picked up by bus) and the site to be visited.

Shanghai

The Shanghai Industrial Tourism Promotion Center has developed quality standards that participating companies have to meet, and provides firms with advice on how they can meet them. The Annual Ticket Book, a voucher book developed by the Center, makes company tours more accessible. Yakult, a Japanese company, has made its tours attractive and accessible for local citizens by investing in a closed glass walkway through the factory (a company policy for all new factories!), arranging shuttle buses to the company and developing special educational programmes for children and older people. Furthermore we found that travel agencies combine factory tours with visits to other, more traditional, tourist attractions nearby.

Rotterdam

Rotterdam will certainly benefit from the opening of the Rotterdam Port Experience: a theme park for the port and industrial complex, and a joint portal for actual visits to the port (by boat, bus or bike) and the port-related companies. Fast connections between the port and the city – notably by boat – are expected to further enhance the accessibility of the industrial tourism product. The experiences of three companies in the food sector demonstrate that so-called 'barriers' for industrial tourism (hygiene, security, and so on) can be turned into attractive and exciting features of the product. We also conclude that particularly non-consumer-oriented firms are able to attract visitors because of innovative production and management methods, with the Happy Shrimp Farm as one of the perfect examples.

Most suggestions mentioned above can easily be applied to any company, although some ideas clearly require more investments than other ones: elevated walkways, bridges and museums are relatively expensive. Quality standards can be very effective, notably if supported by regional and national governments as in the case of Pays de la Loire and Shanghai. National or regional 'models of excellence' can stimulate other companies to improve their offer. It makes sense to make a distinction between 'basic conditions' such as parking facilities, safety procedures, a maximum group size and visitor toilets (that every company should meet) and conditions that should preferably be met to bring products onto a higher quality level, such as multilingual guides and a room for video presentations. Elevated walkways and closed glass walkways can be particularly helpful to reduce conflicts between industrial tourism and the day-to-day production, also in view of hygiene and safety standards. It is cheaper to include these facilities in an original construction than to modify a building afterwards.

One of the most interesting conclusions is that combinations can make industrial tourism more attractive. Packages may include visits to several companies as in the case of St Nazaire (Aker Yards and Airbus). In practice, however, it seems that visitors are more interested in combinations between industrial tourism and other, more traditional, tourism attractions. Also in Rotterdam, the foundation Industrial Tourism gets many requests to develop complete packages in which company visits are just one element. This implies that in terms of promotion, it is advisable to promote company visits not only as an integrated part of 'economic discoveries' (with industrial heritage, industrial museums, and so on) but also as one of the ingredients of the total tourism supply.

10.6   BENEFITS IN TERMS OF INCOME AND IMAGE FOR CITY AND ENTERPRISE

Company visits generate numerous benefits for firms as well as for the cities in which they are located. In this section we discuss the benefits in terms of income and image for city and enterprise, and the convergence of interests between public and private sectors.

10.6.1   What are Costs and Benefits for Companies?

In our research framework we argued that industrial tourism can be an adequate and cost-efficient instrument for marketing (promoting the firm and its brands), public relations (building sustainable relations with society, giving evidence of corporate citizenship), human resources management (attracting and motivating employees) and business development (generating direct and indirect income). Of course these benefits have to outweigh the costs of opening the firm's doors to visitors, such as the required investments in visitor facilities, and safety and security in particular. How does this work out in the case studies?

Wolfsburg

Volkswagen (Wolfsburg) considers factory visits, free of charge, as a cost-efficient and effective tool for promoting the firm and its brands. An internal study has proven that these visits help to improve the company's image and to raise customer loyalty, which in the end leads to higher sales and profits. Similar motives explain the development of Autostadt, since only 70 per cent of the costs are covered by entrance fees.

Cologne

In Cologne the companies we analysed have opened their doors to visitors for free not only because they expect benefits in terms of human resources management (for example Knapsack, Bayer), but also to build good relations with customers and other stakeholders (for example Bayer, Rheinenergie) and to improve the overall image, also giving evidence of corporate social responsibility (for example Bayer).

Pays de la Loire

The selected companies in Pays de la Loire mostly participate in industrial tourism because they expect their image and reputation to improve (also enhancing the relation with the municipality and society in general) as well as better access to qualified labour (Cointreau being an exception; they mainly use company visits to promote the brand). All companies we analysed charge entrance fees for the general public, mainly to cover the costs of professional guides and visitor facilities.

Turin

The three firms in Turin that we investigated recognise industrial tourism as important instruments of public relations and marketing. Interestingly, the main motive for Gufram to participate in Made in Torino is showing good citizenship. For Aurora, company tours are used to emphasise that their products are 'made in Italy', which enables the firm to sell its products in higher segments of the market.

Shanghai

In Shanghai most companies we interviewed (SVW, Yakult, companies at M50) are involved in industrial tourism to promote the company and its brands, expecting (short-term) increases in sales (even on the site, as in the case of M50). Yakult considers industrial tourism more effective and cost-efficient than traditional advertising methods. Baosteel sees industrial tourism also as a method to demonstrate that the firm pays attention to its social and environmental responsibilities.

Rotterdam

The companies that we analysed in Rotterdam expect benefits from company visits in terms reputation and relation management, though with different views on what relations have to be managed. Many firms in the port and industrial complex open their doors to gain access to qualified labour. Schmidt Zeevis expects benefits from all communication with the outside world, and expects company visits to make employees feel proud about their work. The Happy Shrimp Farm makes a direct profit on company visits for business groups, which is partly used to subsidise visits by educational groups.

In general we can conclude that companies expect substantial benefits from industrial tourism in terms of income and image, but also in terms of relation management (including motivating employees). In addition, the case studies demonstrate that consumer-oriented companies are more interested in promoting their brands, while business-to-business companies tend to be triggered by their interest in a good relation with society and the need for well-qualified labour. In some individual examples we have observed that company visits generate direct income, in terms of ticket sales or product sales, but in most cases these revenues are too small to justify the investments and the associated costs. In most cases the income from ticket sales only covers the costs of professional guides. This implies that indirect and intangible benefits are larger and more relevant than direct, tangible benefits. The case studies also confirm that the increasing pressure on the license to operate – companies have to be good citizens – makes companies aware of the need to open their doors to society.

10.6.2   What are the Costs and Benefits for Cities?

For cities, industrial tourism can generate benefits in terms of additional income (attracting more visitors without major investments and using existing attractions to the full), and in terms of a more realistic image (closing the 'perception gap'). What are the main observations in the case studies?

Wolfsburg

In Wolfsburg, Autostadt and the Volkswagen factory generate substantial numbers of business visitors, excursionists and tourists, but most income effects are generated within the industrial theme park which has its own hotel and catering facilities (it functions more or less as an island in the city). More importantly, however, Autostadt has also put Wolfsburg on the mental map of tourists, making it possible to develop new tourist attractions such as the Phaeno Science Centre (2005) and a designer outlet centre (2007) that may generate more spill-over effects for the local economy. The city has no share in the costs of industrial tourism, apart from investments in public space and infrastructure.

Cologne

Cologne prefers to avoid the term 'industrial tourism' because it is associated with the manufacturing industry, which does not exactly fit in the city's image campaign 'Cologne is a feeling'. Nevertheless, the city does expect 'company visits' to generate positive effects, notably when it comes to promoting Cologne as Germany's media capital, showing the successful redevelopment of waterfront areas and attracting inward investment (mentioned by the Chamber of Commerce). Although company visits generate relatively small numbers of visitors, it is considered an interesting niche market, with the event Expedition Colonia (lasting three weeks) acting as a crowd puller in the off season (April). The costs for the city are relatively low.

Pays de la Loire

Pays de la Loire considers industrial tourism – and 'economic discoveries' in general – as a significant segment of the tourism industry, with demonstrated growth potential. Company visits not only generate benefits for the hotel and catering industry, and the retail sector, but also add to a positive and well-balanced image of the region, notably as an attractive alternative location for Paris. Local authorities promote industrial tourism because it is expected to improve the image of their city (for example St Nazaire) and because industrial tourism helps to create better linkages between government, business and knowledge institutions (for example Angers). Governments on several levels (local, regional and national) invest substantial amounts of money in the development of industrial tourism.

Turin

In Turin the development of industrial tourism fits in a long-term strategy which aims to differentiate the Turin economy and improve the city's image. Company visits are promoted to show citizens (in their role as

ambassadors) and visitors the diversity and strength of Turin's manufacturing industry. As for many other developments in the region, the
Olympic Winter Games of 2006 have acted as a catalyst for the development of industrial tourism. With a very limited number of participants, the
income effects of Made in Torino (with an annual budget of €100 000) are
very small, but the image impact is considerable also due to media attention. From a regional perspective, industrial tourism is not considered very
relevant because it hardly ever generates bed nights, which is generally the
main objective for regional tourism bodies. Moreover some discussion
partners expressed their opinion that the association with 'industry' is not
very desirable for tourism promotion, particularly because the region has
much else to offer.

Shanghai
In Shanghai it became clear that industrial tourism fits in the strategy
of 'the government' (on various levels) to demonstrate the performance
of the economy – not only branding the city or region, but also China
as a whole – paying specific attention to corporate citizenship (as in the
case of Baosteel, a state-owned company). Shanghai considers industrial
tourism (in the broadest sense of the word) as a key segment of the tourism
industry, with substantial impacts on the economy. Moreover, company
visits are expected to help in attracting inward investment, showing that
Shanghai is not only strong in manufacturing but other sectors as well.
Although we have no figures about the costs of industrial tourism, the fact
that the city has set up an industrial tourism promotion centre suggests
that considerable investments are made.

Rotterdam
Rotterdam expects that company visits to the port and industrial complex
help to promote the companies involved as employers, also strengthening the link between companies and educational institutions. Industrial
tourism may also help to further improve the image of the city in general
and attract additional visitors, but strategies to take advantage of these
opportunities and associated investments on behalf of the municipality
seem to be lacking. The recently opened theme park Rotterdam Port
Experience, partly subsidised by the municipality, might act as a catalyst
for the development of industrial tourism.

Concerning the (expected) benefits of industrial tourism for cities and
regions we observe interesting differences between the case studies.
Shanghai and Pays de la Loire see industrial tourism – in the broader
definition – as a significant and growing segment of the tourism industry

with positive contributions to place branding. This approach is obviously related to the supply of industrial tourism products, but it also reflects the position of these regions *vis-à-vis* other regions in their countries (China and France). Both regions have to compete against cities such as Paris and Beijing, both endowed with more traditional tourist attractions. Hence, industrial tourism is part of their positioning strategy.

In Turin and Cologne the expected benefits are smaller: industrial tourism is considered a small niche, but it can play a role in place branding though not necessarily towards tourists who might not appreciate the association with industry. Particularly for Turin we observed differences between the city and region. While the city seems to consider industrial tourism as part of a positioning strategy (in competition with cities such as Venice and Rome), the region has clearly identified other key sectors, which makes sense in view of the limited contribution of industrial tourism to the number of bed nights. Cologne, which is blessed with many traditional tourist attractions, has also adopted this latter view.

Rotterdam, Turin and Wolfsburg have in common that their economy and image are strongly linked to one sector: the role of the port in Rotterdam can to some extent be compared with the roles Fiat and Volkswagen play in the two other cities. For this type of city, industrial tourism can be an instrument to demonstrate the diversity of their economies and supply of company visits. Since these key sectors will never disappear from people's perceptions, it could make sense, however, to use these companies in the positioning strategy. The tagline 'Rotterdam World Port – World City' basically says that the city is connected to the port, but also that the city has more to offer. This strategy can be translated to industrial tourism, as demonstrated by Turin: not only promoting company visits to Fiat, but also to other companies (design, food, aerospace, and so on).

It has not been our intention to make a full cost–benefit analysis of investments in industrial tourism. The case studies also explain why it is not very realistic to have this ambition. We have not found any data that demonstrate benefits for local economies, only some indications that industrial tourism generates income (for example substantial shares in the visitor figures), or helps to improve the image of cities and regions. The lack of these data, however, is not specific for industrial tourism, but rather for any investment in tourism or (economic) promotion. What can be said, in general, is that the more benefits expected by cities or regions, the more costs are involved in the investments made in industrial tourism to realise these benefits. As we will see in the next section (10.7), this is also a matter of ambition and strategy.

10.6.3   Are there Converging Interests? How to Benefit All?

City and enterprise have converging interests in industrial tourism: they both have an interest in a better image of the city and its industries. While companies increasingly need good relations with the communities in which they operate, public bodies increasingly realise that they need the involvement of companies to reach their objectives. Although public and private interests tend to converge, companies and public actors may disagree on several issues such as the selection of target groups. This raises the question how to develop industrial tourism in such a way that it benefits all. What lessons can be learnt from the case studies in this respect?

Wolfsburg
In Wolfsburg we found that the bridge between Autostadt and the city centre could be interpreted as an investment that promotes spill-over effects (to the benefit of the local economy), but this effect has not been demonstrated yet.

Cologne
The Cologne case study makes clear that a regional approach could be helpful to benefit all actors involved. Not only tourists but also international investors seem to look at metropolitan regions rather than at cities. Public actors in Cologne seem to understand that visits to companies outside the municipal border (for example Bayer) also generate benefits in terms of income and image. Also excursionists who spend their nights elsewhere in the region are appreciated.

Pays de la Loire
The most important lesson from Pays de la Loire is that the interests of all actors are best served if the selection of specific target groups is handed over to companies and travel agencies (also see next section). The reason is that the problem of different target groups cannot be solved on a regional level. Regional organisations should focus on joint promotion, quality improvement, and the development of networks involving companies, educational and knowledge institutions, governments, and citizen groups.

Turin
One of the lessons from Turin is that the development of industrial tourism requires more sophisticated definitions of the bottom line, not only for companies but for public organisations as well. For both it can be said that if they only look at direct profits (either in terms of sales or bed nights), it is more difficult to reach an agreement. When companies hold

the view that every contact with the outside world can be valuable (as in the case of Aurora), it is easier to let interests converge.

Shanghai
The analysis of industrial tourism in Shanghai demonstrates that it is easier to develop company tours to government-owned companies, because they also serve public interests. To secure a sufficient supply of industrial tourism products, it is recommendable to involve these companies in any effort to develop industrial tourism. They can be an example for other firms.

Rotterdam
The case of Rotterdam shows that (expected) shortages in the labour market and a common policy agenda, in this case on how to anticipate climate change (the Rotterdam Climate Initiative), may act as catalysts for the development of industrial tourism to the benefit of all. Also in Rotterdam we came to the conclusion that converging interests can be realised sooner if companies accept the hypothesis that secondary stakeholders are as important as primary stakeholders.

The case studies produce two lessons that may apply to all cities: investments in accessibility can facilitate spill-over effects and it is advisable to develop industrial tourism on the level of the relevant functional urban region. The other remarks all concern the conflicts that may arise concerning the selection of target groups. While from a city point of view it makes sense to attract a broad audience (including leisure tourists), companies tend to define their target groups more narrowly, focussing on their primary stakeholders (business tourists). Of course, we would certainly advise cities to follow Shanghai's strategy to include public companies in industrial tourism programmes. But the private sector will also have to follow. We expect that companies become more aware of their interest in building sustainable relations with secondary stakeholders too, because of relations between stakeholders (a tourist can be related to a potential business partner) and the fact that one person may fulfil several stakeholder roles (the tourist of today can be a business relation tomorrow). Several examples, in particular from the cases of Rotterdam and Turin, confirm this tendency. Furthermore we think that the distinction between business and leisure tourists is becoming less relevant as both groups are looking for the same combination of content and experience (fun), although in different proportions. This implies that industrial tourism attractions can easily attract both groups, if capacity is no issue and the benefits outweigh the costs for participating actors.

10.7   THE ORGANISATIONAL SET-UP: HOW TO ORGANISE INDUSTRIAL TOURISM?

The development of industrial tourism requires organising capacity, which essentially refers to the ability to create partnerships between actors from various sectors as well as the ability to create an environment in which such partnerships develop. What are the main observations from the case studies?

Wolfsburg

Volkswagen (Wolfsburg) has its own visitor services department – employing about 30 people – with sub-units for specific target groups, enabling the company to develop tailor-made tours and to pay more than average attention to important guests (special visits and press). The board of Volkswagen gives the visitor services department relative freedom without claiming short-term results. Interestingly, the department also gives advice – not for free though – to other companies in the region willing to open their doors, thus helping to create an environment in which industrial tourism can develop (with or without partnerships).

Cologne

In Cologne industrial tourism is an insignificant side activity for both the Tourist Board and the Chamber of Commerce. We even found that the list with companies that open their doors provided by the Tourist Board is not kept up to date. The organisation of industrial tourism is completely in the hands of individual firms that sometimes choose to outsource part of the visits to external parties, as in the case of HGK (visits to Rheinauhafen). An exception is the business park Knapsack where the park management organisation coordinates visits.

Pays de la Loire

The association Visit Our Companies (Pays de la Loire) plays a key role in creating an environment that stimulates companies to open their doors, and to develop an attractive industrial tourism product. This association is financially supported by regional and national funds, but also through membership fees (up to €500 a year) paid by the companies that also invest management time via active participation in the board of managers. In Angers, the university has taken its responsibility by developing a bachelor's programme on 'economic discoveries' in cooperation with companies and the tourism industry. In St Nazaire, the three biggest companies have opted for a model in which the local tourism bureau (the bureau is 70 per cent owned by public shareholders) arranges visits for the general public and invests in visitor facilities on their sites, while the companies take care of receiving professional visitors.

Turin

In Turin we noted that the Chamber of Commerce and the tourism organisation for the Province of Turin have initiated a partnership in which they both take an active share. The industrial tourism programme Made in Torino clearly fits in a long-term strategy which makes it easier to find support among policy makers and firms. Also worth mentioning is the strategy to expand the programme step by step – adding one or two sectors each year – which enables the initiators to convince new participants by showing the results so far, while spreading the organisational efforts (and costs) over several years. In the organisation of Made in Torino companies play a very limited role, however. Apart from their participation in the programme, companies arrange tours for more specific target groups, usually through their marketing and PR departments.

Shanghai

The Shanghai Industrial Tourism Promotion Center is a typical example of a coordinating body in a Chinese context: created by the local government with support from the State and in response to national policies. After its foundation the Center started to cooperate with companies that had already opened their doors, followed by a strategy to involve companies that represent the identity of the region and for that reason are often willing to invest in their relations with the community. Important actors in the case of Shanghai are the travel agencies that organise company tours, notably for leisure-oriented visitors. Several companies (for example SVW) have outsourced the organisation and promotion of industrial tours for leisure visitors to one agency (while keeping the responsibility for receiving primary stakeholders within the organisational structure of the company), and in some cases (for example Baosteel) this agency is owned by the company. For Yakult, industrial tourism plays a key role in the company's marketing strategy, explaining why the reception of visitors is a task of the public relations department. Interestingly, business park managers can also make it compulsory for companies to open their doors, as in the case of M50.

Rotterdam

In Rotterdam many organisations are involved in the development and promotion of industrial tourism, but without any explicit coordinating strategy or vision. Visits to the port and industrial complex are provided by several competing organisations, while there is an undersupply of visits to companies in other sectors. We also found that for companies, the way industrial tourism is organised depends on the objectives (for example recruitment, public relations, and so on).

In general we conclude that the organisation of industrial tourism requires the involvement of companies and other actors that have a stake. Ideally firms do not only open their doors, but also get involved in the development and management of the regional industrial tourism product, as we observed in Pays de la Loire. Other important stakeholders to cooperate with are educational institutions (universities, schools, and so on), research institutes, travel agencies, chambers of commerce, tourism offices, the media and higher-level governments. The research demonstrates that the organisation of industrial tourism – at the company and regional level – very much depends on the ambitions and aims of the actors involved: it is important to develop a vision and strategy in which the main objectives of industrial tourism (for example improving the image, attracting visitors, creating networks) are specified. Such a vision and strategy may help cities and regions to gain support not only from local stakeholders, but also from higher-level governments.

10.8   RECOMMENDATIONS

Our international comparative research has resulted in several lessons for cities that want to develop industrial tourism. Some of these conclusions apply to any city, whereas other conclusions are context-specific (depending on the political, economic, cultural, demographic circumstances). In this final section we shall, with the focus on Rotterdam, translate the conclusions into recommendations. This should not be considered as a blueprint for how to develop industrial tourism, but rather as some helpful guidelines.

10.8.1   Agree on the Main Objectives of Developing Industrial Tourism

Is the aim to generate income, to improve the image of the city and its industries or to strengthen the relation between firms and society? Or are all objectives equally relevant? Some relevant circumstances to take into consideration are:

(a) In comparison with other cities we investigated, there are relatively few consumer-oriented companies located in the Rotterdam region, making it more difficult to generate income by attracting leisure visitors.

(b) Rotterdam is a not a traditional tourist destination and in view of the strong relation between the city and the port it would make sense to define industrial tourism as one of the pillars of a tourism strategy. In comparison with the other case studies Rotterdam is already quite successful with attracting industrial visitors.

(c) Companies in the port and industrial complex of Rotterdam are increasingly concerned about their image and reputation in general, and as employers in particular. From their point of view, the main objectives of industrial tourism should be related to improving perceptions and stakeholder relations.

10.8.2 Define 'Industrial Tourism'

Define the borders of industrial tourism and choose the right 'name' taking into account the perceptions, expectations, needs and demands of potential target groups.

(a) Experiences from the participating cities indicate that the term 'industrial tourism' should be at least reconsidered, because of its association with the manufacturing industry and leisure tourism, as well as with industrial heritage. The term 'company visits' is more neutral, but maybe also less appealing. The challenge is to find a more appealing name with the right associations: good examples (as sources of inspiration) are Visit Our Companies in Pays de la Loire and Made in Torino; Tour the Excellent.

(b) In the definition of industrial tourism (or whatever term is used) the needs and demands of relevant target groups should be leading: their demand for 'discovering firms and the local economy' can also be met by developing communication centres or theme parks, such as Autostadt. Such facilities will never fully replace real company visits but they are very helpful to avoid conflicts between industrial tourism and the daily production process. Cities should consider including such 'showcases' in its definition of industrial tourism.

10.8.3   Build on Strong Assets

The Port is without any doubt the strongest asset of Rotterdam's economy, as well as the city's industrial tourism product. Its importance is comparable with the importance of the automotive sector in Turin. Both cities, however, also have in common that they have much more to offer. Industrial tourism can be used to enrich the image of a city. In Rotterdam the list of companies that open their doors during the World Port Days provides a good, though not yet complete, overview of the city's strong assets and industrial tourism potential. What sectors could be included in the industrial tourism programme, and what are the most important firms? Inspired by the other case studies we look at the region, rather than the city only:[1]

(a) *Port and maritime services and logistics (including ship repair)*: with companies such as the Rotterdam Port Authority, ECT, Boskalis Westminster, SBM Offshore, Smit Internationale, Vopak, Damen Shipyards.

(b) *Energy and climate*: for example the Happy Shrimp Farm, E.On, Shell, ExxonMobil, WATT (Sustainable Dance Club).

(c) *Food*: Unilever, Seabrex, Santas Coffee, Refresco, greeneries, Genever (Schiedam).

(d) *Health*: Erasmus Medisch Centrum, Unilever.

(e) *Water management*: Rotterdam Port Authority, City of Rotterdam (Public Works), TU Delft, Van Oord.

(f) *Design and architecture*: for example OMA, Creative Factory, Netherlands Architecture Institute.

10.8.4   Identify Target Groups that Both City and Enterprise Want to Receive

One of the main problems that other cities have struggled with concerns the selection of target groups.

(a) If the ambition is to use industrial tourism for more than attracting tourists only, companies should be involved in selecting target groups. In view of the fact that many companies listed above are non-consumer-oriented, this implies that the attraction of leisure tourists is probably not the most effective and efficient strategy.

(b) Taking into account the interests of private-sector organisations, Rotterdam would be advised to focus initially on professional visitors (customers, suppliers, investors) and citizens (employees, neighbours), but with the opportunity to attract leisure visitors too (since we expect them to be interested in visiting firms as well).

(c) International professional visitors are also interesting from a tourism point of view, as they spend on average more money during their stay than leisure visitors do.

(d) Some international markets are more interesting to target simply because people from these countries are more familiar with industrial tourism such as Great Britain, France, Germany, Japan and China.

10.8.5 Use Industrial Tourism as a Unique Selling Point for Attracting Tourists and Lengthening their Stay

Although companies may not have a direct interest in receiving leisure tourists, they might still be convinced to open their doors for them, either regularly or occasionally.

(a) The case studies show that particularly companies with strong regional ties are willing to participate in programmes for leisure tourists, simply because they want to secure their relation with the municipality, the chamber of commerce and other local organisations. We also found that more and more companies realise that also secondary stakeholders are important.

(b) An industrial tourism programme for leisure visitors – such as Made in Torino; Tour the Excellent – may not attract thousands of tourists, but can develop into a symbolic image builder for the city as tourist destination and business location.

(c) Showcases such as the Rotterdam Port Experience could play an important role in strengthening the profile of Rotterdam as an industrial tourism destination, attracting many visitors without disturbing production processes. Communication centres and theme parks could be developed into portals for professional and leisure visitors that are interested in 'discovering cities and their industries'. Furthermore, they could help to make cities more attractive for business and leisure tourists, encouraging them to spend more nights in the city.

10.8.6 Introduce Quality Standards for Company Visits

The case studies demonstrate that the introduction of quality standards can not only secure the attractiveness and accessibility of the visits, but also stimulate and help companies to open their doors. The experiences of Pays de la Loire and Shanghai show that national governments can be supportive by introducing quality standards, and giving awards to role model companies, while regional and local organisations can provide advice on how to meet these standards.

10.8.7   Develop an Internet Portal for Industrial Tourism

Shanghai and Pays de la Loire have both developed a website where citizens and (international) visitors can get an overview of all companies that have opened their doors and meet the quality standards.

10.8.8   Cooperate with Travel Agencies, Tourism Offices and Tour Operators

Industrial tourism is a growing segment of the tourism industry. The case studies demonstrate that not only small and medium-sized companies but also large firms lack the human resources and also the expertise to organise company visits: it is not their core business. This implies that specialised travel agencies, tourism offices and tour operators should play a key role in meeting the growing demand.

10.8.9   Use Water Transport to make Rotterdam's Industrial Tourism Product Distinguishing and Accessible

Like the other cities we investigated (and Shanghai in particular), Rotterdam faces the problem of congestion on its roads and the problematic accessibility of industrial tourism attractions. Water transport could play an important role in enhancing the accessibility, while making the product more attractive and distinguishing at the same time. Also the use of other, even more eccentric modes of transport, such as the Maglev train in Shanghai, could create an experience in its own right.

10.8.10   Develop Unique Experiences

An example of a unique experience for visitors to Volkswagen in the industrial area of Wolfsburg is a five-star hotel with an outdoor swimming pool which illustrates that industrial areas can be developed into attractive places for visitors.

To conclude, our international comparative research makes it clear that industrial tourism can produce benefits in terms of income and image for the participating cities and their industries. We have observed that a number of companies in the investigated cities have already made some steps towards an open door policy, but in general firms tend to be passive, emphasizing the barriers and the costs. The case studies demonstrate that a more positive and proactive approach, with the support of public and private actors, can contribute to the competitiveness of individual companies and the city in which they are located.

NOTE

1. This list only gives an indication of what sectors *could* be included. It has not been our ambition to give a complete overview.

REFERENCES

Mader, T. (2003), Produzierende Betriebe als touristische Attraktionen im Ruhrgebiet. Grundlagen, Erscheinungsformen, Probleme. Magisterarbeit, Heinrich-Heine-Universitaet Duesseldorf. Diplomica Gmbh, Hamburg.
Van den Berg et al. (2003), *City and Enterprise: Corporate Community Involvement in European and US Cities*, Euricur Series, Ashgate, Aldershot.

11. An aging population and the economic vitality of Pennsylvania's cities and towns

Peter Karl Kresl

The population of all industrialized economies is aging, frighteningly so in some countries. In a study of the impacts of aging populations the OECD argued that it will be difficult to maintain anticipated increases in living standards, taxes to support age-related programs will reduce productive investment and work effort, and that there will actually be a negative impact on living standards. The report argued that these impacts were not absolutely unavoidable. The solution, it was argued, is focused on older workers, specifically increased efforts at lifelong learning, so as to maintain the skills of older workers, an end to subsidized early retirement, and increasing the labor participation rate of older women (OECD, 2005).

In the European Union, by 2050 the population will be smaller and older, with the working age cohort declining by 48 million, or 16 per cent, and the 65+ cohort increasing by 58 million, or 77 per cent. One of the projected consequences of this demographic change is a decline in potential GDP growth from 2.2 per cent for the current decade to 1.3 per cent for the period 2031–50, with increases in productivity of those who are working, through advances in technology, being the primary source of growth. Another consequence of the increasing age dependency in the EU will be an increase in public sector age-related expenditures of 5 per cent (Economic Policy Committee and the European Commission, 2006). In southern EU countries, such as Italy, declining birth rates, a reluctance to accept a sufficient numbers of immigrants, a reluctance to increase the female labor participation rate, and lengthening life spans mean that by 2050 there will be one retired person for each worker. Clearly the tax burden for health care, pensions, long-term care and other age-related expenses are creating a situation that, unless something changes, will become untenable.

Fortunately the US does accept immigrants and is, in fact, among the leaders of the industrialized countries in foreign-born as a share of the population. The work force today is also about 50 per cent women. Nonetheless, the aging of the US population does have significant consequences. According to the Bureau of the Census: 'The older population is on the threshold of a boom . . . [it] is projected to be twice as large in 2030 [as in 2000], growing from 35 million to 72 million and representing nearly 20 per cent of the total U.S. population at the latter date.' One result of this is the possibility, in the face of increasing age-related expenditures, of 'modifications to Social Security, Medicare, and disability and retirement benefits'.

However, the Census Bureau noted that offsetting this will be the fact that seniors of tomorrow will be better educated, wealthier, healthier and more mobile than has ever been the case (Wan et al., 2005, pp. 1 and 4). It is this conclusion that was in large part the inspiration for the work of which this chapter is one product (Kresl and Ietri, 2010). In spite of the obvious fiscal and other negative consequences of an aging population, the distinctively new socio-economic characteristics of the seniors of tomorrow should lead us to anticipate equally new patterns of behavior, including the ways in which they choose to allocate their time and their money. These new behaviors will be specified and examined in the context of the future for Pennsylvania's cities and towns after we have documented the demographic data with regard to projections of population aging in the Commonwealth.

Among US states Pennsylvania ranks 45th in projected population growth for the period 2000–30, albeit ahead of New York and Ohio (US Census Bureau, 2005). For the period 1990–2020, the Commonwealth is projected to grow by 5.6 per cent, with 25 of 67 counties experiencing population decline. The Philadelphia tri-state MSA (including Philadelphia; Camden, New Jersey; and Wilmington, Delaware) gained 15 186 to 5 838 471 residents during 2000–08, while for the same period the Pittsburgh MSA declined by 2967 to 2 351 192; the two relevant counties both suffered population loss, −4.6 for Philadelphia county and −5.6 for Allegheny county (Pennsylvania State Data Center, 2009). Population growth is concentrated in the south-eastern third of the Commonwealth, the eastern border counties, the university counties Center and Union, and Butler county. Thus many of Pennsylvania's cities and towns are forecast to continue to lose population and, thereby, economic vitality. The picture for the Commonwealth can be most graphically represented by population pyramids, that show the recent and projected shares of the population of all age groups. Figures 11.1 and 11.2, and Table 11.1 indicate the situation for 2000 and 2030. The clear message from them is that the share of the 65 year + cohort grows while that of the working age population, taken here be 20–64 years of age, diminishes. The result of this is a growing age

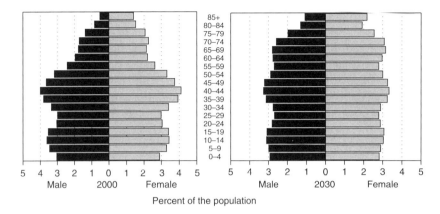

Source: US Census Bureau (2005).

Figure 11.1   Population pyramids of Pennsylvania

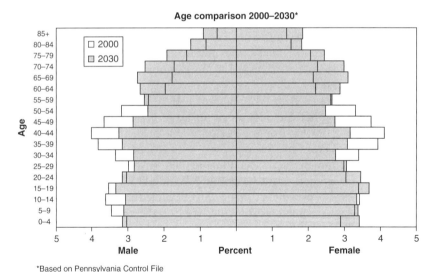

Figure 11.2   Changes in age cohorts, Pennsylvania

dependency ratio and a diminishing youth dependency ratio. This highlights the primary concern of governments in the industrialized nations: a
rising tax burden on the diminishing working population to support the
growing expenditures on pensions and health care. In Pennsylvania this
means that by 2030 there will be 2.75 20–64 year old workers supporting
each 65+ senior. The figure is much more burdensome if one considers

Table 11.1   Pennsylvania age dependency ratios

Demographic Indicator	2000	2030	Change	
Median Age	38.0	42.1	4.1	
Dependency Ratio (1)	73.2	87.2	14.0	
Youth (2)	46.1	44.8	−1.3	−2.8%
Old age (3)	27.1	42.4	15.3	+56.5

Notes:
(1)   Dependency ratio = age under 20 + Age 65 +/Age 20–64 × 100.
(2)   Youth dependency ratio = age under 20/age 20–64 × 100.
(3)   Old age dependency ratio = age 65 +/age 20–64 × 100.

Source: US Census Bureau (2005).

not the 20–64 aged population but rather just those who are in the labor force and working. The overall labor participation rate in Pennsylvania is about 0.67 per cent, so the more relevant figure is that there will be about 1.56 working Pennsylvanians for each senior. This approaches the figure for the worst of the industrialized economies, Italy, which has a 1:1 ratio (OECD, 2000; Eurostat, 2008). Overall, the US figure is about 2.5:1, with other industrialized economies ranging between the US and Italy. Given the needs of a senior population for health care, pensions and other public expenditures, it is easy to see why the aging of the population has been seen to be a 'ticking time bomb' or a 'specter that haunts' societies.

THE POSITIVE SIDE OF AN AGING POPULATION FOR URBAN ECONOMIES

While this negative picture is valid for the national level of government, financially responsible as it is for most of these expenditures, for cities or urban economies there is a brighter element to this picture. The US Bureau of the Census has described the seniors of the decades to come as being 'healthier, wealthier, better educated and more mobile' (Wan et al., 2005) than has ever been the case. Thus we should expect to see behavior on their part that will be different than that of seniors of the past. Specifically, I suggest that there are three aspects of an aging population that portend positive consequences for cities.

First, seniors often relocate residence from a house in the periphery or a rural location to an apartment or condominium in the city center. In the dozen US cities I have visited in the course of a research project, a declining city center is being rejuvenated by a boom in apartment and condominium construction that is to a significant degree led by the inward movement of seniors. In effect, this is a process of 'rejuvenation through aging'.

Second, seniors are disproportionate consumers of education – lifelong learning. All major cities have a university with an Osher Foundation lifelong learning center – 123 such centers are currently being funded.[1] These centers are designed to offer a variety of intellectual experiences to seniors 55 years of age and older. Typically, they are fully subscribed, if not over-subscribed. Most universities and colleges have their own educational opportunities for seniors, ranging from special courses of 4–6 meetings to lecture series to access to the regular academic course offerings. Many urban regions are trying to develop as 'learning regions' and engagement of seniors, as well as university age students, is an essential component of this strategy.

Third, seniors are also disproportionate consumers of cultural activities. Interviews with administrators at symphony orchestras, theaters, performance centers and art museums are uniform in noting that audiences are between 60 and 90 per cent made up of 55 and older individuals and that they are at least as dominant when it comes to being contributors and financial supporters, and, of course, they are responsible for bequests. In other words, most cultural institutions would not be able to survive without the patronage of seniors. This fact is all the more important when we understand that the vitality of a city's cultural institutions is one of a handful of statistically verified determinants of urban competitiveness.

As a final point we should note that the Pew Foundation published a report in 2009 that showed that in the current recession seniors

> are less likely than younger and middle-aged adults to say that in the past year they have cut back on spending; suffered losses in their retirement accounts; or experienced trouble paying for housing or medical care. They're more likely to report being very satisfied with their personal finances. And they're less likely to say the recession has been a source of stress in their family. (Pew Research Center, 2009).

Therefore, far from being a drag on economic performance, seniors can be a key and stabilizing element in a city's economic performance and competitiveness.

THE EXPERIENCES OF SOME US CITIES

These three factors are powerfully present in the dozen US cities I have visited for interviews, and it will be instructive to mention just a few of my observations in this area, before focusing specifically on Pennsylvania.

Relocation to the city center has occurred in Atlanta with development of the Mid-town district between Downtown to the south and Buckhead to the north. Mid-town is the area on the metro subway line that is closest to the Atlanta Symphony and the High Art Museum. In Nashville, the downtown area has been dominated by Grand Ole Opry and the Country Music Hall of Fame. Visitors typically stay at a KOA campground, attend an event, eat some fast food and return home. A few blocks away, the Schemerhorn Concert Hall and the Frist Art Museum have stimulated a boom in condominium and apartment construction in an area that was in decline. Recently a show of these units resulted in the sale of 16 priced at $500000, predominantly to seniors. Out-of-town seniors attending the symphony or art museum typically stay in a hotel, spend money on retail and eat in restaurants. Americans for the Arts is an organization that has done economic impact of the arts studies for 156 US communities and regions, showing that the multiplier tends to be roughly 2.6:1 (Americans for the Arts, 2007). Denver considers itself to be the 'boomer' capital of the US. Residential construction is on the upswing and the Denver Center for the Performing Arts brings boomers and other seniors to the city as residents or as visitors. The DCPA was successful several years ago in convincing the Mayor that cultural activities have a greater positive impact on the Denver economy than do sports. Finally, in Charlottesville the mile strip between the University of Virginia and the Historic District is in the midst of construction of 1000 residential units, again stimulated by relocation of seniors partly to a University of Virginia alumni targeted complex near the University and partly to commercial developments closer to the historic district.

In these and other US cities, seniors are fueling a boom in residential construction in the city center, they are engaged in many learning activities and they are enthusiastic participants in, and financial supporters of, the city's cultural institutions.

THE ECONOMIC CONSEQUENCES FOR PENNSYLVANIA'S CITIES AND TOWNS

In Pennsylvania we have four categories of cities and towns with regard to aging. First, the largest cities, Philadelphia and Pittsburgh, have been actively seeking to induce periphery to center relocation of residence among seniors. These cities also have rich complements of learning opportunities and cultural institutions and they have strategies to ensure they capture the positive benefits from a senior population. Pittsburgh has been developing its Culture District for the past 25 years and Philadelphia is now doing the same with Arts Avenue. Second, Pennsylvania has over 150 colleges and universities and as a consequence we have dozens of 'college towns.' These cities and towns have ample cultural and learning assets, they are often very attractive in terms of housing and architecture, many have excellent health care facilities, and they are usually endowed with parks, walking trails and athletic facilities. Many have good restaurants and vibrant retail and can, as I am sure David Maurrasse will tell us, serve as bases for economic development. Both of these two categories of cities have their own resident senior population, but they also draw from other parts of the Commonwealth, or from other states, seniors who are looking for a place to retire with just these amenities.

Third, there are many towns that are between the largest cities and the college towns. These are towns that are large and diverse enough so that a university or college does not have a dominating influence.

Fourth, we have many other cities and towns in declining parts of the Commonwealth which, having lost their industry and then their young people, find themselves populated by a senior population that is anything but healthy, wealthy, better educated and mobile. These are the cities and towns that, other things being equal, will experience the increased costs of a senior population in need of health care, income support, housing and living facilities that will impose severe fiscal strains, without any of the positive benefits the large cities and college towns have the potential to realize. The same is, of course, also true for large areas of the larger cities of the Commonwealth.

Rejuvenation through Aging

Since relocation of residence to the city center varies so much by type of city, I will look at these four types of Pennsylvania cities in turn, beginning with our two largest cities.

Pittsburgh

Pittsburgh has, of course, had a troubled past quarter century. In part the city is handicapped by things that it cannot change and in part by things it has done to itself. The two rivers that become one create a topographical difficulty, and the escarpment south of the Monongahela creates another (Figure 11.3). But Pittsburgh has done negative things to itself. North of the Allegheny are two sports stadiums that make it difficult for people to gain access to the Golden Triangle, while between the Triangle and the escarpment to the south are railroad lines. To the east is a major interstate highway, I-579, that blocks access to the Triangle from the city's major residential areas, Oakland and Squirrel Hill. In actuality the Triangle is

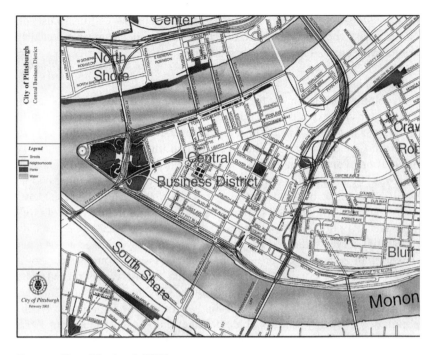

Source: City of Pittsburgh (2003).

Figure 11.3   Downtown Pittsburgh

surrounded by a wall of transportation corridors that preclude easy access
to it. This is in sharp contrast to Lyon, France, another city with two rivers
that become one and a downtown triangle. However, Lyon is bordered
across the Saone river by a vibrant UNESCO-recognized Renaissance
historic district, across the Rhône river by a densely populated plain
and on the third by the old silk district hill that allows easy access to the
downtown triangle. Thus Pittsburgh is severely challenged in its efforts to
develop its Golden Triangle.

   However, recently the downtown is showing signs of a revival. There
are only 2500 non-student residents living in the Triangle today but 300
residential units were being built in 2008, with another 600 projected for
the next 2–3 years. The cultural institutions are now in place, the restaurants have followed and now the last piece, residential units, is being
addressed. Many of the new residents are seniors who are moving in from
areas of the city to the east of the Triangle, Squirrel Hill and Oakland
(Pittsburgh Downtown Partnership, 2008). They tend to be relatively well

off and educated people who seek the amenities of the Cultural District. Nevertheless, the movement into the city center, while promising, is clearly not as robust as it is in many other US cities.

Philadelphia
Philadelphia has none of the topographical handicaps of Pittsburgh. The center city extends without hindrance to the north and the south, and across the Schuylkill River to the University of Pennsylvania area to the west. One official noted that the city had the third largest center city population of any city in the US. The City Center District centered on City Hall has 20000 residents and a slightly larger city center that most people would consider to be the downtown area has 57000. The 20000 residents who 'routinely walk to work support new retail and animate streets well after dark'. Eighty-eight per cent of respondents to a 2006 Center City residential survey indicated they had at least a college degree and 47 per cent had an advanced or professional degree. Twenty-four per cent of a 2007 Center City condo owner survey listed themselves as retired. The residential survey of 2008 stated that Center City households are smaller, more affluent, childless, and increasingly retired. The stimulus to recent population growth was a tax abatement act that was introduced in 1997. In the City Center area, about half of all owners of residential units are 55 years of age or older. Linked together with an excellent transportation system, which offers free rides to those who are 65 and older, access to Philadelphia's considerable cultural and educational opportunities is not a significant deterrent to participation by seniors. During the past decade the movement of seniors to downtown has increased, with some developments targeted specifically at them. For the past decade there has been construction of an additional 1155 residential units in the city center, many of which have one or two bedrooms and are suited for young people and seniors.

Philadelphia is rich with cultural activities, from the Symphony and Art Museum to its many theaters and the city government has linked culture and residential construction. Along Avenue of the Arts new buildings are required to have some link to cultural activity. For example, Symphony Court is a residential building, and has Broad/Avenue of the Arts and Pine Street with the Suzanne Roberts Theater on the ground floor and ample parking as well. Many of the units are priced at $500000 and above and are designed with empty nesters/young seniors in mind.

College towns
College towns have been touted as particularly attractive places to retire and are prominent on lists of the country's best retirement communities.

In the college town in which I live, Lewisburg, realtors tell me that the town attracts seniors from the Boston to Virginia agglomeration and from states as far away as California who want a congenial place to set up a shop or a bed-and-breakfast or just to establish their residence. Here as well as in the two larger cities it is not necessary to have a resident population of seniors who are, in the words of the US Census Bureau, 'healthier, wealthier, better educated and more mobile than ever before'; these seniors will search far from their suburban house for the ideal place to retire. As in the movie *A Field of Dreams*, 'if you build it they will come'. This suggests the wisdom of designing a strategy to develop the desirable urban amenities that will attract this cohort of the population. I believe the situation is similar for other college towns such as Meadville, Grove City, Gettysburg and Carlisle. Private colleges are more likely to be able to justify expenditures on community relations than are public institutions since the budgets of the latter have to pass the scrutiny of the Commonwealth authorities. As is the case with many college towns, Lewisburg has a Downtown Neighborhood Corporation that brings the University and the town together for improvement projects, and the University is moving its bookstore to Market Street with the objective being in part that of increasing the retail flow downtown. Private universities have an interest in having a downtown that is vibrant if only to give a positive impression to potential students and their parents. This also makes the town increasingly attractive to mobile seniors seeking a place to retire.

Several of Pennsylvania's cities and towns fall between the large cities and the college towns. Lancaster, Bethlehem, Harrisburg, Easton, Williamsport, Reading, State College and York all have educational institutions but are too large and diverse for their universities and colleges to dominate the economy and community life. Nonetheless these institutions do enrich the intellectual and cultural life of their city or town and do draw to it a senior population that has the sort of positive impact that is the subject of this chapter. State College is the anomaly here as Pennsylvania State University is a public university and it is so large that it does in fact dominate the local economy. Each of the universities in these towns attracts seniors who want to retire in a congenial environment, although with State College it seems to be more athletic than cultural and intellectual.

Pennsylvania's other cities and towns

The rest of Pennsylvania's cities and towns have to chart their own course, trying to take advantage of whatever assets or amenities they have. It is not true that all successful cities have to follow the same path of being a center of bio-pharmaceutical or information-communication technology, or a learning region, or a professional services center, or whatever the flavor of the day for consultants happens to be. Many cities are quite successful in that their residents have the jobs, income, degree of social exclusion and town amenities they seek – as centers of logistics, or cities of recreation and culture or regional medical centers. To pick just one, in Tioga county, in North-central Pennsylvania, Wellsboro is successful as a town close to the Pine Creek 'Grand Canyon of Pennsylvania', as a regional medical center, and as a town that has preserved a charming 19th century character complete with gas street lights. Needless to say, this mixture of health care, recreation and architecture is attractive to those seniors who seek something other than a large city or a college town. The challenge for any of these towns is to examine what they have, and to make a concerted effort to capitalize on it. Easier said than done, but it is in fact being done in many towns throughout the Commonwealth.

Education and Lifelong Learning

Pennsylvania cities are rich in educational opportunities for seniors. The Bernard Osher Foundation gives grants of $100 000 to a promising university lifelong learning center and if it meets certain criteria then awards it an endowment of one million dollars. In Pittsburgh, both Carnegie Mellon University and the University of Pittsburgh have well established Osher centers with over 2000 members together, and each is experiencing growth in its membership. Temple University, in Philadelphia, has had a lifelong learning center since 1976, and began to receive Osher funding in 2007. Its membership is currently at 700 and, although the current financial crisis has slowed growth this year, it is anticipated that as the population ages membership will regain its growth. Pennsylvania State University and Widener University also have Bernard Osher Foundation centers of lifelong learning.

Many other colleges and universities have their own less ambitious learning programs and/or offer seniors admission to regular classes, usually at reduced tuition. However, lifelong learning programs are usually quite different from the usual university offerings in that these courses may meet for 4–6 times with sessions lasting an hour and a half or two hours, and they may meet once a week or less frequently, rather than the typical university course of 13 weeks and three hours of meeting per week. One other component of many of these educational programs is that of physical education activity. This may take the form of walking and hiking, Tai-chi, exercise and weight equipment, team sports and swimming. Given the growing number of seniors who can add something positive to a municipality's economy and given the fact that many of these seniors hunger for intellectual engagement, it is probably safe to predict that these learning programs of universities and colleges will become more popular in the years to come.

While data is hard to come by, health care professionals, from my personal physician to professionals in offices of aging, are convinced that seniors who are intellectually and physically active have longer lives in good health, and shorter periods of infirmity and of costly health care. Thus, while of a different order than relocation of residence to the city center, active engagement in educational activities does bring a benefit to the city in that there are reduced health care costs; seniors are not confined to, and deteriorating in, their apartment; they contribute to the community as volunteers in social, cultural and educational institutions; and they continue to be active consumers of goods and services.

Cultural Life

I got started on this project when I noticed that in my empirical studies of urban competitiveness, one of the statistically verified determinants of urban competitiveness is the vitality of a city's culture and arts institutions. The link was that a highly skilled and educated labor force would not work in a city that lacked such institutions; not necessarily for the long-working skilled workers themselves, but they demanded it for their children. When I looked closely at the vitality of this sector, it became clear that the city's culture and arts activities were heavily dependent upon the participation of seniors, both as audience and participants and as financial supporters. Typically, orchestra, art museum and theater audiences are 60 per cent or more composed of seniors. In Venice, Italy, the Teatro Goldoni audience is over 90 per cent seniors. These institutions are even more dependent upon seniors for their financial contributors and sponsors – often seniors account for 80 per cent or more of this funding. Without seniors most cultural institutions would be financially non-viable. Without seniors who support these institutions a city would suffer in its competitiveness, with regard to a skilled labor force, plant location, headquarters functions, retail, and so forth, in relation to other cities.

Very good data for the cultural sector is available for Philadelphia and Pittsburgh, two cities that have been the subject of economic impact studies by Americans for the Arts, an organization that has done similar studies for dozens of US cities. In Pittsburgh the average age of subscribers is 55, and audiences have always been dominated by this age group. Over 55 per cent of ticket and subscription revenues for all cultural organizations comes from the 55 and older population. The organizations in this comprehensive study include entities that appeal to children, families, young people and professionals, as well as seniors. The Pittsburgh Symphony takes the approach of investing in its audience and its patrons. The objective is that of bringing a new person along from audience member to subscriber to patron in 4–5 years. Ninety per cent of the 'super patrons', the biggest financial supporters, are seniors. Many have developed such a strong commitment to the orchestra that they continue to contribute even when immobility precludes attendance at concerts. This lifelong commitment is the result of the development of a community among the supporters of the orchestra and a social environment that they find rewarding and satisfying. Given the already mentioned topographical challenges of the Golden Triangle, parking and transportation access remain among the largest problems the cultural institutions face.

In Philadelphia, the situation is similar. Younger residents support smaller-scale entities such as the annual Fringe Fest, but seniors tend to support the larger institutions – the museums, musical entities, and theaters – of the city center. This sector is responsible for 21 000 jobs in the cultural sector and an additional 19 000 as a consequence of expenditures of those who attend events and spend money in restaurants, hotels and shopping. Each dollar spent by the local government on culture and the arts brings in $5.00 in local tax revenue and for the state $1 brings in $2.50. Other figures also confirm the economic importance of the culture and arts sector (Greater Philadelphia Cultural Alliance, 2008). While the city proper is losing population, the city center is growing and this growth is tied to the focus of the city's economic development strategy on 'eds and meds', that is on education and health care. The labor force in these industries demands an extensive array of first-rate cultural institutions. Since the demand for cultural goods and services is related to the educational attainment of the population, this combined with the growth of the senior population should add to the strength of Philadelphia's culture and arts vitality.

However, one criticism of the approach taken in Philadelphia is precisely the lack of direct connection between the cultural and arts entities and the economic development of the city, especially since the dissolution by a recent mayor of the Office of Arts and Culture. While both the public sector and the city's major corporations give lip service to the importance of cultural life, neither follows this up with financial support to the degree that is found in other cities (McCarthy et al., 2007).

It goes without saying that college and 'in between' towns offer an array of cultural and intellectual activities, from the college orchestra, theater and dance company to a performance hall for touring group to lectures and other events that are open to the public. While the variety and quality are not that of the larger cities, they are usually adequate to satisfy seniors who want to combine cultural activities with intellectual and learning opportunities and recreational facilities. Of course, for those seniors who want a symphony evening every week or a first run play, the typical college town may not suffice.

The other non-college towns will have to make do with the other amenities that are available. Their economic development will be of a different character. Excellent recreational amenities, hiking, rock-climbing, cycling and winter sports, may in fact attract a younger and more active population, one that can provide a different way to achieve the economic and social objectives of the town's residents. Not all towns have to be cultural and intellectual centers.

AN INTERGENERATIONAL BATTLE?

One possible outcome of this aging of the population will be in inter-generational battle over income, wealth and expenditures. Clearly for many seniors, not as healthy, wealthy, educated and mobile as some of their fellow seniors, their final decades will be one in which they are net recipients of transfers from young workers, as has been noted above. For them, expenditures on pensions, health care and long-term care will have to be exclusively tax financed. Other seniors will have been able to set aside funds in private accounts that will be dedicated to these expenditures. The current collapse in the equity market has made many of these accounts incapable of providing for retirement to the degree that had been planned. As a consequence of this, many seniors will extend their working lives into their late 60s or later, thus reducing their need for these transfers.

It must also be noted that there is another side to the question of fiscal transfers. Parents generally pay for most of the educational expenses of their children, in some cases through graduate or professional school. They also often transfer resources to their children when the latter purchase a home; they transfer ownership or use to their children of an apartment, automobile or furniture. Many seniors lend money to their children until they are established professionally and in life. There are also many transfers in kind, through child care, and so forth. Thus intergenerational transfers are more complex than the tax-transfer mechanism would suggest.

Finally, traditional patterns will certainly shift, both for the positive and the negative, through changes in living styles, the labor market and other factors. This is already true in the US and is going to become so in the EU in years to come. Seniors are likely to find that their children will no longer work and live in close proximity to them. Jobs take workers to all parts of the country and abroad. The traditional 'family home' may no longer exist in a meaningful way for many seniors. Instead of children staying 'near home', many seniors end up moving across the country to live near their children and grandchildren. Thus the relationship between parents, their children and 'home' will probably be quite different as we move through the 21st century than it was in the 20th. In many parts of Pennsylvania, the traditional pattern of the family home has been a powerful force and reality. However, in recent years many of these areas, formerly towns of mining and heavy manufacturing, have seen an out-migration of young people and a corresponding deterioration of the local economy. Seniors in many instances will then be trapped in a situation of isolation and of dependency on public support. While some of these towns may find it impossible to reverse the downward trajectory, for others the choice of an economic-strategic plan to capitalize on the local assets and amenities they do have is close to a decision of life and death. As we have been discussing changes that are dynamic in nature, it is clear that there is no time to be wasted.

PENNSYLVANIA CITIES AND TOWNS AND THE AGING POPULATION – WHAT TO DO?

The conclusion that is to be drawn from this presentation is simple – seniors can be a source of positive economic benefits for a city or town that adopts the policies that will make it attractive to them. The seniors of today are, and tomorrow will be, better educated, wealthier, in better health longer, and much more mobile than has been the case in the past. This being the case, we should expect them to evince patterns of behavior that are quite different, as well. The three consequences of an aging population that have been highlighted in this chapter – the relocation of residence to the city center, support for culture and the arts and a commitment to lifelong learning – have the potential to have positive impacts on the economies of four categories of cities and towns in Pennsylvania. For the large cities, college towns and 'in between' cities there is a potential for beneficial economic impact that is theirs if they adopt policies and initiatives to develop the potential of resident seniors and to attract relatively mobile seniors from other parts of the Commonwealth or the nation. These policies should work on enhancing the urban amenities that make for an urban space and community that will be attractive to seniors. Rather than simply building 'senior citizen residences' and health care facilities, the amenities desired by the new cohort of seniors include opportunities for cultural and intellectual engagement for well-educated people, pedestrian ways and parks for physically active seniors, high quality retail and restaurant options, and an engaging street life and architecture.

With regard to urban competitiveness, it was noted above, first, that the vitality of a city's cultural sector is one of eight or ten of its statistically verified determinants. The participation of seniors in the cultural life of a city, both as audiences and as financial supporters, makes the case that this cohort of seniors is key to a city's competitiveness in relation to other competing cities. Second, the role of seniors in the rejuvenation of declining city centers of most of the cities in this study identifies a second way in which seniors enhance the attractiveness, and ultimately competitiveness, of a city. Third, intellectually active seniors engaged in, among other things, lifelong learning experiences, will have better health further into their life, lower health costs and a shorter period of intensive care. In addition, intellectually active adults and seniors are an important component in any city's strategy to become a technologically-based economy or a learning region.

If cities and towns in Pennsylvania do not continue their past efforts to create an attractive urban *milieu*, their counterparts in other states will, and these potential benefits of an aging population will be lost to us. This poses a clear challenge to officials and city leaders throughout the Commonwealth. Much that is very good has been done and in many cities and towns there are current efforts to move further down this path. The current economic crisis will jeopardize further progress in the short run, but we must return to the strategy of capturing the potential inherent in the demographic and economic facts of the growing senior population of the years to come.

ACKNOWLEDGEMENT

I would like to thank the International Center for Economic Research in Turin, Italy, for its financial support of my work in this area.

NOTE

1. http://www.osherfoundation.org.

REFERENCES

Americans for the Arts (2007), *Arts and Economic Prosperity III*, Washington: Americans for the Arts, p. 3.

Central Philadelphia Development Corporation (2008), *Residential Development, 2008*, Philadelphia: Central Philadelphia Development Corporation and the City Center District, September.

Economic Policy Committee and the European Commission (2006), 'The impact of ageing on public expenditure projections for the EU25 Member States on pensions, health care, long-term care, education and unemployment transfers (2004–2050)', *European Economy*, Special Report No. 1, pp. 8–15.

Eurostat (2008), *Europe in Figures – Eurostat Yearbook 2006–2007*, Brussels: Eurostat.

Greater Philadelphia Cultural Alliance (2008), *Arts, Culture and Economic Prosperity in Greater Philadelphia*, Philadelphia: Greater Philadelphia Cultural Alliance, pp. 3 and 4.

Kresl, Peter Karl and Daniele Ietri (2010), *The Aging Population and the Competitiveness of Cities*, Cheltenham: Edward Elgar.

McCarthy, Kevin F., Elizabeth Heneghan Ondaatje and Jennifer L. Novak (2007), *Arts and Culture in the Metropolis: Strategies for Sustainability*, Santa Monica, CA: Rand Corporation, pp. 80–81.

OECD (2000), *Reforms for an Aging Society*, Paris: Organisation for Economic Cooperation and Development, ch. 10.

OECD (2005), *Ageing Populations: High Time for Action*, Background paper for the Meeting of G8 Employment and Labour Ministers, London, 10–11 March 2005, Paris: Organisation for Economic Cooperation and Development.

Pennsylvania State Data Center (2009), *2008 Pennsylvania County Population Estimates*, Harrisburg: Pennsylvania State Data Center, Penn State Harrisburg, March 19.

Pew Research Center (2009), 'Not Your Grandfather's Recession – Literally', Pew Research Center, May 14.

Pittsburgh Downtown Partnership (2008), *2008 Downtown Market Survey*, and *Residential Population – from the 2008 PDP Resident Survey*, Pittsburgh: Pittsburgh Downtown Partnership.

US Census Bureau (2005), *Interim State Population Projections, 2005*, Washington: US Census Bureau, April 21, Table 1.

Wan He, Manisha Sengupta, Victoria A. Velkoff and Kimberly A. DeBarros (2005), *65+ in the United States: 2005*, Washington: US Department of Commerce, US Census Bureau, December.

12. The repositioning of cities and urban regions in a global economy

Saskia Sassen

The impacts of global processes on major urban areas are far more diverse than is commonly asserted. The much talked about homogenizing of urban economies due to globalization is only half of the story. The other half is that the specialized differences of cities matter more today than they did in the Keynesian period. To begin to address these issues this chapter examines two major sets of processes. One concerns actual shifts in the scales, spaces and contents of economic activity. The second concerns the needed shifts in our interpretations and policy frameworks to adjust to these novel trends and maximize their benefits and distributive potential.

First, the chapter examines some of the key components of 'globalizing processes' and what this means for different types of cities and urban regions. Rather than reviewing all components, the chapter singles out three types of processes as critical. The ongoing formation of global cities is one of these, but as this is a well-documented trend, the chapter will touch on it only when it intersects with two other developments which are examined in more detail. One is the novel trend towards the formation of mega regions tends to be a cross-border process. The other is the expansion of cross-border flows connecting cities at diverse levels of the urban hierarchy. To capture the growth and diversification of these inter-city flows, I will examine a sample of cities in terms of 60 variables organized into seven major indicators. This allows us to recognize the diverse ways in which cities are today positioned in the global economy.

These formations – mega regions and global urban circuits – are very different. It will be argued that it is possible, analytically, to identify a distinct dynamic at work in both of these very diverse components of globalizing cities and urban regions. This dynamic is the interaction between geographic dispersal and new kinds of agglomeration economies. Specifying a common analytic ground for these two very diverse spatial forms should enable us to develop a sharper approach to policy and, secondly, to establish the actual negotiating power of urban/regional actors, as well as novel types of inter-governmental actors. These very diverse spatial forms also should help in assessing the extent to which policy decisions can encourage greater economic integration between a country's more globalized city (or cities) and its other metropolitan areas currently performing subordinate functions within the national urban hierarchy. In other words, it might help in connecting the 'winners' and the 'laggards' to take a mega-regional scale, which is to say, a scale that includes both globalizing and 'laggard' cities and metropolitan regions. But this connecting of winners and laggards can also be extended to cross-border intercity networks by strengthening the connections between winners and laggards across borders.

One consequence is that not only winners get privileged, as is becoming common with 'targetting' of resources to enable the formation of world-class cities, but also laggards insofar as they are dynamically interconnected within a mega region and/or within a cross-border network. It might mean that rather than pursuing only economic policies focused on the most advanced sectors there is also a strong case for concentrating upon the poorer regions, not as charity but as a recognition that they are part of the new economic dynamic that combines a need for dispersed, lower-cost areas and dense high-cost areas. To mention just one of several examples, this type of framing would bring value to poorer areas within the richer (OECD) countries as these might be developed to become advantageous for the location of activities that are now being outsourced to low-wage countries. The aim would be to avoid a race to the bottom and to provide alternative development paths rather than only privileging development concepts that target high-end economic activities, such as bio-tech parks and luxury office parks.

Secondly, the chapter will examine some of the key challenges these developments generate for globalizing cities and urban areas, from economic to social. A critical question here is what will happen if current policy and development trajectories are simply allowed to continue? To address this question the chapter uses the case of the 'knowledge economy' as a window onto a whole range of issues confronting cities and urban regions. What is the role of cities in regional competitiveness and how can current territorial and urban policies be drawn together more effectively? This focus can also add to our understanding of 'soft' policy instruments – for example in higher education, skills, innovation, enterprise and social policy areas – that can be reconfigured in order to face these challenges more effectively, and to get a sense of what needs to change and why. For instance, even the most advanced sectors need a range of jobs (truckers, cleaners, and so on) and economic sectors ('urban manufacturing' and certain components of the new types of informal economy) we usually fail to recognize as belonging to an advanced economy. Identifying these types of articulations should help in identifying how sector-specific policies should be working together in many cases where they are not; we need to recognize that a strong advanced services sector may need a well-functioning urban manufacturing sector. Another type of articulation that needs to be recognized is that certain non-urban policies actually can have strong effects on cities and urban regions.

CORE ELEMENTS IN TODAY'S CITIES AND URBAN REGIONS

Here I introduce the main lines of analysis developed in this chapter. I first briefly address the two novel spatial formations referred to above and their implications for policy and the socio-economic reality of cities and urban regions. Next I briefly address the knowledge economy and the soft policy issues it engenders. These two in short are a summary of respectively the first and second half of this chapter.

Novel Spatial Formations: (a) Mega Regions

One major tendency evident throughout the world is the formation of increasingly large urban scales, which at some point are best described as mega regions. Often these are merely seen as more of the same – more people, more endless urban landscapes. At its most elemental the mega region results from population growth in a geographic setting where cities and metro-areas blend into each other. And this does indeed call for cross-regional infrastructures, notably transport and electricity, and various forms of regional planning and coordination, as can be seen today. But are these conditions, which amount to an expanded version of urbanization economies, all there is to consider?

The mega region emerges as a sufficiently internally diverse territory, where novel development strategies might be explored to the advantage of both the more advanced and the least advanced areas within the region. It takes innovative governance umbrellas and new types of private–public arrangement. Familiar advantages of scales larger than that of the city, such as metropolitan and regional scales, come from sharing transport infrastructures for people and goods, enabling robust housing markets and, possibly, supporting the development of office, science and technology parks. More complex and elusive is whether the benefits of mega-regional economic interaction can go beyond these familiar scale economies. There is no definitive research on this subject. Thus empirical specification can only be partial as the available evidence is fragmentary for the urban level, a shortcoming that becomes acute when dealing with the novel category of the mega region.[1] There is, however, enough analysis and evidence on one particular component of this subject – the advantages for global firms and markets of particular types of agglomeration economies at the urban level – that we can begin to use it as a lens onto the mega-regional scale. Agglomeration economies are to be distinguished from familiar urbanization economies. They involve complex interactions of diverse components, not simply, for instance, more people using a train line and the scale economies this might enable.

The specific advantages of the mega-regional scale consist of and arise from the co-existence within one regional space of multiple types of agglomeration economies. These types of agglomeration economies today are distributed across diverse economic spaces and geographic scales: central business districts, office parks, science parks, the transportation and housing efficiencies derived from large (but not too large) commuter belts, low-cost manufacturing districts (today often offshore), tourism destinations, specialized branches of agriculture, such as horticulture or organically grown food, and the complex kinds evident in global cities. Each of these spaces evinces distinct agglomeration economies and empirically at least, is found in diverse types of geographic settings – from urban to rural, from local to global.

The thesis is that a mega region is sufficiently large and diverse so as to accommodate a far broader range of types of agglomeration economies and geographic settings than it typically does today. This would take the advantages of mega-regional location beyond the notion of urbanization economies. A mega region can then be seen as a scale that can benefit from the fact that our complex economies need diverse types of agglomeration economies and geographic settings, from extremely high agglomeration economies evinced by the specialized advanced corporate services to the fairly modest economies evinced by suburban office parks and regional labor-intensive low-wage manufacturing. It can incorporate this diversity into a single economic mega zone. Indeed, in principle, it could create conditions for the return of particular (not all) activities now outsourced to other regions or to foreign locations.[2]

Thus the critical dimension for the purposes of this chapter is not just a question of the contents of a mega region, such as its economic sectors, transport infrastructure, housing markets, types of goods and services that get produced and distributed, exported and imported – a sort of x ray of a mega region. Also critical is the specification of economic interactions within the mega region in order to detect what could be re-incorporated into that region (for example, factories or routine clerical work that is now outsourced to other national or foreign areas) as well as to detect emerging mega-regional advantages.

Novel Spatial Formations: (b) Cross-border Economic Networks

To get at the question of cities and the global economy, it helps to specify the multiple global circuits through which cities are connecting across borders. Particular networks connect particular groups of cities. This allows us to recover details about the diverse roles of cities in the global economy. The formation of inter-city geographies is contributing a socio-technical infrastructure for a new global political economy, new cultural spaces and new types of social networks. Some of these inter-city geographies are thick and highly visible – the flows of professionals, tourists, artists and migrants among specific groups of cities. Others are thin and barely visible – the highly specialized electronic financial trading networks that connect particular cities depending on the type of instrument involved. A bit thicker are the global commodity chains for diverse products that run from exporting hubs to importing hubs.

The sample of cities examined comes from a study of 75 cities studied in terms of 60 variables ranging from economic to social.

The Knowledge Economy and Place

The deep economic history of a place is actually one critical variable in the development of a competitive knowledge economy. If this is so, then one of the things that matters in a global economy is the specific difference of a city and of a region. This positions cities and urban regions in terms of their specific differences rather than, as it is common to assert, in direct competition with all kinds of cities which are all becoming similar. The argument goes against two very common notions: (i) that 'the' knowledge economy is some sort of standardized, no matter how state-of-the-art, entity, which reduces policy to the effort to capture some of that knowledge economy that seems to float above everything, and bring it into an area; and (ii) that for the knowledge economy to take hold in an area, and to develop, it has to overcome/surpass/destroy its older material economies (manufacturing, mining, agriculture, and so on). My research suggests that the strongest knowledge economies have complex imbrications with the deep economic history of a place (city, region).

The second argument is that the knowledge economy depends on a larger social and economic infrastructure that has mostly been rendered invisible and been devalued. Knowledge economies are easily reduced to their 'knowledge' components. Yet they (a) require non-knowledge-economy components: for example producing a financial instrument requires not only knowledge and software, but also a range of material conditions, including truckers to bring the software, and (b) knowledge economies are often embedded in non-knowledge economy sectors: for example the knowledge economy component might be embedded in rather elementary manufactured goods (a toaster, a washing machine), and not only high-tech goods or non-material goods.

Both arguments signal that much more complex understandings are needed of the parameters and conditionalities of knowledge economies, and of its implications for urban and regional development. There are policy implications for each of these arguments, and they can go in unexpected directions or directions that do not correspond to many of the widespread notions about the knowledge economy and the policies that seek to promote it.

SCALING AND ITS CONSEQUENCES

Moving from the scale of the city to that of an urbanized region alters the analytics. A region easily contains sites that evince agglomeration economies and sites that offer the option of geographic dispersal of activities. Beyond this, questions of power and inequality play out rather differently when regions and cities are compared. To sharpen the focus, the discussion in this section of the chapter is confined to global cities and global-city regions. The concept of the global-city region adds a whole new dimension to questions of territory and globalization.[3] This type of comparison illustrates some of the issues developed in the more analytic discussion of the preceding sections. And it makes the argument in a more descriptive manner, so even if a reader rejects the analytics of the preceding section it still leaves room for the empirics.

A first difference concerns the question of territory. The territorial scale of the region is far more likely to include a cross-section of a country's economic activities than the scale of the city. For instance, it is likely to include as key variables manufacturing and a range of standardized economic sectors that are at the heart of the national economy. This, in turn, brings with it a more benign manifestation of globalization. The concept of the global city introduces a far stronger emphasis on strategic components of the global economy, typically subject to extreme agglomeration economies in top level management functions and specialized corporate servicing; this in turn can lead to extreme forms of power and inequality in the global city. Secondly, the concept of the global city will tend to have a stronger emphasis on the networked economy because of the nature of the industries that tend to be located there: finance, media and other specialized services. And, thirdly, it will tend to have more of an emphasis on economic and spatial polarization because of the disproportionate demand for very high and very low income jobs in these cities compared with what would be the case for the region which would have far more middle range firms and workers.

Overall, the concept of the global city is more attuned to questions of power and inequality. The concept of the global-city region is more attuned to questions about the nature and specifics of broad urbanization patterns, a more encompassing economic base, more middle sectors of both households and firms, and hence to the possibility of having a more even distribution of economic benefits under current economic growth dynamics, including economic globalization. In this regard, it could be said that the concept of the global-city region allows us to see the possibilities for a more distributed kind of growth and a wider spread of the benefits associated with economic growth, including growth resulting from globalization.

Secondly, both concepts have a problem with boundaries of at least two sorts, the boundary of the territorial scale as such and the boundary of the spread of globalization in the organizational structure of industries, institutional orders, places, and so on. In the case of the global city I have opted for an analytic strategy that emphasizes core dynamics rather than the unit of the city as a container – a container being an entity that requires territorial boundary specification. Emphasizing core dynamics and their spatialization (in both actual and digital space) does not completely solve the boundary problem, but it does allow for a fairly clear trade-off between emphasizing the core or center of these dynamics and their spread institutionally and spatially. In my work I have sought to deal with both sides of this trade-off by emphasizing, on the one side, the most advanced and globalized industries such as finance, and, on the other side, how the informal economy (typically seen as local) in major global cities is articulated with some of the leading industries. In the case of the global-city region, it is not clear to me how Scott (2001) specifies the boundary question both in its territorial sense and in terms of its organization and spread.

A third difference is the emphasis on competition and competitiveness, much stronger in the global-city region construct. The nature itself of the leading industries in global cities strengthens the importance of cross-border networks and specialized divisions of functions among cities in different countries and/or regions rather than international competition per se. Further, though competitiveness is a necessary condition, it is far less prominent in these sectors which tend to flag 'talent' as their key rather than competence, than it would be in developing regional rapid rail where the question of competence (rather than speculative talent, for instance) is essential. Global finance and the leading specialized services catering to global firms and markets – law, accounting, credit rating, telecommunications – constitute cross-border circuits embedded in networks of cities, each possibly part of a different country. It is a *de facto* global system, centered in more than competition and competitiveness.

The industries that will tend to dominate global-city regions are less likely to be networked along these lines. For instance, in the case of large manufacturing complexes, and of final and intermediate consumption complexes, the identification with the national is stronger and the often stronger orientation to consumer markets brings to the fore the question of quality, prices and the possibility of substitution. Hence competition and competitiveness are likely to be far more prominent. Further, even when there is significant offshoring of production and in this regard an international division of production, as in the auto industry, this type of internationalization tends to be in the form of the chain of production internal to a given firm, which today can cross borders. Insofar as most firms still have their central headquarters associated with a specific region and country, the competition question is likely to be prominent and, very importantly, sited – that is, it is the US versus the Japanese auto manufacturers, though even this is changing.

The question of the competitiveness of a region is deeply centered in its conventional infrastructure – transport of all sorts, water and electricity supply and distribution, airports, and so on. To some extent this is also a crucial variable in the case of global cities, but it is a far more specialized type of infrastructure in the latter. The regional scale brings to the fore questions of public transport, highway construction and kindred aspects in a way that the focus on global cities does not. Again, it reveals to what extent a focus on the region produces a more benevolent representation of the impacts of the global economy. A focus on the regional infrastructure is far more likely to include strong consideration of middle class needs. In contrast, a focus on the global city will tend to bring to the fore the growing inequalities between highly provisioned and profoundly disadvantaged sectors and spaces of the city, and hence questions of power and inequality.

A fourth difference, connected to the preceding one, is that a focus on networked cross-border dynamics among global cities also allows us to capture more readily the growing intensity of such transactions in other domains – political, cultural, social and criminal.[4] There is growing evidence of greater cross-border transactions among immigrant communities and communities of origin and a greater intensity in the use of these networks once they become established, including for economic activities that had been unlikely until now. There is also evidence of greater cross-border networks for cultural purposes, as in the growth of international markets for art and a transnational class of curators; and for non-formal political purposes, as in the growth of transnational networks of activists around environmental causes, human rights, and so on. These are largely city-to-city cross-border networks, or, at least, it appears at this time to be simpler to capture the existence and modalities of these networks at the city level. The same can be said for the new cross-border criminal networks. Dealing with the regional scale does not necessarily facilitate recognizing the existence of such networks from one region to the other. It is far more likely to be from one specific community in a region to another specific community in another region, thereby neutralizing the meaning of the region as such.

One key implication of this comparison is the need to control for some of the inevitable differences that are a function of scale per se. There is a risk of reifying the spatial organization of a bounded terrain, whether that is a city, a region or a mega region. Comparing a city and a region does add important information to our effort of understanding the variability of location and of the advantages of proximity. But it is also a fact that the reality of a mega region may well rest on dynamics that underlie both of these – city and region.

Part of the task of specifying mega regions needs to get at these sharp differences within a region and at the possibly shared dynamics underlying these differences; thus the multipolarity and geographic dispersal that characterize these mega regions may in part also feed agglomeration economies in these regions' cities arising precisely out of that dispersal. A critical question is whether some of these diverse formations – multipolarity, dispersal, agglomeration – can be re-regionalized. This can take two forms, one more elementary and one more complex. The elementary one is increasing the range of formations that could be incorporated within a mega region, rather than only thinking in terms of the high end of an economic sector or a firm's operations, as is often done. The complex form is to increase the range of formations that are part of a given growth sector or a firm's multi-sited chain of operations. Such a re-regionalizing of the components of economic growth could emerge as a major advantage of mega regions.

MEGA REGIONS

The chapter seeks to identify possible types of intraregional economic interactions that could be enabled by the mega-regional scale. The concern is to understand two things: first, whether such interactions might mean moving beyond economic planning styles that search to capture only the most advanced economic sectors, such as 'knowledge economies', and begin to find value in areas within a region that are not advanced economic spaces; and second, whether this might in turn give mega regions particular advantages in today's global economy. If both of these are indeed the case, it is useful to ask whether and how novel types of mega-regional coordination and governance could be helpful. The central effort is to take the benefits of mega regions beyond the familiar scale economies.

One critical dimension in this effort is to examine whether a mega region is a scale that can benefit from the fact that our complex economies evince diverse types of agglomeration economies and geographic setting, from very high (for example the specialized advanced corporate services) to fairly modest (for example suburban office parks and labor-intensive low-wage manufacturing). A mega region can incorporate this diversity into a single economic mega zone. Indeed, in principle, it could create conditions for the return of particular (not all) activities now outsourced to other regions or to foreign locations. This would expand the project of optimizing growth beyond the usual preference for state-of-the-art sectors (such as office and science parks) and include a greater diversity of economic sectors. A second critical dimension examined concerns the growth effects resulting from the interactions of a firm's diverse types of sites: from the perspective of a mega region this means that both a firm's top level headquarters and its low-cost routine work add yet another specific source of growth for the region, one beyond the mere sum of the jobs involved.

One way of specifying some of this empirically is to establish whether agglomeration economies (not just urbanization economies) matter for developing the spatial organization of a mega region. Examining the question of agglomeration economies in the current period is framed by two facts that are potentially in tension with each other. On the one hand, the new information technologies enable firms to disperse a growing range of their operations, whether at the metro, regional, or global level, without losing system integration;[5] this has the potential to reduce (though not eliminate) the benefits of urbanization economics for such firms. On the other hand, the evidence clearly shows the urbanizing and densifying of massive regions, including scale-ups to the mega-regional level as identified for instance by RPA for the case of the US.[6]

The chapter first addresses the most extreme instance – globalized firms with considerable digitization of their production process and their outputs. In this case there are conceivably fewer and fewer agglomeration advantages, especially for the most advanced sectors, typically high-value producing, able to buy the latest technologies, and highly globalized, that is, with multiple operations across the world.

Contesting this technologically-driven explanation, the chapter describes how and why precisely these firms are subject to extreme agglomeration economies in some – not all – of their components.[7] This fact matters for understanding mega-regional advantage because mega regions also contain extremely dense cities with diverse resources and types of talent. A second implication for the mega region is that the 'multi-sited' character of the leading economic sectors includes cities as one key site, but these advanced sectors also have other sites – some marked by medium and even low or no agglomeration economies, with some economies of scale, but strong preferences for low-cost, often underdeveloped areas.

What gives this added meaning is a third implication for the mega-regional scale which has to do with the growth effects resulting from interactions of a firm's diverse types of sites: a firm's central headquarter functions expand as a result of that multi-sidedness (whether national or global).[8] This is a growth potential that builds on the second point above in that the co-presence of a firm's top level headquarters and low-cost routine work adds yet another specific source of growth for a mega region that contains both; that is to say, this is a growth effect that goes beyond the mere addition of jobs resulting from that mega region capturing more sites of a firm's chain of operations.

Now the question becomes: can a mega region seek to accommodate a larger range of the operations constituting a firm's value chain – from those subject to agglomeration economies to those that do not evince such economies? Practically speaking this points to the possibility of bringing into (in some cases, back to) a mega region some of the services and goods now produced offshore to get at lower wages and less regulations. Can these be reinserted in the low-growth, low-cost areas of a mega region? What type of planning would it take, and can it be done so as to optimize the benefits for all involved, not only firms, but also workers and localities? This would expand the project of optimizing growth beyond the usual suspects – office and science parks being one notable example – and move across far more diverse economic sectors. It would use the lever of the mega-regional scale to provide diverse spaces catering to different types of activities, ranging from those subject to high to those subject to low agglomeration economies. And, finally, the mega-regional scale would help in optimizing the growth effect arising from the interactions of some of these diverse agglomeration economies. This growth effect would be optimized by re-regionalizing some of the low-cost operations of firms today spread across the country and/or the world.

If this type of thesis does indeed capture a potential of mega regions, it would be the making of new economic history. The possibility of this type of potential is easily obscured by the prevalence of national level economic indicators, data sets, and policies. Identifying the mega region produces an intermediate level, one that even though partly dependent on national macro-policies also inserts a far more specific set of issues into the economic picture.[9] A mega region can combine a very large share of the diverse economies that are very much part of our current era. And it can incorporate growth effects arising from the interactions of some of these diverse economies.

This way of thinking about the mega-regional scale raises the importance of planning and coordination to secure optimal outcomes for all parties involved, including the challenge of securing the benefits firms are after when they disperse their operations to low-wage areas. This would work for some types of economic sectors and types of firms, not for all. Some activities that have been outsourced to other countries have not worked out and have been repatriated – they range from airline sales agents to particular types of design work in industries as diverse as garments and high-tech. But many of these outsourced activities are doing fine as far as the firms are concerned. Research and specific policies are needed to establish the what, how and where of the advantages for the pertinent firms of accessing low-wage workers in the US; this includes understanding how the location of these low-cost components in the mega region where a given firm is headquartered could compensate for higher costs. This may require mega-regional investment in developing low-cost areas for such jobs – a kind of rural enterprise zone.

There is possibly a positive macro-level effect from repatriating some of these jobs if a race to the bottom can be avoided and a certain level of consumption capacity secured via reasonable wages or particular indirect subsidies. This brings a specific positive effect for a mega region's less developed areas insofar as lower-wage households tend to spend a much larger share of their income in their place of residence – they lack the investment capital of the upper income strata who can wind up allocating most of their income on overseas investments. Finally, this is also one element in the larger challenge of securing more equitable outcomes.[10] It is important to ask about the distributive effects of the current configuration and of (potentially) optimized outcomes as described in this chapter; there is sufficient evidence of how extreme ill distribution of the benefits of economic growth is not desirable in the long run.

These ways of specifying the meaning of a mega region (or a region) take us from a 'packaging' approach to a more dynamic concept of the mega region: beyond urbanization advantages, a mega region may well turn out to be sufficiently large scale to optimize the benefits of containing multiple and interacting agglomeration economies.

PROXIMITY AND ITS ADVANTAGES: DOES IT HOLD FOR MEGA REGIONS?

Today's information technologies and communication capabilities can deliver system integration no matter how far-flung the operations of a firm or sector might be. If all firms and sectors can buy/use these technologies to reduce or neutralize agglomeration economies/advantages, the result would be a decline in the benefits of locations that deliver agglomeration economies, most notably global cities. Such a decline would be further strengthened by the possibility of rising shares of e-commuters – working online from home.

In its most extreme version this scenario suggests that the advantages of locating in a mega region would be limited to urbanization economies. Firms need to locate somewhere and so do their workers, so why not a mega region; and, secondly, regardless of whether there are or not specific mega-regional locational advantages, there would be a demand for local suppliers of final and intermediate goods and services that need to be produced *in situ* – that cannot be imported from far away, or at least not yet. The fact itself of population growth – a fact in most of the RPA mega regions – is enough to feed this type of demand.

Under these conditions, the specificity of mega-regional locational advantages comes down to the fact that there is a market, or rather a whole range of markets, for needed goods and services, both final and intermediate. Transport, housing, office buildings, factory buildings, and so on, all meet a real demand by households, governments and their multiple instances, from schools to courts, institutions of all sorts, and firms. As populations and distances grow, novel types of demand emerge: for speed-rail, super highways, more diversity in the housing supply. No matter how complex the components of this final and intermediate demand, this is, in some ways, a very elementary version of the advantages of the mega-regional scale.

ARE THERE MORE COMPLEX ADVANTAGES FOR MEGA-REGIONAL LOCATION?

The starting point is that location is a variable. The firm that can replace agglomeration advantages with the new information technologies represents one extreme case on the location variable: it evinces minor if any agglomeration economies. The fact of population growth and the associated need for housing and all that comes with it, is in many ways the same type of point on that variable; the difference is that it is subject to urbanization advantages. At the other end of these two cases is high agglomeration economies; this is well-established for very specialized branches of global finance and the most innovative branches of high-tech industries, with global cities and silicon valleys the respective emblematic spatial forms.

The advantages of location in a mega region in these three diverse types of instances need to be specified empirically. In the first two cases the particular advantage is some very broad, and geographically expanded, notion of urbanization advantages – the bundle of infrastructures, labor markets, buildings, housing, basic institutional resources, amenities. In a mega region these advantages spread over a vast geographic terrain, engendering its own specific components of final and intermediate demand, for example rapid-transit systems.

The question then becomes how to enhance these urbanization advantages, how to avoid excess growth/expansion/spread and its negative effects on congestion, prices, costs, and so on. Whether markets or planning are the desirable instruments to optimize 'urbanization' economies (broadly understood in that they include not only urban locations) will depend on a range of variables. One potentially innovative line of analysis here is the extent to which the mega region enables novel ways of handling negative externalities.

On the other hand, in the case of sectors subject to agglomeration economies, it may well be the case that the mega region does not contain distinctive advantages over other scales, notably cities and metro areas. What these sectors seem to need is a bundle of resources that correlate with high density and, at its extreme, very dense central places – such as global cities and silicon valleys. The question then becomes whether there is one or several specific types of agglomeration economies that can develop, and be enhanced, at the scale of the mega region. Mega regions contain high-density locations; a firm subject to agglomeration economies may well find the mix of highly specialized diverse resources it needs in one of those locations. But does it need a whole mega region attached to that location?

Here, a new theoretical and empirical territory opens up. One critical hypothesis developed for the global city model is that insofar as the geographic dispersal of the operations of global firms (whether factories, offices, or service outlets) feeds the complexity of central headquarter locations, the more globalized a firm the higher the advantages its headquarters derive from central locations (see note 8).[11] One inference is that the advantage of a mega-regional scale is that it could, in principle, contain both the central headquarters and at least some of those dispersed operations of global firms. In other words, is a mega region a scale at which such firms can actually also 'outsource jobs' and suburbanize headquarter functions – both in search of cheaper costs – and benefit from the region's major city(s), including in some cases, global cities, or cities with significant global-city functions?

Can mega regions deliver particular advantages if they can also contain some of the geographically dispersed operations of a firm? The evidence shows that increasingly the spatial organization of firms and economic sectors contains both points of spatial concentration and points of dispersal. Further, the evidence also shows that in many cases these points of spatial concentration contain segments in a firm's chain of operations that evince rather strong agglomeration economies. One underlying (and disciplining) trend here, becoming visible already in the 1970s, is that spatial concentration is costlier for many firms so that the push is to disperse whatever operations can be dispersed; this contrasts with earlier periods when even large headquarters kept all functions in one place. This dispersal of a firm's operations can be at a regional, national and/or global level, and agglomerations might vary sharply in content and in the specifics of the corresponding spatial form.[12] For instance, just to refer to US cases, Chicago's financial center, Los Angeles' Hollywood, Northern California's Silicon Valley, each deliver agglomeration economies to firms and sectors which also contain often vast geographic dispersal of some of their other operations.

A focus on the fact that much economic activity contains both spatial concentration and trans-local chains of operations helps us situate the specifics of a city, a metro area, or a mega region in a far broader systemic condition, one that might include both points subject to sharp agglomeration economies and points that are not – where geographic dispersal is an advantage. What the mega region offers in this context is a bigger range of types of locations than a city or a metro area – from locations subject to high agglomeration economies all the way to locations where the advantage comes from dispersal.

Taking it a step further, most globalized and innovative firms were characterized by the fact that agglomeration economies are themselves partly a function of dispersal. That is to say, the more globalized and thus geographically dispersed a firm's operations, the more likely the presence of agglomeration economies in particular moments (the production of top-level headquarter functions) of that firm's chain of operations.[13] For the purposes of this chapter, it underlines the fact of a single dynamic with diverse specializations, that is both agglomeration and dispersal, across diverse geographic scalings; a mega region would then conceivably be a scaling that can incorporate these different settings.

One way of specifying some of this empirically is to posit a direct

relation between growth in a mega region's locations for dispersed economic activities and locations for activities subject to high agglomeration
economies. The more the former grow, the more the latter will also grow.
The trick is then to maximize the co-presence in a given mega region of
these two types of locations. It is important to notice that this also sets
limits to the advantages of urbanization economies. The latter turn out to
be a curve: they grow with scale, but up to a point. That point is typically
specified in terms of negative externalities. But what my analysis here suggests is that this point can also be specified in terms of the economic losses
derived from not allowing the 'development' of dispersal locations; since
this means locations where firms can send their low-wage jobs requiring
little education, it clearly goes against the prevailing aims of most places,
which is to get high-wage, high-capital-intensive jobs. Finally, if what is
today the point on the curve where familiar negative externalities set in
(for example excess congestion) can be made to coincide with that development of 'dispersal locations' for firms, an advantage could be made out
of what is now a disadvantage.

In practical terms there are, clearly, massive challenges for a mega
region to achieve this type of co-presence – maximizing the extent to which
a mega region can contain both the agglomeration and dispersal segments
of a firm's chain of operations. For one, it is a countersensical, counterintuitive proposition. It is not easy to see why a mega region's highly
dynamic economic spaces (the central areas of its global cities and silicon
valleys), anchored by the headquarters of global and national firms, might
actually be partly fed and strengthened by developing the 'dispersal locations' of those same firms. Thinking of developing such dispersal locations
as one way of making the most of negative externalities might make it
more acceptable to the sceptics – you might as well go for activities that
benefit from geographically dispersed arrangements once you hit excess
congestion disadvantages. But one option at this point is of course such
items as golf courses and ex-urban luxury housing. This is an argument
that could be countered since mega regions tend to contain much land that
is not optimal for such uses, but that could be optimal for developing dispersal locations; further, and critical to some of my substantive concerns
for disadvantaged areas, these could benefit from such development, if a
race to the bottom is avoided.

The mega region can then be seen as an interesting scalar geography: it
can contain some of the dispersals of a firm's operations that feed these
new kinds of agglomeration economies. It would suggest that strategic
regional planning could aim at maximizing the combination of different
locational logics. It is this combination that in my view marks the specificity of the 'project' contained in the notion of the mega region. This

kind of region cannot be looked at simply as an outcome: there it is, and let us then find a packaging that brings a lot of this together under one umbrella. As a term, mega region has a certain passivity attached to it. Mega-regional agglomeration economies, on the other hand, is a notion that captures a dynamic that produces outcomes. This in turn opens up a research agenda: for instance, to understand at what territorial scales such economies are enhanced or become weaker. Mega region is, however, a catchy term, describing a self-evident condition, and in that sense is an acceptable and digestible term (something that cannot be said about mega-regional agglomeration economies).

The hypothesis here could be framed as follows: the more an urban region is being shaped by the new economic dynamics, the more its spatial organization will involve agglomeration economies as a function of geographic dispersal of economic activities under conditions of systemic integration, no matter the scale – regional, national or global.

The next section examines one critical aspect of such a co-presence: does geographic dispersal feed agglomeration economies? I take the extreme case – the most digitized and globalized firms – as a natural experiment to understand the parameters of the articulation between geographic dispersal and agglomeration economies, and what it would mean to regionalize this articulation.

DOES GEOGRAPHIC DISPERSAL FEED AGGLOMERATION ECONOMIES?

A good starting point is to focus on why the most advanced firms of the knowledge economy are subject to what seem often extreme agglomeration economies, even when they function in electronic markets and produce digitized outputs. Another way to ask it is by focusing on the most globalized and digitized of all knowledge sectors: Why does global finance need financial centers? Or, more generally, why do highly specialized global corporate services that can be transmitted digitally thrive in dense downtowns? This means inserting place in an analysis of knowledge economies that are usually examined in terms of their mobility and space–time compression. Looking at the knowledge economy and, more broadly, global firms, from the optic of regions, cities or metro-areas, brings in different variables.[14]

Much is known about the wealth and power of today's global firms. Their ascendance in a globalizing world is no longer surprising. Similarly, with the new information and communication technologies, much attention has focused on their enormous capacities for worldwide operations without losing central control. Less clear is why cities or regions should matter for global firms, particularly global firms that are rich enough to buy whatever the technical innovations that free them from place, its frictions and its costs. There are several logics that explain why cities matter to the most globalized (dispersed) and digitized firms and sectors in a way they did not as recently as the 1970s. Here three of these logics are taken into account.[15]

The first one is that no matter how intensive a user of digital technology a firm is, its operational logic is not the same as the engineer's logic for designing that technology. Confusing these two potentially very diverse logics has produced a whole series of misunderstandings. When the new information and communications technologies (ICTs) began to be widely used in the 1980s, many experts 'forecasted' the end of cities as strategic spaces for firms in advanced sectors. Many routinized sectors did leave cities, and many firms dispersed their more routine operations to the regional, national and global scale. But the most advanced sectors and firms kept expanding their top-level operations in particular types of cities.

Why were those experts so wrong? They overlooked a key factor: when firms and markets use these new technologies they do so with financial or economic objectives in mind, not the objectives of the engineer who designed the technology. The logics of users may well thwart or reduce the full technical capacities of the technology.[16] When firms and markets disperse many of their operations globally with the help of the new technologies, the intention is not to relinquish control over these operations. The intention is to keep control over top-level matters and to be capable of appropriating the benefits/profits of that dispersal.[17] Insofar as central control is part of the globalizing of activities, their top-level headquarter functions actually have expanded because it is simply more complicated and riskier to function in 30 or 50 or more countries, each with distinct laws, accounting rules and business cultures.

As these technologies are increasingly helpful in maintaining centralized control over globally dispersed operations, their use has also fed the expansion of central operations. The result has been an increase in high-level office operations in major cities and a growth in the demand for high-level and highly-paid professional services, either produced in-house or bought from specialized service firms. Thus the more these technologies enable global geographic dispersal of corporate activities, the more they produce density and centrality at the other end – the cities where their headquarter functions get done.

A second logic explaining the ongoing advantages of spatial agglomeration has to do precisely with the complexity and specialization level of central functions. These rise with globalization and with the added speed that the new ICTs allow. As a result global firms increasingly need to buy the most specialized financial, legal, accounting, consulting and other such services. These service firms get to do some of the most difficult and speculative work. It is increasingly these corporate service firms that evince agglomeration economies, as their work benefits from being in complex environments that function as knowledge centers because they contain multiple other specialized firms and high-level professionals with worldwide experience. Cities are such environments –with the 40 plus global cities in the world the most significant of these environments, but a growing number of other cities strong in particular elements of such environments. In brief, cities or central places provide the social connectivity which allows a firm to maximize the benefits of its technological connectivity.[18]

A third logic concerns the meaning of information in an information economy. There are two types of information. One is the datum, which may be complex yet is standard knowledge: the level at which a stock market closes, a privatization of a public utility, a bankruptcy. But there is a far more difficult type of 'information', akin to an interpretation/ evaluation/judgment. It entails negotiating a series of data and a series of interpretations of a mix of data in the hope of producing a higher-order datum. Access to the first kind of information is now global and immediate (even if often for a high fee) from just about any place in the highly developed world and increasingly in the rest of the world thanks to the digital revolution.

But it is the second type of information that requires a complicated mixture of elements – the 'social infrastructure' for global connectivity – which gives major financial centers a leading edge. When the more complex forms of information needed to execute major international deals cannot be gotten from existing data bases, no matter what one can pay, then one needs to make that information; it becomes part of the production process in specialized corporate service firms, including financial services both as service providers and as firms in their own right. That making includes as critical components interpretation, inference and speculation. At this point one needs the social information loop and the associated *de facto* interpretations and inferences that come with bouncing off information among talented, informed people. It is the importance of this input that has given a whole new importance to credit rating agencies, for instance. Part of the rating has to do with interpreting and inferring. When this interpreting becomes 'authoritative' it becomes 'information' available to all. For specialized firms in these complex domains, credit ratings are but one of these inputs; the making of authoritative information needs to be part of a production process, either in-house or bought from specialized firms. This process of making inferences/interpretations into 'information' takes an exceptional mix of talents and resources. Cities are complex environments that can deliver this mix.

The key implication of this analysis for mega regions is the possibility of containing both (at least some of) the dispersed operations of a given firm and the central headquarter operations. The feedback effects of containing both can be significant, feeding simultaneously growth in a mega region's low-cost possibly marginal areas and in its global cities, or cities that are national business centers.

THE ONGOING IMPORTANCE OF CENTRAL PLACES

Cities have historically provided national economies, polities and societies with something that can be thought of as centrality. The usual urban form for centrality has been density, specifically the dense downtown. The economic functions delivered through urban density in cities have varied across time. But it is always a variety of agglomeration economies, no matter how much their content might vary depending on the sector involved. While the financial sector is quite different from the cultural sector, both evince agglomeration economies; but the content of these benefits can vary sharply. One of the advantages of central urban density is that it has historically helped solve the risk of insufficient variety. It brings with it diverse labor markets, diverse networks of firms and colleagues, massive concentrations of diverse types of information on the latest developments and diverse marketplaces. The new information and communication technologies (ICTs) should have neutralized the advantages of centrality and density. No matter where a firm or professional is, there should be access to many of the needed resources. But in fact, the new ICTs have not quite eliminated the advantages of centrality and density, and hence the distinct role of cities for leading global firms.[19]

Even as much economic activity has dispersed, the centers of a growing number of cities have expanded physically, at times simply spreading and at times in a multi-nodal fashion. The outcome is a new type of space of centrality in these cities and their metro-areas: it has physically expanded over the last two decades, a fact that can actually be measured, and it can assume more varied formats. The geographic terrain for these new centralities is not always simply that of the downtown; it can be metropolitan and even regional. In this process, the geographic space in a city or metro area that becomes centralized often grows denser as measured in number of firms, though not necessarily households, than it was in the 1960s and 1970s. This holds for cities as different as Zurich and Sydney, Sao Paulo and London, Shanghai and Buenos Aires (although population density is not necessarily the best indicator of this type of density).

The global trend of expanded newly built and rebuilt centralized space suggests an ironic turn of events for the impact of ITCs on urban centrality. Clearly, the spatial dispersal of economic activities and workers at the metropolitan, national and global level that began to accelerate in the 1980s actually is only half the story of what is happening. New forms of territorial centralization of top-level management and control operations have appeared alongside these well-documented spatial dispersals. National and global markets as well as globally integrated operations require central places where the work of globalization gets done, as analyzed in the preceding section.

Centrality remains a key feature of today's global economy. But today there is no longer a simple straightforward relation between centrality and such geographic entities as the downtown, or the central business district (CBD). In the past, and up to quite recently in fact, centrality was synonymous with the downtown or the CBD. Today, partly as a result of the new ICTs, the spatial correlates of the 'center' can assume several geographic forms, ranging from the CBD, the metro area, to the new global grid comprising global cities.[20]

Particular urban, metro and regional spaces are becoming massive concentrations of new technical capabilities. A growing number of buildings are the sites for a multiplication of interactive technologies and distributed computing. And particular global communication infrastructures are connecting specific sets of buildings worldwide, producing a highly specialized interactive geography, with global firms willing to pay a high premium in order to be located in it. For instance, AT&T's global business network now connects about 485000 buildings worldwide; this is a specific geography that actually fragments the cities where these buildings are located as you need to be in a 'member' building to access the network. The most highly valued areas of global cities, particularly financial centers, now contain communication infrastructures that can be separated from the rest of the city, allowing continuous upgrading without having to spread it to the rest of the city. And they contain particular technical capabilities, such as frame relays, which most of the rest of the city does not. Multiplying this case for thousands of multinational firms begins to give us an idea of this new inter-city connectivity, largely invisible to the average resident.

One question is whether some of these trans-local operations are actually located within some of the mega regions that concern this chapter.

This is an empirical question, but one with policy/planning implications. Similarly, if these globally networked spaces of centrality are seen as platforms for global operations of firms and markets, it is important to ask what components of these platforms are contained within a given mega region. Finally, these platforms consist of a variety of specific geographic sub-national spaces but also electronic spaces. Hence it is important to ask what are the implications for mega regions of the fact that a growing number of sub-national scales – from cities to precisely such mega regions – emerge as strategic territories that contribute to articulate a new global political economy, and new national and regional political economies.

CROSS-BORDER NETWORKS: AN URBANIZED SPATIAL FORM

One way of thinking about the global economy is in terms of the many highly specialized circuits that make it up. Different circuits contain different groups of countries and cities. Viewed this way, the global economy becomes concrete and specific, with a well-defined geography. Globally traded commodities – gold, butter, coffee, oil, sunflower seeds – are redistributed to a vast number of destinations, no matter how few the points of origin are in some cases. With globalization, this capacity to redistribute globally has grown sharply.

These circuits are multidirectional and criss-cross the world, feeding into inter-city geographies with both expected and unexpected strategic nodes. For instance, New York is the leading global market to trade financial instruments on coffee even though it does not grow a single bean. But a far less powerful financial center, Buenos Aires, is the leading global market to trade financial instruments on sunflower seeds. Cities located on global circuits, whether few or many, become part of distinct, often highly specialized inter-city geographies. Thus if I were to track the global circuits of gold as a financial instrument, it is London, New York, Chicago, Zurich, that dominate. But if I track the direct trading in the metal, Johannesburg, Mumbai, Dubai and Sydney all appear on the map.

This networked system also feeds unnecessary mobilities, because the intermediary economy of specialized services thrives on mobilities. Thus in the case of the UK economy, a study by the New Economics Foundation and the Open University of London found that in 2004, the UK exported 1500 tonnes of fresh potatoes to Germany, and imported 1500 tonnes of the same product from the same country; it also imported 465 tonnes of gingerbread, but exported 460 tonnes of the same product; and it sent

10 200 tonnes of milk and cream to France, yet imported 9900 tonnes of the same dairy goods from France.

One way of tracking the global operations of firms is through their overseas affiliates. The top 100 global service firms have affiliates in 315 cities worldwide. For all multinational firms, the figure jumps to 1 million overseas affiliates.

The global map tightens when financial networks are examined – for instance, when what is getting traded is not the butter or coffee as such, but financial instruments based on those commodities. The map of commodity futures shows us that most financial trading happens in 20 financial futures exchanges. These 20 include the usual suspects, New York and London, but in perhaps not so familiar roles as well. Thus London, not necessarily famous for its mining, is the largest futures trader in the metal palladium. But besides these two major financial centers, these 20 also include Tokyo as the largest trader in platinum, Sao Paulo as one of the major traders in both coffee and gold, the already mentioned case of Buenos Aires as the major trader in sunflower seeds, and Shanghai in copper. Finally, some of these centers are highly specialized in unexpected ways: London controls potatoes futures.

The map tightens even further when the 73 commodities thus traded are aggregated into three major groups. Five major global futures exchanges (NYME, LME, CBOT, TCOM and IPE) located in New York, London, Chicago and Tokyo concentrate 76 per cent of trading in these 73 commodities futures traded globally. Aggregated into three major groups, one single market clearly dominates in each. For agricultural commodities futures, the CBOT (Chicago) controls most global trading, for energy it is the NYME (New York) and for metals, the LME (London).

This escalation in the capacity to control a vast multi-sited network of locations makes visible the diversity of global economic spaces that are being generated. Thus the commodities themselves come from well over 80 countries and are sold in all countries of the world, even as only about 20 financial exchanges control the global commodities futures trading. This tighter map of commodities futures trading begins to show us something about the role of cities in today's globalizing and increasingly electronic economy.

It is here that global cities enter the picture. They are not the places where commodities are produced but they are the places where commodity futures are invented so as to facilitate the global trading of these commodities and partly manage some of the associated risks, and they are the places where these futures are traded. It brings to the fore the distinction between the sites and networks for producing the actual good, and the sites and networks for managing and coordinating the trading of the actual good and the financial instruments they support. And it makes concrete what is one of the main counterintuitive trends evident in today's global economy: that the more globalized and non-material the activity (trading in financial instruments), the more concentrated the global map of those activities.

There are other such global maps, beyond commodities, commodities futures and finance in general. A focus on the global networks of global service firms, migration flows and flight patterns, shows us a far more distributed global map.

Mapping the global operations of specialized service firms shows almost the opposite of the sharp concentration of the financial futures exchanges mentioned above. The servicing operations of these firms are in demand everywhere. When countries open up to foreign firms and investors and allow their markets to become integrated into global markets, it is often foreign service firms that take over the most specialized servicing; it happened in cities as diverse as Buenos Aires and Beijing. This is, clearly, one particular mapping of interconnectivities among a group of very diverse cities. The most detailed information about these kinds of patterns comes from a study covering 315 cities by Peter Taylor (2004; see generally the GAWC website) who have generously put the data in the public domain. What the numbers capture is the extent to which these cities are connected through the office networks of those 100 firms. This information is one microcosm of a pattern that repeats itself over and over with a variety of other types of transactions, such as the almost meaningless measure of a city with McDonald's outlets or the extreme concentration of the commodities futures discussed earlier. Against this background, the connectivity measures of such office networks are a middle ground, very much a part of the infrastructure for the new inter-city geographies.

Elsewhere (Sassen, 2006b) I have examined a subsample of inter-city connections among 24 cities distributed over the top half of the global rankings of these cities. This allowed me an in-depth examination of a sort of small world sample that escapes the overwhelming weight of the top ranked cities and makes more visible the particular circuits that connect cities at much lower rankings among themselves.

The global map produced by the operations of the top 100 service firms is dramatically different from that produced by the financial trading of commodity futures, which is in turn different from that of the trading in the actual commodities. The extreme concentration evident in finance would stand out even more if a map were drawn of goods trading and the innumerable criss-crossing circuits connecting points of origin and destination. It does suggest that the specialized services are a sector that seeks out cities, the more the better.

THE SPECIALIZED DIFFERENCES OF CITIES MATTER: THERE IS NO PERFECT GLOBAL CITY

There is today a network of over 70 cities worldwide that is a sort of organizational platform managing and servicing the global operations of firms, investors and markets. These major and minor global cities have the wherewithal to handle and enable the cross-border flows of people, capital, information, and generally the instruments of the knowledge economy – from finance and accounting to design and information. A key feature of this network is that as globalization expanded in the 1990s and onwards, the number of global cities grew and came to include more and more regions of the world. It has become a worldwide organizational architecture. The financial crisis has affected the levels but not necessarily the patterns that characterize these cities. Many of the deepest effects of the crisis have been on households rather than firms, with the millions of foreclosures on homes of low-income and low–middle-income households in the US the most dramatic example (Sassen, 2008a).

A major study of 75 cities has identified a number of novel trends, some expected, others not. First, the much discussed shift from a uni- to a multi-polar world can also be detected in these findings. Thus Asia, not surprisingly, but also Europe, more surprisingly, have consolidated their global positions in the worldwide network of global cities. Each has done so through a handful of cities that are in the top global echelon of 15 cities. In contrast, the United States has been left with two cities (New York and Chicago) in that top echelon. Los Angeles, until recently the tenth ranked in the world, has now fallen to 17, with several other US cities also losing ground. In contrast Asia has four cities in the top echelon –Tokyo, Singapore, Hong Kong and Seoul. Probably most surprising is the ascendance of several European cities into the top echelon. Besides London, Paris and Frankfurt, long in the top echelon, Amsterdam and Madrid have now joined the top ranks. Below this top group of 11 we have Toronto, Sydney, Zurich and Copenhagen.

Second, the number of cities that can now deliver global city functions has kept expanding with the expansion of the global economy since the 1980s. Thus cities that may have been put to pasture, so to speak, by global firms and markets, have now become reinserted into global circuits. An example is Buenos Aires, which saw firms and professionals leave as its severe economic downturn and bankruptcy erupted in 2000 and the ensuing years saw the largest sovereign bankruptcy in modern history. Yet now it has become reincorporated. This also brings to the fore that global cities are built, developed, partly made. Much investment and effort from local governments and firms and foreign firms goes into them. Since global firms and markets need a vast network of spaces of operation, reintegrating cities into the global network is desirable.

Third, there is no perfect global city – no city ranks at the top in all the 100 data points, aggregated into seven variables, on which the study is based. There is sharp variability. This also points to the fact that global firms and markets need many global cities, no matter that some are rather so-so. Better many than a single perfect one, as might have been the case in earlier empires, when the capital was the city of the empire. Thus New York, one of the most important global cities, ranks rather low in a whole range of variables, which is not going to shock anybody. But more surprising are some of the very low rankings on various aspects of London, now the top global city in the world. A somewhat different pattern is evident in many of the megacities of the global south that have now emerged as global cities. These tend to rank high in global corporate aspects and very low in social issues. Thus Mumbai and Sao Paulo are financial and economic powerhouses and have high rankings in financial indicators, but they have very low rankings in basic services and general social conditions and livability. Yet, they are critical to the global economy – the latter can (regrettably) overlook all these social negatives and continue happily on its own way.

Fourth, a new type of city is emerging as a significant platform for global firms and markets. These are cities in small countries, where foreign firms locate not to invest in these countries but to use them as a platform. They have all the resources, the best legal and political frameworks, and basic services for all. They are veritable global platforms. Dubai is this in a spectacular fashion in the Middle East, as is Singapore. But what stands out here is how the European cities have ascended in this domain. Thus Copenhagen, with its strong legal and political framework, is emerging as a platform. For investors to go to Copenhagen is not necessarily about investing in that relatively small economy. Frankfurt, which in the 1980s rose fast to become one of the top financial centers in the world, also emerged as such a platform. Locating in Frankfurt was not about investing in the city. Amsterdam, which ascended to tenth, is another such platform in what is a very small country.

Fifth, Zurich, long and still today the capital of international private banking, has lost ground to Amsterdam and Madrid as a financial center. Madrid, on the other hand, is reinserting itself in its old imperial geography, with heavy investments throughout Latin America. This has given Spanish firms and investors a strong base for significant financial gains which in turn have enabled the acquisition of, among others, one of the largest UK banks and the British Airports Corporation. It indicates to what extent private banking is not quite the power base it was in today's global economy, while old imperial geographies can be reactivated.

Why is this expansion of the worldwide network of global cities happening? The general answer often heard is that most people now live in cities. But that is far too general to explain the fact that our global economy, increasingly based on knowledge capital that can circulate electronically, has produced a 'systemic' demand for a growing number of global cities over the last 20 years. Let us recall that as recently as the 1970s many of our most powerful cities had become poor, and some had actually gone bankrupt – New York City, London and Tokyo among them.

The network of global cities has expanded as more and more firms go global and enter a growing range of national economies. The main business centers in each of these economies have begun to evolve as global cities – they are the bridge between global firms and markets and the specifics of national economies. This then also explains the multi-polar character of the network of global cities. And the rebuilding of central areas, whether downtown and/ or at the edges, we see in all of these cities is part of this new economic role. It amounts to rebuilding cities as platforms for a rapidly growing range of globalized activities and flows, from economic to cultural and political. This also explains why architecture, urban design and urban planning have all become more important and visible in the last two decades.

GLOBAL IMMIGRATION CITIES

Finally, and very briefly, given the heightened importance of immigration, the top 33 immigrant-receiving cities (in terms of share in their total population) in the world were selected. One of the main utilities is to show to what extent European cities, notwithstanding the emotions the topic causes there, are not among the top recipients, and further, that some of the very high recipient cities are generally considered to be well-functioning cities (Table 12.1). Only Amsterdam, Geneva and The Hague are among the top ten in terms of share of immigrants in the population, but the absolute numbers are relatively small. There is a similar combination in the bottom ten, with Frankfurt, London, Brussels and Zurich.

REGIONAL SPECIFICITY AND KNOWLEDGE ECONOMIES: ANY LINKS?

How much a region's specificity matters will vary, partly depending on that region's economy. The point is that a region's specificity matters more than is usually assumed, and that it matters in ways that are not generally recognized. The policy implications of the argument are that too great a

Table 12.1   Global immigrant cities: foreign born percentages and total population for selected cities

	City	Year	City Population	Foreign Born Population	% Foreign Born
1	Dubai	2002	857233	702931	82.00
2	Miami	2000	2253362	1147765	50.94
3	Amsterdam	2002	735328	347634	47.28
4	Toronto	2001	4647960	2091100	44.99
5	Muscat	2000	661000	294881	44.61
6	Vancouver	2001	1967475	767715	39.02
7	Auckland	2001	367737	143417	39.00
8	Geneva	2002	427700	164118	38.37
9	Mecca	1996	4467670	1686595	37.75
10	The Hague	1995	441595	161509	36.57
11	Los Angeles	2000	9519338	3449444	36.24
12	Tel Aviv	2002	2075500	747400	36.01
13	Kiev	1992	2616000	941760	36.00
14	Medina	2000	5448773	1893213	34.75
15	New York	2000	9314235	3139647	33.71
16	San Francisco	2000	1731183	554819	32.05
17	Riyadh	2000	4730330	1477601	31.24
18	Perth	2001	1336239	422547	31.62
19	Sydney	2001	3961451	1235908	31.20
20	Jerusalem	2002	678300	208700	30.77
21	Melbourne	2001	3367169	960145	28.51
22	Frankfurt	2000	650705	181184	27.84
23	Tbilisi	1999	1339105	370932	27.70
24	London	2001	7172091	1940390	27.05
25	Brussels	2002	978384	260040	26.58

Source: The top 33 cities were selected out of a total of 100. For the full list see Benton-Short et al. (2005), and http://gstudynet.com/gwcsg/publications/OPS/papers/CSGOP-04-32.pdf.

focus is put upon competition – between cities, between regions, between countries – and not enough on the emergence of new types of networked systems and the partly associated emergence of an increasingly specialized global division of functions. These networked systems arise partly out of the multi-sidedness of firms and out of the evolution of global markets into global platforms open to many and from many different places. And the increasingly specialized global division of functions arises from the multiplication of specialized economic sectors and the increasing complexity of many of these sectors.

Among the key implications for mega regions of these combined trends is that their scale can allow them to capture a large share of those networks and, secondly, that the specialized economic strengths of a region increasingly matter. Yes there is competition, but it accounts for far less than is usually assumed. What really matters is the specialized difference of a city or region. This section examines the connection between regional economic specificity and the formation of advanced knowledge economies. And in the ensuing section I examine the question of increasingly homogenized landscapes and built environments to understand how regional or urban specificity can co-exist with that homogenizing.

How does a city or a region become a knowledge economy? The case of Chicago may prove helpful to illustrate the point. It is common to see Chicago as a latecomer to the knowledge economy (and thus to global city status). Why did it happen so late – almost 15 years later than in New York and London? Typically the answer is that Chicago had to overcome its agro-industrial past; that its economic history put it at a disadvantage compared to old trading and financial centers such as New York and London.[21]

But its past was not a disadvantage. It was one key source of its competitive advantage. The particular specialized corporate services that had to be developed to handle the needs of its agro-industrial regional economy gave Chicago a key component of its current specialized advantage in the global economy.[22] While this is most visible and familiar in the fact of its preeminence as a futures market built on pork bellies, so to speak, it also underlies other highly specialized components in its global city functions. The complexity, scale and international character of Chicago's historical agro-industrial complex required highly specialized financial, accounting, legal expertise, quite different from the expertise required to handle the sectors New York specialized in – service exports, finance on trade, and finance on finance. Today there are other sectors that are, clearly, also critical to Chicago's advanced service economy, notably the conventions and entertainment sector and cultural industries. But the point here is that Chicago's past as a massive agro-industrial complex gave the city some of its core and distinctive knowledge economy components.

But for this specialized advantage to materialize requires a repositioning of that past knowledge to a different set of economic circuits. It entails, then, dis-embedding that expertise from an agro-industrial economy and re-embedding it in a 'knowledge' economy – that is to say, an economy where expertise can increasingly be commodified, function as a key input and, thereby constitute a new type of intermediate economy. Having a past as a major agro-industrial complex makes that switch more difficult than a past as a trading and financial center. This then also partly explains

Chicago's 'lateness' in bringing that switch about. But that switch is not simply a matter of overcoming that past. It requires a new organizing logic that can revalue the capabilities developed in an earlier era (Sassen 2008b; chs 1 and 5).[23] It took making to execute the switch. Through its particular type of past, Chicago illuminates aspects of the formation and the specifics of knowledge economies that are far less legible in cities such as New York and London, which even though they did have manufacturing were dominated by predominantly trading and banking economies. A first issue is then that Chicago's past as an agro-industrial economy points to the mistake of assuming that the characteristics of global cities correspond to those of such old trading and banking centers.

A second issue raised by the Chicago case is that while there are a number of global city regions today with heavy manufacturing origins, many once important manufacturing cities have not made the switch into a knowledge economy based on that older industrial past. Along with Chicago, Sao Paulo, Tokyo, Seoul and Shanghai are perhaps among today's major global city regions with particularly strong histories in heavy manufacturing. But most once important manufacturing cities, notably Detroit and the English manufacturing cities, have not undergone that type of switch. They were to some extent dominated by a single or a few industries and shaped up more like mono-cultures. This points to the importance of thresholds in the scale and diversity of a region's manufacturing past to secure the components of knowledge production I identify in Chicago's case – specialized servicing capabilities that could be dislodged from the organizational logic of heavy manufacturing and relodged in the organizational logic of today's so-called knowledge economy.

The specialized economic histories of major cities and regions matter in today's global economy because they are the main way in which national economies are inserted in variable ways in multiple globally networked divisions of functions. It never was 'the' national economy that articulated a country with the international division of functions. But today it is even less so because the global economy consists of a vast number of particular circuits connecting particular components of cities and regions across borders. It is at this level of desegregation that it is best to understand how cities and regions are globally articulated. It is also in this context that it is possible to see how much more the specialized economic histories of a region matter today than they did in the Keynesian period marked by national territorial convergence, rather than today's targeting, and by mass production rather than today's proliferation of increasingly specialized and diverse services.

Thus, returning to the Chicago example, the city today has a specialized advantage in producing certain types of financial, legal and accounting instruments because financial, legal and accounting experts in Chicago had to address in good part the needs of the agro-industrial complex; they had to deal with steel and with cattle produced for regional, national and international markets. It is this specialized type of knowledge that matters for Chicago's competitive situation in the global market. Chicago, Sao Paulo, Shanghai, Tokyo and Seoul are among the leading producers of these types of specialized corporate services, not in spite of their economic past as major heavy industry centers, but because of it.

The fact that these distinctions and differences in the specialized economic histories of cities and regions has become increasingly prominent and value-adding in today's global, and also national, economy is easily obscured by the common emphasis on competition and cross-border standardization. Competition and standardization have been rescaled partly to the subnational level of cities and regions – this is a reality that is difficult to avoid. But the emphasis remains on competition, notably inter-city competition, and on standardization – the notion that globalization homogenizes standards of all kinds, business cultures and built environments (no matter how good the architecture). The economic trajectory and switching illustrated by the case of Chicago contests the thesis of the homogenizing effects of today's advanced economic sectors; a thesis which also brings with it an emphasis on inter-city and inter-regional competition. This thesis and its implications could also be extended to certain types of regions and mega regions with similarly specialized economic trajectories, albeit very different contents. The Chicago case shows that becoming part of a knowledge economy is not simply a question of dropping a manufacturing and agro-industrial past, and then proceeding to converge/homogenize on the headquarters–services–cultural sector axis. It is critical to execute the switch described earlier – whatever might be the specifics of an area's past.[24]

Further, Chicago also indicates that the meaning of homogenized urban and regional landscapes needs to be examined empirically. It becomes critical to establish the particular specialized sectors that might inhabit that homogenized landscape.

HOMOGENIZED BUILT ENVIRONMENT: OBSCURING ECONOMIC DIFFERENCE

The homogenized and convergent state-of-the art urban and increasingly regional landscapes are actually functioning as an 'infrastructure'. As an infrastructure, these homogenized built environments guarantee the provision of all advanced systems and luxuries needed/desired by the firms and households in leading economic sectors are in place. Office districts, high-end housing and commercial districts, conventional and digital connectivity, cultural districts, security systems, airports, and so on, are all in place and they are all state-of-the-art.

Comparative analyses rely on similarities and differences to make their point. Contemporary urbanization, whether at the urban, metro or regional level, is often seen as marked by a homogenizing of the urban landscape and a growing range of its built environments. This is especially so in the case of global cities and global city-regions due to the intensity and rapidity of urban reconstruction in such areas. And yet this obscures the fact of the diversity of economic trajectories through which cities and regions emerge and develop (as discussed in the preceding section), even when the final visual outcomes may look similar. Out of this surface analysis based on homogenized landscapes and built environments, comes a second possibly spurious inference, that this homogenizing is a function of economic convergence, for instance, the notion that there is a general move to (the same) knowledge economy. Both propositions – that similar visual landscapes are indicators of both similar economic dynamics and of convergence – may indeed capture various situations. But these propositions also obscure key conditions that point to divergence and specialized differences; in fact, divergence and specialized difference is easily rendered invisible by such notions. Such spurious inferences need to be taken into account when understanding the character of these mega regions.

At the most general level it is possible to start with developments at the macro-economic level which can easily lead observers to buy into the homogenization thesis. An important structural trend evident in all reasonably working economies is the growing service intensity in the organization of just about all economic sectors, including rather routine and often non-globalized sectors. Whether in mining and agriculture, manufacturing, or service industries such as transport and health, more firms are buying more producer services. Some of this translates into a growing demand for producer services in global cities, but much of it translates into a demand for such services from regional centers, albeit often less complex and advanced versions of those services. The growth in the demand for producer services is then, in the analysis, a structural feature of advanced market economies which affects most economic sectors. It is not just a feature of globalized sectors.[25] What globalization brings to this trend is a sharp increase in the demand for complexity and diversity of professional knowledge.[26] It is this qualitative difference that leads to the heightened agglomeration economies evinced by firms in global cities compared to other types of urban areas. But the basic structural trend is present in both types of areas. This perspective also clarifies what is in my view a somewhat misguided interpretation about the higher growth rates of producer services in cities that are not global. The trend is to assume *ipso facto* that these higher growth rates of producer services reflect decline and/or the departure of producer services from global cities. Those higher growth rates are actually in good part the result of lagged growth of these services throughout the national economy; global cities had their extremely high growth rates much earlier, in the 1980s.[27] The lower growth rates evident in global cities compared with other cities should thus not necessarily be interpreted as losses for the former, but rather as the latter entering this new structural phase of market economies.[28] Looking at matters this way recodes some common interpretations of growth and decline.

What is critical for the analysis in this section is that the growth of this intermediate economy across diverse urban areas amounts to a kind of structural convergence that explains a homogenizing of built environments and spatial patterns even when the sectors serviced are radically different. Regardless of economic sector and geographic location, firms are buying more of these services. A mining firm, a transport firm, and a software firm all need to buy legal and accounting services. To some extent these services may be produced in the same city and in similar built environments, even though they are feeding very different economic sectors and geographic sites of the larger economy, including the mega-regional economy. Thus 'old economy' sectors such as manufacturing and mining are also feeding the growth of the intermediate economy.

This structural convergence does filter through and homogenizes spatial organization and the visual order of the built environment. It does account for key patterns evident in cities small and large, notably the well-documented growth of a new type of professional class of young urbanites and the associated high-income gentrification and growth of the cultural sector. This convergence and homogenizing of the visual order easily obscures the specific trajectories and contents through which a region develops a knowledge economy, as discussed in the preceding section of this chapter.

Seen this way, it is possible to begin to qualify the homogenization and convergence thesis. There is a kind of convergence at an abstract systemic level, and at the level of the needed built environments for the new intermediate economy and the new kinds of professional workforces. But at the concrete, material interface of the economy and its built environments, the actual content of the specialized services that inhabit that built environment can vary sharply.

From here, then, my proposition that critical components of the homogenized/convergent urban and regional landscape frequently presented as today's quintessential new advanced built environment, are actually more akin to an infrastructure *for* economic sectors. This unsettles the concept (and the reality) of the built environment as it is generally used. The critical question becomes what inhabits that 'infrastructure'. Looking similar does not necessarily entail similar contents, circuits, moments of a process. This illustrates the thesis that different dynamics can run through similar institutional and spatial forms, and vice versa.[29] Thus the substantive character of convergence in the global city model, for instance, is not the visual landscape per se but its function as an infrastructure; and it is, above all, the development and partial importation of a set of specialized functions and the direct and indirect effects this may have on the larger city, including its built environment.

One question here is whether this distinction between homogenized built environments and the often highly diverse contents they house also need to become part of our understanding of what is specific to a city, an urban region or a mega region.[30] State of the art office buildings or speed rail or airports can look very similar yet serve very different economic sectors. These types of differences are becoming increasingly important to understand a city's, a region's and possibly a mega region's place in the global economy. There are two reasons for this. One is the shift from a Keynesian spatial economy striving for national territorial convergence to a post-Keynesian space economy oriented towards territorial targeting (global cities, silicon valleys, science parks, and so on). The second is that a city's, a region's and possibly a mega region's advantage in the global economy is a function of positioning in multiple highly particularized, and often very specialized, economic circuits; it is not helpful to think of 'the' place of 'the' mega region in 'the' global economy.

CONCLUSION

Beyond the familiar policy suggestions, these comments point to policy implications that go beyond ensuring that the most dynamic sectors of developed economies are targeted for support. It is also needed to counter excessive targeting to ensure more territorial convergence. Developed countries have entered a distinct phase of territorial organization, away from Keynesian convergence and towards territorial targeting: from global cities to silicon valleys and technopoles. Much of this territorial targeting is linked to the development of knowledge economies. This raises several questions about the actual content of these knowledge economies and the relationship between that content and the older economic histories of a place.

Secondly, knowledge economies are merely one (albeit critical) component of national, regional, or urban economies. Prioritizing only advanced sectors is a critical mistake, and it risks furthering a 'plantation economy'; no matter how fancy the crop, depending on a monoculture is not a good way to proceed. Further, the most advanced sectors require a vast array of types of firms, workers and products/services that are not usually seen as 'advanced'. A key policy implication is that the knowledge economy should not be reified as something that exists by itself. It is embedded in multiple other sectors.

The soft underbelly of the knowledge economy is the vast array of low-wage jobs, low-profit and low-tech firms, and under-resourced economic spaces that are part of the knowledge economy, even though rarely coded as such. If addressing this undesirable condition requires 'soft' policy, that is fine. But the objective has to be upgrading those jobs, firms and spaces. This is one way of counteracting the strong tendencies towards polarization wired into the knowledge economy. Low-growth sectors may also contain such tendencies towards growing inequality (though in a much narrower range) but rarely contain the resources to even begin to counteract polarization. One policy objective should be to avoid the outcomes of the US, where a third of workplaces are below standards, and the incidence of workplace injuries and fatalities is the highest of all developed countries.

Finally, if the relationship between older material economies (manufacturing, mining, agriculture, and so on) and today's knowledge economy is rethought, it is possible to see that this is not one of conflict as is typically thought, but rather that the former can feed the latter. This relationship is usually overlooked or not addressed in analyses of the knowledge economy because the latter is new and hence it is easily assumed that it had to overcome the older economies of a place.

One key policy implication of rethinking that relationship is that a city or region can build strengths in terms of its 'specialized difference'. For example, Chicago's knowledge economy is strong because its agro-industrial past was strong. Law, accounting, finance, and so on all had to be developed to address the needs of large manufacturing and agro-business. This view goes against the common view that Chicago had to overcome that agro-industrial past. On the contrary! That past gave it its specialized advantage in the national and global economy. Thus a city or a region needs to build on the specifics of its economic history in order to achieve specialized differentiation (high levels of complexity) in developing a knowledge economy. This also means distinguishing the formats of the knowledge economy from its contents (for example both are leading financial centers, but NY's financial knowledge economy is built on trade and finance, Chicago's on agro and manufacturing). It is essential to develop more encompassing understandings of the parameters and conditionalities of knowledge economies, and of the implications for urban and regional development.

NOTES

1. For one of the definitive examinations of the shortcomings of the data on sub-national scalings see the report by the National Academy of Sciences (2003). See also generally, OECD (2006, 2007).
2. Besides 'regionalizing' various segments of a firm's chain of operations, one might also propose to regionalize more segments of various commodity chains. See, for instance, Gereffi et al. (2005).
3. For a development of this concept see Scott (2001).
4. I cannot resist referring to a book that breaks new terrain in this regard: Hagedorn (2006).
5. For one of the best data sets on the dispersal at the global scale of the operations of firms in corporate services see Globalization and World Cities Study Group and Network (1998).
6. See Regional Planning Association (2007).
7. A parallel issue here, not fully addressed in this chapter, is the articulation of technical connectivity with social connectivity. See, for instance, Garcia (2002).
8. This is a type of agglomeration economy I found in my research on global cities, but it can also be applied to national or regional scales. The hypothesis was that the greater the capabilities for geographic dispersal a firm has, the higher the agglomeration economies it is subject to in some of its components, notably top level headquarter functions. (See Sassen, 2001, for a brief explanation of the nine hypotheses that specify the global city model.) It is the most specialized functions pertaining to the most globalized firms which are subject to the highest agglomeration economies. The complexity of the functions that need to be produced, the uncertainty of the markets such firms are involved in, and the growing importance of speed in all these transactions, is a mix of conditions that constitutes a new logic for agglomeration; it is not the logic posited in older models, where weight and distance (cost of transport) are seen to shape agglomeration economies. The mix of firms, talents and expertise in a broad range of specialized fields makes a certain type of dense environment function as a strategic knowledge economy wherein the whole is more than the sum of (even its finest) parts.
9. The region, the metro area and the city are scalings that enable research to capture the many highly specialized cicuits that comprise 'the' global economy. Different circuits contain different groupings of regions and cities. Viewed this way, the global economy becomes concrete and specific, with a well defined geography. Goods and services are redistributed to a vast number of destinations, no matter how few the points of origin are in some cases. With globalization, this capacity to redistribute globally has grown sharply. By focusing on a scale such as the region and on the diverse types of economic spaces it contains, it is possible to capture many of these points of redistribution, as well as points of origin. For a definitive treatment of some of these issues as they apply to service industries see Taylor (2004).
10. For an analysis of options see Henderson (2005).
11. But there is a caveat. A second key hypothesis used to specify the global city model is that the more headquarters actually buy some of their corporate functions from the specialized services sector rather than producing them in house, the greater their locational options become. Among these options is moving out of global cities, and more generically, out of dense urban environments. This is an option precisely because of

the existence of a networked specialized producer services sector that can increasingly handle some of the most complex global operations of firms and markets. It is precisely this specialized capability to handle the global operations of firms and markets that distinguishes the global city production function in my analysis, not the number per se of corporate headquarters of the biggest firms in the world, as is often suggested.

12. One of the best and most detailed analysis comparing two different formats for high-tech districts is Saxenian (1996).

13. And, indeed, certain very contemporary forms of dispersal are a function of particular capacities developed in settings marked by high agglomeration economies (exemplified by global cities). And they are not only happening in the narrowly understood sphere of the economy: it is possible to identify the growth of an international curatorial class, and major museums allowing their most valued collections to go on tour in a foreign country.

14. This spatial lens is also to be distinguished from the more common angle of firms and markets (see, for example, Ernst, 2005).

15. For a full development of this subject please see Sassen (2008b).

16. For a detailed explanation of this thwarting of technical logics by the economic, financial, or for that matter cultural and political logics of users see Sassen (2008b: ch. 7).

17. Today's multinationals have over one million affiliates worldwide. Affiliates are but one mode of global operation. For empirical details about the range of formats of global operations see Sassen (2006a), Taylor (2004) and World Federation of Exchanges (2007).

18. For a detailed examination of the importance of the subnational scale for a global market, see Harvey (2007).

19. See, for instance Rutherford (2004).

20. For a full development of these patterns see Sassen (2008b: ch. 5).

21. For one of the most detailed examinations of the current and past economic patterns of Chicago and its region see Greene (2006).

22. This brings to the fore the specialized division of functions in the global economy, one partly constituted and implemented through a proliferation of specialized cross-border city networks. The critical mass of these networks has expanded to include about 40 major and minor global cities. There are many networks and different types of functions/positions for cities. Detecting this has required developing new methodologies (see Taylor, 2004, Alderson and Beckfield, 2004, and the illuminating debate on questions of method between Taylor and Alderson and Beckfield). The global network of cities is much more than just a set of cross-border flows connecting cities. It is a complex, highly specialized organizational infrastructure for the management and servicing of the leading economic sectors.

23. Sassen (2006a) develops this notion of switching (existing capabilities switching to novel organizing logics) in order to understand the formation of today's global economy as well as today's partial denationalizing of state capacities

24. For very different types of cities and economic trajectories, see for example Amen et al. (2006) and Gugler (2004).

25. For one particular aspect – artistic practice as it feeds into commercialized design – see Lloyd (2005).

26. In developing the global city model I posited that a critical indicator is the presence of a networked, specialized producer services sector capable of handling the global operations of firms and markets, whether national or foreign. Given measurement difficulties, a proxy for this networked sector is the incidence and mix of producer services in a city. This is frequently reduced to the share of producer services employment as the indicator of global city status. This is fine, though it needs empirical specification as to the quality and mix of the producer services industries. More problematic is to interpret a small share, or a declining share, or a falling growth rate, or a lower growth rate than in non-global cities, as an indicator of global city status decline or as signaling that the city in question is not a global city. Similarly problematic as a variant on this indicator is the share a city has of national employment in producer services and whether it has

grown or fallen; the notion here is that if a city such as New York or London loses share of national employment in producer services, it loses power.

27. On that earlier phase, see, for example, Drennan (1992).
28. Thus the high growth rates of producer services in smaller cities as compared with global cities is not necessarily a function of relocations from global cities to better priced locations. It is a function of the growing demand by firms in all sectors for producer services. When these services are for global firms and markets their complexity is such that global cities are the best production sites. But when the demand is for fairly routine producer services, cities at various levels of the urban system can be adequate production sites. The current spatial organization of the producer services reflects this spreading demand across economic sectors.
29. In Sassen (2008b) a parallel argument is posited for the liberal state as it is subjected to the forces of economic and political globalization. The outcome does not necessarily mean that these states lose their distinctiveness, but rather that they implement the necessary governance structures to accommodate global projects and that they do so through the specifics of their state organization.
30. For a detailed examination of this mix of visual, urban engineering, architectural, and economic issues across 16 major cities in the world see Burdett (2006) and Sudjic (1993, 2005).

REFERENCES

Alderson, Arthur S. and Jason Beckfield (2004), 'Power and Position in the World City System.' *American Journal of Sociology* **109**(4): 811–51.
Amen, Mark M., Kevin Archer and M. Martin Bosman (eds) (2006), *Relocating Global Cities: From the Center to the Margins.* New York: Rowman & Littlefield.
Benton-Short, Lisa, Marie Price and Samantha Friedman (2005), 'Globalization from Below: The Ranking of Global Immigrant Cities.' *International Journal of Urban and Regional Research*, **29**(4): 945–59.
Burdett, Ricky (ed.) (2006), *Cities: People, Society, Architecture.* New York: Rizzoli.
Drennan, Mathew P. (1992), 'Gateway Cities: The Metropolitan Sources of U.S. Producer Service Exports.' *Urban Studies* **29**(2): 217–35.
Ernst, Dieter (2005), 'The New Mobility of Knowledge: Digital Information Systems and Global Flagship Networks.' In *Digital Formations: IT and New Architectures in the Global Realm*, edited by Robert Latham and Saskia Sassen. Princeton: Princeton University Press, pp. 89–114.
Garcia, D. Linda (2002), 'The Architecture of Global Networking Technologies.' In *Global Networks/Linked Cities*, edited by Saskia Sassen. New York and London: Routledge, pp. 39–69.
Gereffi, Gary, John Humphrey and Timothy Sturgeon (2005), 'The Governance of Global Value Chains.' *Review of International Political Economy (Special Issue: Aspects of Globalization)* **12**(1): 78–104.
Globalization and World Cities Study Group and Network (GAWC) (1998), http://www.lboro.ac.uk/departments/gy/research/gawc.html.
Greene, Richard P. (2006), *Chicago's Geographies: Metropolis for the 21st Century.* Washington, DC: Association of American Geographers.
Gugler, Joseph (2004), *World Cities Beyond the West.* Cambridge: Cambridge University Press.

Hagedorn, John (ed.) (2006), *Gangs in the Global City: Exploring Alternatives to Traditional Criminology.* Chicago: University of Illinois at Chicago.

Harvey, Rachel (2007), 'The Sub-National Constitution of Global Markets.' In *Deciphering the Global: Its Spaces, Scales and Subjects*, edited by S. Sassen. New York and London: Routledge.

Henderson, Jeffrey (2005), 'Governing Growth and Inequality: The Continuing Relevance of Strategic Economic Planning.' In *Towards a Critical Globalization Studies*, edited by R. Appelbaum and W. Robinson. New York: Routledge, pp. 227–36.

Lloyd, Richard (2005), *NeoBohemia: Art and Bohemia in the Postindustrial City.* London and New York: Routledge.

National Academy of Sciences (2003), *Cities Transformed: Demographic Change and its Implications in the Developing World*, Washington, DC: Panel on Urban Population Dynamics, National Academies Press.

OECD (2006), *OECD Territorial Reviews: Competitive Cities in the Global Economy*. Paris: OECD Publishing.

OECD (2007), 'What Policies for Globalising Cities? Rethinking the Urban Policy Agenda.' Proceedings from the OECD International Conference, Madrid, 29–30 March, http://www.oecd.org/document/16/0,3343,en_21571361_3767395 4_40078672_1_1_1_1,1,00.html.

Regional Planning Association (RPA) (2007), *Economic Megaregions*, Princeton: Policy Research Institute for the Region, Woodrow Wilson School of Public and International Affairs, Princeton University.

Rutherford, Jonathan (2004), *A Tale of Two Global Cities: Comparing the Territorialities of Telecommunications Developments in Paris and London.* Aldershot, UK and Burlington, VT: Ashgate.

Sassen, Saskia (2001), *The Global City*, Princeton: Princeton University, 2nd edn; original edition 1991: New Preface.

Sassen, Saskia (2006a), *Cities in a World Economy*, 3rd edn, Sage/PineForge.

Sassen, Saskia (2006b), *Why Cities Matter*. 2006 Venice Biennale of Architecture Catalogue, New York: Rizzoli.

Sassen, Saskia (2008a), 'Mortgage Capital and its Particularities: A New Frontier for Global Finance.' *Journal of International Affairs*, Fall/Winter, **62**(1): 187–227.

Sassen, Saskia (2008b), *Territory, Authority, Rights: From Medieval to Global Assemblages*. Princeton, NJ: Princeton University Press.

Saxenian, Anna-lee (1996), *Regional Advantage: Culture and Competition in Silicon Valley and Route 128*. Cambridge, MA: Harvard University Press.

Scott, Anthony J. (2001), *Global City-Regions*. Oxford: Oxford University Press.

Sudjic, Deyan (1993), *The Hundred Mile City.* New York: Harvest/HBJ.

Sudjic, Deyan (2005), *The Edifice Complex: How the Rich and Powerful Shape the World*. Harmondsworth: Allen Lane/Penguin.

Taylor, Peter J. (2004), *World City Network: A Global Urban Analysis*. New York: Routledge.

World Federation of Exchanges (2007), *Annual Statistics for 2006*. Paris: World Federation of Exchanges (and annual updates).

Index

absolute competition 135
active population 246
advanced corporate services 252
aerospace 48
age dependency 232, 234
age-related programs 232
agglomeration economies 249, 252, 254, 259, 263
aging population 1, 19, 232
agricultural commodities 272
Airbus 203
Aker Yards 203
Alliance NumériQC 56
Americans for the Arts 237, 244
anchor institutions 26, 33
area vasta 108
Asian financial crisis 133
Association des producteurs en multimédia du Québec 60
Association for Community and Higher Education Partnerships 33
associations 126
Atlanta 237
Aurora 215, 217
Avenue of the Arts 240

Baosteel 208, 220
Bari 99
Barletta 98
Bartlett, Randall 2
Bassanini laws 91
Bayer 203, 214, 217
benchmarking 16
benefits of industrial tourism 220
bio-tech parks 250
biotechnology cluster 86
Brookings Institution 3
Bureau of the Census 233
business environment 200
business park, Knapsack 224
business sociology 125
business tourists 223

Carbonaro, G. 75
Cassidy, E. 39
categories of cities and towns 237
central places 263
central urban density 269
centrality 269
centralized control 267
Centre d'Expertise et de Services Application Multimédia 60
Charlottesville 237
chemical business park 203
Cheshire, Paul 75
Chicago 20, 278, 279
China Development Institute 149
Chinese Academy of Social Sciences 16
Chinese competition 106
Cité du multimédia 57, 63
cities in Northeastern US 16–17, 181
CLUNET (Cluster Network) 49
clusterization 53
clusters 38, 44
CMM economic development plan 48
Coalition for Urban Serving Universities 32
codified knowledge 74
Cointreau 217
college or university towns 18, 238, 241
colleges and universities 243
Cologne 203, 205, 207, 210, 214, 217, 219, 222, 224
commercial opening 117, 124
company visits 202
competition and cooperation 201
competitive performance of nations 121
competitiveness 74, 94, 121, 128, 153, 178, 248, 256
concertation 94, 99
connectivity 81
consumers of cultural activities 236
coordinator 163
core dynamics, 255

cost–benefit analysis 221
counter urbanization 112
creative capacity and innovation 44
creative industries 153
creative media complex 87
cross-border criminal networks 256
cross-border flows 249
cross-border flows of people 273
cross-border networks 256
cultural district 170
  Pittsburgh 240
cultural institutions 236
cultural policy 65
customer-based knowledge 74

decentralization 119
decision making power 188
de-industrialization 165
de-location 124
demand for industrial tourism 208
demographic change 13, 232
Denver 237
Department of Community and
  Economic Development 3
determinants of urban competitiveness
  236
differential urbanization 112
dispersal locations 265
division of public power 199

economic capital 26
economic development level 184
economic discoveries 205
economic growth 183
education and health care 245
electronic spaces 270
embededness 125
employment rates 186
engagement in educational activities
  244
enterprises 191
equitable outcomes 260
Euricur 201
European Union 84, 232
European urban and regional planning
  award 98
external economies 185

factory of the world 204
female labor participation 232

Fiat 15, 160, 162, 206
film and audiovisual production 38,
  43, 48, 50
FIM, information highway and
  multimedia forum 59
financial services grouping 87
financial trading networks 253
fiscal evasion 104
fiscal transfers 245
Florida, Richard 84, 88
forces of globalization 19
Fordist paradigm 160
Forum des inforoutes et du multimédia
  61
Functional Urban Regions 75
furniture industrial district 98

GDP per capita 184
geographic dispersal 254, 264
geographic scalings 264
geographic space 269
Glaeser, Ed 8, 88
global cities 177, 249, 261, 272, 276
global city 256, 273
global city functions 273
global-city regions 254
global competition 188
global connectivity 197
global firms 252
global map 271
global pipelines 42
global urban circuits 249
Global urban competitiveness index
  179, 180
Global Urban Competitiveness Project
  (GUCP) 3
global urban system 177
global urban value system 177
globalized city 250
globalized industries 256
Gottlieb, Joshua 8
governance 12
government 91
Government of Canada 51, 62
Government of Québec 38, 51, 62
Greater Montreal Innovation system
  46

Happy Shrimp Farm 206, 209, 212,
  215, 218

hard environment 194
health sciences 47, 50
high-capital intensive jobs 264
high-end economic activities 250
higher education 32, 85, 153
higher education/community
    partnerships 30
higher educational institutions (HEIS)
    9
Hong Kong 133
Hong Kong Airport Authority 137
Hong Kong/Shenzhen co-operation
    141
Hong Kong Special Administrative
    Region 134
human capital 25, 42, 74, 81
human resource competitiveness 193

IBM Consulting Services 3, 11, 18
Ietri, Daniele 16
illegal migration 151
image and identity 204
image and reputation 218
immigrant communities 256
immigrants 232
immigration 276
import substitution model 119, 129
index 24
index system 178
industrial clusters 10
industrial heartland 3, 15
industrial heritage 206, 218
industrial tourism 201, 222
Industrial Tourism Promotion Center
    206, 211, 215
industrial upgrading 199
industry structure 192
information and communication
    technologies 48, 269
information economy 267
infrastructural transformations 165
innovation 102, 194
innovation and creative capacity 39
innovation and knowledge 125
Innovation Systems Research Network
    40
innovative milieux 39
innovative regions 168
input competitiveness 178
intercity competition 132

inter-city connections 272
intercity cooperation 133
inter-city geographies 253
intergenerational battle 245
international commerce 122
international competition 177
international linkage 31
International Turin Association 165
intraregional economic interactions
    257
Italia 150, 171
Italian municipalities 90

Keystone Innovation Zone 35
knowledge base 79, 85
knowledge capital 23, 25
knowledge economies 258, 283
knowledge economy 26, 250, 253, 266,
    275, 280
knowledge sector clusters 11
knowledge-base 87, 88
knowledge-based industries 73
Kondratieff cycles 73
Kresl, Peter Karl 18, 75

labor participation rate 235
L'atlas industriel du Québec 46
learning 43
learning regions 236, 242
leisure tourism 205
lengthening life spans 232
Les grappes industrielles 46
Lever, William 11, 75
lifelong learning 236
Lingotto 161
living environment 196, 200
Local Development Agency 101
local governments 94
location quotients 120
locational advantages 261
Lok Ma Chau river 143
low-wage manufacturing 252

macroeconomic environment 121
Made in Torino 213, 217
Maglev 206
Malecki, Ed 114
manufacturing industry 205
Marga Incorporated 22
market share 182

Markusen, Ann 7
Marshall, Alfred 10
Marshallian district 39
Master Card World Centers of
    Commerce 11
Mastercard Worldwide Centers of
    Commerce 76
Matera 96, 107
mature industrial economies (MEIs) 1,
    8
Maurrasse, David 8
mega regional scale 260
megalopolis 114
mega-region 20, 249, 251, 257, 262, 283
mega-regional scale 250, 252
Memorandum of Enhancing Hong
    Kong-Shenzhen Cooperation 134
Mercer Index 82
metamorphic agenda 172
Metamorphic Turin 165
metroplex 114
Metropolitan forum of the film
    industry 51
Mexico 115
Mexico City 13, 116
Mexico City Metropolitan Area
    (MCMA) 116
Mezzogiorno 164
migration 83, 129
migratory experiences 13
Mirafiori 162
mobilities 270
Mollica, Stefano 12
mono-cultures 278
Montréal 37
Montréal International 47
Montreal Metropolitan Community
    48, 51
Morrill Act 35
movie industry 170
multimedia occupations 56
multimedia sector 38, 56
multinational companies 189, 197
multipolarity 257

Nashville 237
national macro-policies 260
National Research Council 40
National Science Foundation 33
negative externalities 262

Negrete, María Eugenia 125
net migratory balance 117
networked systems 276
networks 125, 126
new enterprise formation 75
Ni Pengfei 16, 122
nominal exchange rate 190
non-globalized sectors 280
Nord Barese Ofantino Territorial Pact
    98, 108
North American Free Trade
    Agreement 13, 47, 119
Northeastern US cities 182

OECD 73
Office of University Partnerships 33
Olympic Winter Games 203, 220
Osher Foundation 236, 242
out-migration 246
output index system 178

partnerships 22, 28
Pays de la Loire 203, 205, 208, 211,
    217, 219, 220, 222, 224
Pearl River Delta 152
Pennsylvania 4, 26, 83, 181
Pennsylvania
Pennsylvania's cities and towns 233
Pesaro 101, 108
Pew Foundation 236
pharmaceutical industry 46
Philadelphia 6, 233, 237, 240, 244
Piano, Renzo 96
Picard Report 46
Piedmont 161, 168, 203
Pittsburgh 7, 233, 238, 239
Pittsburgh Symphony 244
planning 259
plantation economy 283
platform 275
polarization reversal 112
polycentric urban regions 114
polytechnic 167
polytechnic agenda 172
population 83, 116
population pyramids 234
Porter Diamond of performance 41
Porter, Michael 46
positive economic benefits 246
PPP exchange rate 190

price and cost advantages 189
primate city 112, 114
private wealth and philanthropy 34
problems that confront the cities and towns 7
productivity gaps 187
Public Engagement Exercise 151
public money 39
pyrotechnic 167
pyrotechnic agenda 172

Québec Film and Television Council 50, 52

realistic image 221
recreational amenities 246
regional innovation system 169
rejuvenation through aging 236, 238
relocate residence 235
Rendell, Ed 2
reorganisation process 103
resource limitations 32
resurgent city 2
Rheinenergie 210, 217
RLA 143
Rotterdam 204, 207, 209, 212, 216, 220, 223, 227
Rotterdam Climate Initiative 223
Rotterdam Port Experience 209, 221
rural enterprise zone 260
rust belt 6

Sassen, Saskia 20
Sassi 96, 107
Sassi Law 97
Saucier Commission 46
Schrock, Greg 7
Schumpterian model 73
science museums 206
science parks 167, 171
Scotland 83
Scott, Allan 2
Scottish Executive 88
senior citizen residences 247
Shanghai 204, 206, 208, 211, 215, 218, 220, 223, 225
Shen Jianfa 14
Shenzhen 133
Shenzhen Airport Company Ltd 137

Shenzhen-Hong Kong Economic Development Foundation 149
Silicon Valley 22, 37
Singh, Balwant 75
slow food movement 170
'Smart Successful Scotland' 88
smuggling 151
Sobrino, Jaime 12
social capital 25, 42
social connectivity 267
social infrastructure 267
social security 200
socio-territorial capital 42, 65
soft environment 195
soft policy instruments 251
southern EU countries 232
space-time compression 265
spatial organization 263
spatial polarization 254
spatialization 255
specialized advantage 283
specialized circuits 270
spill-over effects 225
sticky capital 23
strategic planning 15
Strategic Plan(s) 165, 171, 173
STRIVE 23
structural convergence 281
subway line 167
success@montreal 47
survey of public opinion 145
sustainable competitiveness 182

tacit knowledge 74
tax burden 234
Taylor, Peter 272
Teatro Goldoni 243
technical knowledge 74
technical visits 205
technological and cultural clusters 10
technological innovation 188
technopoles 282
territorial embeddedness 45
territorial homogeneity 98
territorial pacts 98
theme park 215
ticking time bomb 235
Torino Film Festival 170
Torino internazionale 174
traditional patterns 246

Trans-European Network 167
trans-local operations 269
Tremblaly, Diane-Gabrielle 10
Tremblay, Gérard 46, 47
Turin 15, 160, 165, 203, 206, 208, 211,
    215, 217, 219, 221, 222, 225
Turok, Ivan 8

Ubisoft 57
UNESCO 97
Unique Office for Productive Activities
    105
universities 85
University of Pennsylvania 28, 35
urban decline 8
urban regeneration 95, 98
urban renaissance 83
urbanization advantages 262
urbanization economies 252, 259
urbanized region 254
US Metropolitan Statistical Areas 4
US Senate committee on Banking,
    Housing and Urban Affairs 2

van den Berg, Leo 17
Vaugeois, Sylvain 58
Visit Our Companies 203, 206, 212,
    216, 226
visitor numbers 209
Volkswagen 202, 207, 210, 213, 217,
    224

Washington Consensus 117
Wharton School of Business 3
White House Office on Social
    Innovation and Civic Engagement
    32
Winter Olympic Games 165, 169
Wolfsburg 202, 205, 207, 210, 213, 217,
    219, 222
World Cities Research Group 75
World Development Indicators 180
world economic centers 189
World Port Days 213
Wright, Robert 84

Yakult 208